Why It Sells

DATE DUE

Why It Sells

Decoding the Meanings of Brand Names, Logos, Ads, and Other Marketing and Advertising Ploys

Marcel Danesi

ROWMAN & LITTLEFIELD PUBLISHERS, INC.
Lanham • Boulder • New York • Toronto • Plymouth, UK

ROWMAN & LITTLEFIELD PUBLISHERS, INC.

Published in the United States of America
by Rowman & Littlefield Publishers, Inc.
A wholly owned subsidiary of The Rowman & Littlefield Publishing Group, Inc.
4501 Forbes Boulevard, Suite 200, Lanham, Maryland 20706
www.rowmanlittlefield.com

Estover Road, Plymouth PL6 7PY, United Kingdom

British Library Cataloguing in Publication Information Available

Library of Congress Cataloging-in-Publication Data

Danesi, Marcel, 1946–
  Why it sells : decoding the meanings of brand names, logos, ads, and other marketing
and advertising ploys / Marcel Danesi.
    p.   cm.
  Includes bibliographical references and index.
  ISBN-13: 978-0-7425-5544-0 (cloth : alk. paper)
  ISBN-10: 0-7425-5544-5 (cloth : alk. paper)
  ISBN-13: 978-0-7425-5545-7 (pbk. : alk. paper)
  ISBN-10: 0-7425-5545-3 (pbk. : alk. paper)
  1. Advertising. 2. Marketing. 3. Consumer behavior. 4. Brand names. 5. Signs and
symbols I. Title.
  HF5823.D255 2008
  658.8001'9—dc22

                                                                     2007016167

Printed in the United States of America

∞™ The paper used in this publication meets the minimum requirements of American
National Standard for Information Sciences—Permanence of Paper for Printed Library
Materials, ANSI/NISO Z39.48-1992.

Contents

Preface

To say that consumer product *advertising* has become the twentieth century's most ubiquitous means of mass communication is an understatement. The implicit messages, styles of presentation, and visual images of advertisers have become integral categories of the grammar of modern-day society, so to speak. They are found in all media—on posters, in magazines, in radio and television commercials, on Internet sites, on pamphlets, on catalogs, and the list could go on and on. Given their ubiquity and great appeal, the question becomes, Are they indelibly shaping the thoughts, personalities, and lifestyle behaviors of countless individuals by tapping into the one need that distinguishes the human species from all others—the need for *meaning*? The purpose of this book is to address this question. It will do so indirectly by addressing the more concrete question of "Why it sells." To do so, I will employ mainly the science of *semiotics*, as will be discussed throughout this book, although I will also rely on cognate disciplines for insight and comparison.

This book is written for a general audience and, thus, requires absolutely no background knowledge about either advertising or semiotic analysis. It is based in large part on research I have conducted on advertising practices over the many years of teaching at the University of Toronto. Some of the ideas found herein are scattered in other publications of mine, but there are also many new concepts discussed here, many of which have emanated from follow-up research and from in-class discussion with my own students. My debt to my students is immeasurable. They are the source of all my ideas. As such, therefore, this book is recommended as a classroom text for courses in advertising, pop culture, and various other disciplines concerned with advertising. I have shaped this book to make it as "user friendly" an explication of advertising as I possibly could. Nevertheless, I have made reference to appropriate research documents and to theories in scholarly ways that cannot be avoided, even in a text like this one. So, some effort may be required to get through some of the pages of this book. To facilitate cross-references, I have added a glossary of technical terms at the back. For those wishing to pursue the topic further, I have also added a list of further readings and a list of online resources.

This is not a critical book about advertising, although it does reflect some of my own views on the effects of advertising that I interspersed in other publications. There are many excellent works currently on the market that look at the psychological and social implications of advertising that the reader can consult. Some of these are listed in the further readings section at the back. Nor is this book designed to be a comprehensive, in-depth analysis of advertising methods. It is intended, simply, as a practical guide on how messages and meanings can be woven into and extracted from advertising representations, from brand naming, logo design, to the strategy of placing brands as props in movies and television programs. The approach I have employed, discussed, and illustrated throughout is intended to give only an initial glimpse into what semiotics has to offer to the study of advertising, at least as I see it. It can also be used in high school, college, and university courses preparing students for careers in advertising, marketing, and media.

I wish to thank the many advertisers, marketers, and companies who have allowed me to conduct research on their ad campaigns. There are too many to list here. I also wish to thank Victoria College of the University of Toronto, where I teach and direct its Program in Semiotics and Communication Theory, for all the support that it has given to the serious study of semiotics over the years and the countless number of students I have had the privilege of meeting and interacting over the almost four decades of teaching. In addition, I wish to thank Bruce Owens for a wonderful copyediting job and Janice Braunstein for her work on the production of this book. Finally, I must thank my wonderful family for putting up with me and my constant pontifications about the state of the world. I dedicate this book to them.

1

What Is Advertising?

Ideally, advertising aims at the goal of a programmed harmony among all human impulses and aspirations and endeavors. Using handicraft methods, it stretches out toward the ultimate electronic goal of a collective consciousness.

—Marshall McLuhan, 1911–1980

Print ads fill the pages of newspapers and magazines. Posters appear in buses, subways, and trains and on city walls. Streets and roadsides are dotted by neon signs and billboards. Commercials interrupt television and radio programs constantly. Ads pop up unwanted on Web pages. There are even television channels, magazines, and other media that are exclusively concerned with advertising. In a phrase, advertising is everywhere. No wonder that brand names, logos, trademarks, jingles, and slogans have become part and parcel of the mental lexicon of virtually everyone who lives in a modern-day society. Since the early 1960s, advertising has even become the main vehicle for publicizing matters of social concern, from antismoking to antipoverty campaigns. And, needless to say, the use of advertising in the political arena seems to know no bounds. Politicians at all levels of government now communicate their platforms during political campaigns and their personal perspectives on social issues regularly through sleek persuasive forms of advertising.

To say that advertising has become a ubiquitous form of message making in today's global market culture is an understatement. It is estimated that the average American is exposed to over 3,000 advertisements a day and watches three years' worth of television commercials over the course of a lifetime (Kilbourne 1999). Using both verbal and nonverbal techniques to make its messages as persuasive as possible, advertising has become an integral category of modern-day life designed to influence attitudes and lifestyle behaviors by covertly suggesting how we can best satisfy our innermost urges and aspirations.

The study of advertising has become a hugely popular one in various disciplines, including psychology, semiotics, anthropology, culture studies, communication science, and sociology—each approaching it from its own particular purview. The basic focus of this book is semiotics—the discipline that focuses on how signs (such as brand names) and texts (such as ads and commercials) generate meaning and how they connect with the network of meanings present in a culture. This chapter has two main purposes (among a few others): to sketch a history of advertising as a backdrop to the discussion that will ensue and to introduce some basic notions that will be used throughout.

DEFINING ADVERTISING

The term **advertising** has come down to us from the medieval Latin verb *advertere*, "to direct one's attention to." In line with its etymology, it can thus be defined as any type or form of public announcement intended to direct people's attention to the availability, qualities, and cost of specific commodities or services. The emergence of advertising in social life has a straightforward explanation—people need to know about the existence of products and services and what they offer to them. And indeed, sales of a product are enhanced in relation to the amount and type of public exposure that it receives. Modern advertising has, however, progressed considerably beyond the use of simple techniques for announcing product or service availability. In the twentieth century, it evolved into a form of persuasion intended to influence how people perceived products, not on their own terms but in terms of what they signified psychologically or socially. Over the century, it became (and has remained) a form of rhetorical discourse that rose to challenge (and in various ways even replace) the more traditional forms of discourse—sermons, political oratory, proverbs, wise sayings, and the like—that in previous centuries had rhetorical force and moral authority. Advertising discourse exalts and inculcates Epicurean values. And this has had concrete consequences. The French semiotician Roland Barthes (1915–1980) coined the term *neomania* to refer to the consequences of living in a consumerist society bombarded constantly by advertising messages, defining it as an insatiable appetite for new objects of consumption, regardless of whether they are needed or not. Neomania has been induced by the subtexts that uphold advertising messages: buy this or that, and you will be happy, successful, beautiful, safe, and so on.

The overarching message in such subtextual messages is that solutions to human problems can be found in buying and consuming. As Barry Hoffman (2002: 4) has aptly observed in this regard,

> Most people who grew up in the last fifty years find it hard to get a clear fix on what's old and what's new. It feels like the only thing that is constant is the ever-increasing rate of change. Fads, fashions, trends and movements blow through our days like wind through an unstable weather system. Lines that were etched in stone become lines drawn in the sand.

Advertising has evolved into a combination of art and science. It is an art because it employs the same types of techniques that artists, musicians, and poets do; it is a science because it relies on marketing science, psychological research methods, and statistics to assess the effects of its techniques on consumer behavior. Advertising and marketing agencies are now one enterprise. They conduct extensive and expensive surveys to determine the efficacy of various strategies such as brand names and ad campaigns. This partnership is the reason why today the term *advertising* refers to not only the activity of making ads, commercials, and ad campaigns but also any other activity that will enhance the appeal and potential sales of a product, including the creation of a name for the product, the design of a logo for it, the creation of a slogan for it, and the like. It would indeed be meaningless to advertise products without some distinctive identifier or identifiers like a brand name and a trademark.

Propaganda and Public Relations

Advertising is only one of the modern-day persuasive crafts. Two other common ones are propaganda and public relations:

- **Propaganda** is the craft of spreading and entrenching doctrines, views, beliefs, and so on reflecting specific interests and ideologies (for example, political, social, or philosophical).
- **Public relations** is the profession employing activities and techniques designed to establish favorable attitudes and responses toward organizations, institutions, and/or individuals on the part of the general public or special groups.

Like advertising, propaganda is one-sided communication designed to influence people's views, opinions, beliefs, and actions. Often the line between the two is a blurry one. A television commercial or a poster urging people to vote for a political candidate might be much more than an advertising text.

Depending on its method of persuasion or overall subtext, it might be a form of propaganda designed to reflect a particular political ideology. In this book, propaganda and advertising will be considered as distinct modes of persuasion. However, there is much overlap between the two.

Public relations, commonly abbreviated to PR, is the craft that aims to increase communication and understanding between some organization or individual and the public (or some segment thereof). The mode of communication can range from a simple news release to a sophisticated campaign featuring films, advertisements, and the like. PR is practiced through corporate departments, agencies, and public information departments. PR specialists use several methods to communicate with the public. Among these are advertising, lobbying, and publicity. The same kinds of techniques used by advertisers of products are used by PR specialists to impart a positive attitude toward their organization or individual. Lobbying is the craft of influencing legislators to support the interests of a group. Publicity involves promoting an organization or individual by getting favorable coverage in the media.

PR originated in the late 1800s, when rapid and unchecked industrial expansion had brought about the perception that some businesses did not operate with the best interest of the public in mind. Severe criticism of business practices ensued. As a consequence, corporations began to set up programs designed to win the public's favor. Since the 1950s, PR has been incorporated into the organizational fold by every large corporate and nonprofit organization. And the growth and expansion of mass communication media have tended to make PR a more powerful strategy than ever before.

Main Types of Advertising

Advertising falls into three main categories: 1) **consumer advertising**, which is directed toward the promotion of some product or service to the general public (or market segment thereof); 2) **trade advertising**, which is directed to dealers and professionals through appropriate trade publications and media; and 3) **political-social advertising**, which is used by special-interest groups (such as antismoking groups) and politicians to advertise their platforms. The focus of this book is on the first type, which can be defined more specifically as any strategy designed to promote the sale of marketable goods and services.

Consumer advertising gave birth to the first agency for recording and analyzing data on advertising effectiveness in 1914 with the establishment of the Audit Bureau of Circulations in the United States, an independent organization founded and supported by newspaper and magazine publishers wishing to obtain circulation statistics and to standardize the ways of presenting them. Then, in 1936, the Advertising Research Foundation was established to conduct research on advertising techniques so that they could be made to be more effective and to gauge the effects of advertising on people. Today, the increasing sophistication with statistical information-gathering techniques, along with sophisticated online technology, makes it possible for advertisers to target audiences on the basis of where people live, what income they make, what educational background they have, and so on in order to determine their susceptibility to or inclination toward certain advertising pitches, styles, and messages.

A HISTORICAL SKETCH

It is believed that outdoor signs displayed above the shop doors of ancient cities of the Middle East were among the first ads of human civilization. As early as 3000 B.C.E., the Babylonians, who lived in what is now Iraq, used such signs to advertise the stores themselves. Few people could read, and so the merchants used symbols carved in stone, clay, or wood for the signs. The drawing of a bush, for example, indicated a wine shop, and the figure of a boot advertised a shoemaker's shop. These were the first *trademarks*. Trademarks can be deciphered by anyone, literate or not. They were, literally, "marks" of the "trade" so that people could easily identify the nature of the goods sold in shops. The ancient Greeks and Romans also hung signs outside their shops. Among the best-known trademarks surviving from the medieval period are the striped pole of the barbershop and the three-ball sign of the pawnbroker shop. Some products, such as swords and pottery, were also marked with identifiable visual marks so that buyers could trace their origin and determine their quality.

A poster found in Thebes in 1000 B.C.E. is a relic of one of the world's first print ads. In large letters, it offered a whole gold coin for the capture of a runaway slave. Archaeologists have found similar kinds of posters scattered all over ancient societies. On a wall in Pompeii, for example, a poster was found that called the attention of travelers to a tavern located in a different town. Throughout history, poster advertising in marketplaces and temples has, in fact, constituted a popular means of disseminating information and of promoting the barter and sale of goods. In addition, word-of-mouth praise of products by so-called town criers (who went to the market square on behalf of shops or businesses), was also used to great advantage. In ancient Egypt, for instance, criers walked through the streets of cities broadcasting the arrivals of ships and their cargo at the tops of their voices.

The Age of Print

The use of shop signs, posters, and criers continued uninterrupted right into medieval times, to the great advantage of the merchants of that era. But it was the invention of the modern printing press by Johannes Gutenberg (ca. 1400–1468) in the fifteenth century that transformed advertising into a craft of persuasion once and for all. Gutenberg's invention made the printed word available to masses of people. Fliers and posters could be printed quickly and cheaply and posted in public places or inserted in books, pamphlets, newspapers, and so on. The printing press also spawned a new form of advertising known as the *handbill*. This had an advantage over a poster or sign because it could be reproduced and distributed to many people living near and far apart. But more important, as the "Age of Print" progressed, advertising texts were being stylized so as to make them more attractive and persuasive.

By the latter part of the seventeenth century, when newspapers were beginning to circulate widely, print advertising was being used, more and more, in tandem with publications designed for other purposes. Advertising was fast becoming an intrinsic part of the "Gutenberg Galaxy," as the Canadian communications theorist Marshall McLuhan (1911–1980) characterized the radical new social order that ensued from print technology. The written page, with its edges, margins, and sharply defined characters organized in neatly layered rows or columns, induces a linear-rational way of thinking in people. Advertising texts thus came to be viewed as *rational* statements about the *objective* qualities of products, independently of the makers of these products and of their pecuniary motives.

The *London Gazette* became the first newspaper to reserve a section exclusively for advertising. So successful was this venture that by the end of the seventeenth century several agencies came into existence for the specific purpose of creating newspaper ads for merchants and artisans. In general, they designed the texts in the style of modern classifieds, without illustrative support. But the ads nonetheless had all the persuasive rhetorical flavor of their contemporary descendants. The ad makers of the era catered to the wealthy clients who bought and read newspapers, promoting the sale of tea, coffee, wigs, books, theater tickets, and the like. The following advertisement for toothpaste dates back to a 1660 ad published in the *Gazette*. What is captivating about it is the fact that its rhetorical style is virtually identical to the one used today for the promotion of this type of product (cited by Dyer 1982: 16–17):

> Most excellent and proved Dentifrice to scour and cleanse the Teeth, making them white as ivory, preserves the Tooth-ach; so that being constantly used, the Parties using it are never troubled with the Tooth-ach. It fastens the Teeth,

sweetens the Breath, and preserves the Gums and Mouth from cankers and Im-
pothumes, and the right are only to be had at Thomas Rookes, Stationer.

The creator of the ad describes the dentifrice not simply in terms of its ingredients and qualities but also as being "excellent" and "proved," implying
that scientific testing has been conducted on the product. For this reason, the
dentifrice will make teeth "white as ivory" and allow the user to overcome
toothache, cankers, and other buccal maladies. The ad also suggests, by innuendo, that the dentifrice will enhance the social life of its users because it
"sweetens the Breath."

Print advertising spread rapidly throughout the eighteenth century in both
Europe and America, proliferating to the point that the writer and lexicogra-
pher Samuel Johnson (1709–1784) felt impelled to make the following statement in *The Idler*: "Advertisements are now so numerous that they are very
negligently perused, and it is therefore become necessary to gain attention by
magnificence of promise and by eloquence sometimes sublime and sometimes pathetic" (cited by Panati 1984: 168).

With the advent of industrialization in the nineteenth century, rhetorical advertising took on an increasingly important role as a means for manufacturers to coax people into buying their products in an increasingly competitive
marketplace. Ad layouts were created more and more to be eye-catching. The
words were set out in attractive fonts; compact sentences were employed to
make a pitch sound more informal, colloquial, humorous, and personal; and
illustrations were added to emphasize the ad's message visually. Advertising
copy was being designed more and more, as Dyer (1982: 32) notes, "to attract
attention to a product." Advertising was slowly evolving into an art of persuasion, surreptitiously starting even to influence everyday discourse, as
more and more people became exposed to ad messages in newspapers, in
magazines, and on posters, using the particular phraseology of ad slogans to
refer to all kinds of topics.

As print advertising started becoming a fixture of the social landscape in the
preindustrialized world, ad creators began paying more attention to the design
and layout of the ad text. With the advent of industrialization in the nineteenth
century, *style of presentation* became increasingly important in raising the persuasive efficacy of the ad text. The syntactically cumbersome and visually un-
interesting ads of the previous century were replaced more and more by layouts using words set out in blocks, compact sentences, and contrasting type
fonts. New language forms were coined regularly to fit the needs of the manufacturer. As a consequence, advertising was surreptitiously starting to change
the very structure and use of language and verbal communication as more and
more people became exposed to advertising in newspapers, in magazines, on

posters, and the like. Everything from clothes to beverages was being promoted through ingenious new techniques that included the following:

- Strategic repetitions of the firm's name or of the product in the composition of the ad text
- The use of compact phrases set in eye-catching patterns (vertically, hor-
  izontally, and diagonally)
- The use of contrasting font styles and formats, along with supporting illustrations
- The creation of slogans and neologisms designed to highlight some quality of the product

As the nineteenth century came to a close, American advertisers in particular were, as Dyer (1982: 32) aptly points out, using "more colloquial, personal and informal language to address the customer" and also exploiting certain effective rhetorical devices including "the uses of humour to attract
attention to a product." So persuasive had this new form of advertising become that, by the early decades of the twentieth century, it started changing
the perception of commodities from practical objects to "signs" standing for
lifestyle, social values, and other such things. The era saw the institutional-
ization of the advertising agency, which was essentially an organization
whose goal it was to ensure that products were perceived to be more than just
products. By the first decades of the century, such agencies had become themselves large business enterprises, constantly developing new techniques and
methods to get people to think of products as signs of great value to their
lives. The following advice, given by one of the early advertising agents (a
man named Claude Hopkins) to prospective ad copywriters in the early part
of the century, is typical of the mind-set of advertising that was fomenting
(cited in Bendinger 1988: 14):

> Don't think of people in the mass. That gives you a blurred view. Think of a typi-
> cal individual, man or woman, who is likely to want what you sell. The advertising
> man studies the consumer. He tries to place himself in the position of the buyer. His
> success largely depends on doing that to the exclusion of everything else.

Modern Advertising

The first advertising agency was established by Philadelphia entrepreneur
Volney B. Palmer in 1842. By 1849, Palmer had offices in New York, Boston,
and Baltimore in addition to his Philadelphia office. In 1865, George P. Rowell began contracting with local newspapers as a go-between with clients. Ten

years later, in 1875, N. W. Ayer and Son, another Philadelphia advertising agency, became a rival of Rowell and Palmer. In time, the firm hired writers and artists to create print ads and carried out complete advertising campaigns for clients. It thus became the first ad agency in the modern sense of the word. By 1900, most agencies in the United States were writing ads for clients and were starting to assume responsibility for complete advertising campaigns. From the 1920s on, everything from product name, design, and packaging came gradually within the purview of the ad agency—and it still is, although many firms now have their own advertising departments. Aware of the growing power of advertising, the American government established the Federal Trade Commission in 1914 to help monitor advertising practices. The "Age of Advertising" had crystallized and is still going strong.

In the 1920s, the increased use of electricity led to the possibility of further entrenching advertising into the social landscape through the use of new electronic media. Electricity made possible the illuminated outdoor poster; photo-engraving and other printing inventions helped both the editorial and the advertising departments of magazines create truly effective illustrative material that could be incorporated into ad texts. The advent of radio, also in the 1920s, led to the invention and widespread use of a new form of advertising known as the *commercial*—a mininarrative or musical jingle revolving around a product or service and its uses. The commercial became immediately a highly entertaining form of advertising since it could reach masses of potential customers, print literate or not, instantaneously. Early commercials, such as Folger's coffee's pseudoscientific sales pitches, Mum Deodorant's satires of spy movies, and Pepsodent toothpaste's snappy jingles, became so familiar that perception of the product became inextricably intertwined with the style and content of the commercials created to promote it. The commercial also created the first advertising personalities, from Mr. Clean (representing a detergent product of the same name) to Speedy (a personified Alka-Seltzer tablet).

Advertising quickly became an intrinsic part of television in the 1950s, giving visual form to the commercial. And, of course, the Internet has itself spawned a whole new array of advertising forms and strategies, from pop-ups to banners (as will be discussed in chapter 2). The Internet is where advertising is starting to move more and more. The big ad campaign philosophy of marketers, spreading the message through large media campaigns, is probably a thing of the past. As Andrew Goodman (2005: 5) perceptively writes, "Thanks in large part to Google's efforts, search engine advertising is now the leading engine of growth." Off-line advertising currently eclipses online advertising by a considerable margin (as I write in early 2007). But this will change. It is, in fact, a salient characteristic of advertising strategy to adopt new technology in a creative way and to jump ahead of the line, so to speak,

in mass communications. Advertisers were among the first to use print technology creatively, as we saw previously, and, of course, they were among the
first to use the new electronic technologies, the radio and television, which
were used as creative canvases to promote their advertising aesthetics. There
has always been a synergy between advertisers and technology.

Overall, modern-day advertising has turned shopping into a form of recre-
ation rather than a means of acquiring essentials for daily living. It is becoming more and more an end in itself. No wonder, then, that the shopping malls
are filled with thrill seekers who would otherwise become stir crazy. And all
this has been brought about, arguably, by the type of persuasion techniques
used by advertising, many of which are designed to speak indirectly to the unconscious level of mind where the Freudian id—the unconscious part of the
psyche actuated by fundamental impulses toward fulfilling instinctual
needs—can be accessed unwittingly. The sense of touch and smell, which are
largely downplayed in our culture, are frequently evoked in an ad text through
synesthesia—as we shall see in a subsequent chapter—so as to induce an unconscious desire for the product by sensory association. As Freudian psycho-
analysis has always emphasized, any one of the unconscious tendencies that
a culture represses systematically can be manipulated and actuated easily by
persuasion techniques into motivating forces and drives. As Berger (2005: 75)
aptly points out, advertising works on the id because that is where desires ("I
want it now") gain force:

> Advertising agencies and companies involved in consumer products appeal to
> the id elements of people, seeking to generate an emotional appeal that leads in-
> dividuals to overcome the strictures of their superegos and purchase things be-
> cause they get pleasure (or anticipate pleasure) from doing this.

The superego, in Freudian theory, is the conscience part of the psyche ("You
can't afford it"), and the ego is the reflective intellect ("Why don't you think
about it before buying it?").

ADVERTISING AND SOCIETY

Already in 1922, newspaper columnist Walter Lippmann published a controversial book, *Public Opinion*, in which he illustrated how slogans and other
advertising devices shaped public perception. Following on Lippmann's coat-
tails, in 1957, Vance Packard wrote *The Hidden Persuaders*, which warned
people about advertising's power as a surreptitious form of persuasion. It became a best-seller, initiated a spate of studies about advertising's effects on
society, and inspired movements against advertising and mass consumerism.

Although no consensus has yet been reached as to advertising's effects on the ethos and mores of people living in consumerist cultures, it is certainly true that the modern world would be vastly different if advertising had not evolved into the art of persuasion that it has become. Ironically, advertising started being used, shortly thereafter, by both right-wing groups, who attacked it for promoting secular humanism and promiscuity, and left-wing ones, who attacked it instead for deceitfully influencing and promoting stereotypical role models and unabashed consumerism. Measures were soon taken. In 1971, for instance, tobacco ads were banned from television. They were banned from billboards in 1998. All this proves, paradoxically, that advertising is indeed an effective form of persuasion. The language of advertising has become the language of all—even of those who are critical of it. As Twitchell (2000: 1) aptly puts it, "Language about products and services has pretty much replaced language about all other subjects." Advertising has become one of the most ubiquitous, all-encompassing forms of persuasion ever devised by humans.

Advertisers are also among the most creative users of new technologies. Since young people are highly expert Internet users, advertisers are using this new medium in ways that are pushing advertising techniques in new and interesting directions. On the site for Barbie dolls, for instance, visitors are invited to design their own doll and then buy it. At the Hot Wheels website, visitors are invited to play games and then buy the toy cars. No wonder, then, that advertising has become an issue of debate and a target of legislation across the world. For example, in some countries, the law prohibits or restricts the use of women simply to attract attention in advertisements unless the product is relevant for women as consumers. In other countries, advertising for sanitary products and toilet paper is forbidden. Clearly, in the global village some cultures are scrambling to protect themselves against the images that emanate from the advertising image factory—images that emphasize sex, attractiveness, youth, and pop culture trends that have become routine and part of the global village.

Synergy

The term *synergy* is used a lot these days, especially in the business world. Although it has variable meanings, in advertising it alludes to a simple strategy—tapping into cultural trends and then mirroring them in the style and content of advertising forms and strategies, from brand naming to the design of ads. Already in the 1920s, advertisers started to pay close attention to trends in the ever-expanding pop culture world, often using, in the form of jingles and slogans, the same kinds of popular musical and linguistic styles found in that world. In that era, people listened to radio as much for the commercials as for the programs.

Today, advertising has established itself a virtually complete synergy with cultural trends. This synergy makes it possible for advertising to be in a constant "adaptive mode," so to speak, creating a dynamic interplay between advertising style and social lifestyle whereby one influences the other through a constant synergy. This macrostrategy today thus makes it possible for manufacturers to ensure that any fad can be reflected in the product as well and that changes in social trends (fashion, music, values, popularity of media personalities, and so on) can be reflected in ads and commercials.

Modern-day advertising can be defined as persuasion attained through synergy. This can take many forms and manifest itself in many ways. Common synergistic ploys used by advertisers include the use of endorsements by celebrities to make a product appear reliable, the incorporation of social trends (in fashion, music, and so on) into ad campaigns, and a general socially sensitive approach to advertising. The sensitivity can be demographic (responding to the worldviews of baby boomers, teenagers, and so on) or geographic—for example, the use of sexual themes in the promotion of a product would be attenuated or removed in a global advertising campaign so as to avoid offending societies where sexuality is not expressed openly.

The concept of *emergent code* is sometimes used to describe the overall effects of the synergy that now characterizes advertising—a concept taken from the work of the late culture critic Raymond Williams (1921–1988). The concept is based on the fact that cultural behaviors and codes can be subdivided into *dominant*, *residual*, and *emergent*. The dominant code is the set of ideas, values, lifestyles, and so on that define the current or middle-of-the-road norms, residual codes are those that were dominant in the past but are still around in minor ways, and emergent codes are those that will dictate future norms but that reveal their elements in bits and pieces at the present time. The most effective ad campaigns are those that tap into the emergent codes of a culture (in lifestyle, in music trends, and so on). The idea is to incorporate them directly into ads and ad campaigns so that the brand is always up to date.

Coca-Cola was one of the first brands to use an early and basic form of synergy—namely, by imprinting its logo on drinking glasses and providing them to diners and other eateries that featured foods meant to be eaten quickly and cheaply. Since then, Coca-Cola has used the simple yet effective strategy of co-opting any emergent code. It has consistently kept itself in synch with relevant cultural trends, such as the brotherly love and peace theme that was relevant in the counterculture era of the late 1960s and early 1970s with its "I'd like to teach the world to sing in perfect harmony" campaign and its "Coke is the real thing" campaign shortly thereafter.

Mirroring humor styles and the emergent comedic formulas has also been an intrinsic part of the ad campaign strategies of many brands for at least three decades. Examples in 2005 were Dairy Queen's commercials of a baby trying to steal his father's Cheesecake Sundae, a man who started fires after eating a Flamethrower Burger, the Six Flags commercials featuring a bald old man in a tuxedo driving his vintage bus into neighborhoods and then dancing joyfully to the catchy tune "We want to party," and Budweiser's "Whassup?" series of commercials.

These techniques have become so intrinsic to the art of advertising that they are no longer recognized consciously as synergistic stratagems. Advertising has become, in effect, an integral component of an entertainment-based society that seeks artifice, fantasy, and spectacle as part of its routine of escapism from the deeper philosophical questions that would otherwise beset it. Advertising is powerful because it offers the hope of more money and better jobs, security against the hazards of old age and illness, popularity and personal prestige, praise from others, more comfort, increased enjoyment, social advancement, improved appearance, better health, erotic stimulation, and so on. The effectiveness of the techniques used to generate such messages is limited only by the ingenuity of the advertiser, by the limits of the various channels of communications, by certain legal restrictions, and by standards self-imposed by the advertising industry.

The synergy between advertising and society is, arguably, the cause for many (if not most) fads. Without effective advertising, fads such as hula hoops, troll dolls, pet rocks, smurf toys, Teenage Mutant Ninja Turtles, Mighty Morphin Power Rangers, sudoku, and iPods would never have come about in the first place. Some fads are so intertwined with the advertising–society synergistic nexus that they have the capacity to generate mass hysteria. A case in point is the Cabbage Patch doll craze of 1983. Scalpers offered the suddenly and unexplainably out-of-stock dolls (a marketing ploy?) for hundreds of dollars through the classified ads. Grown adults fought each other in lineups to get one of the few remaining dolls left in stock at some mall toy outlet. In a *Newsweek* article of that year, titled "Oh, You Beautiful Dolls," we read the following (cited in Berger 2005: 82):

> It was as if an army had been turned loose on the nation's shopping malls, braving the *Ficus* trees, sloshing through the fountains, searching for the legendary stockrooms said to be filled with thousands of the dough-faced, chinless, engagingly homely dolls that have become the Holy Grail of the 1983 Christmas shopping season: the Cabbage Patch Kids. Clerks were helpless before the onslaught.

How could a simple doll have caused such mass hysteria? It is instructive to note, incidentally, that the Cabbage Patch dolls came with "adoption papers." Each doll was given a name—taken at random from 1938 state of

Georgia birth records—which, like any act of naming, conferred on it a humanlike personality. And, thanks to computerized manufacturing, no two dolls were alike. Each doll was an ersatz child who was adopted into the family as a sibling. No wonder, then, that the Cabbage Patch episode was fraught with so much hysteria. Parents did not buy a simple doll; they bought their child another member of the family, in much the same way that Egyptian parents got their children a doll for companionship.

Although the Cabbage Patch episode was extraordinary, it was not out of whack with the faddish nature of toy-giving generally. Toys, as the name of a major toy chain overtly puts it, are indeed Us. It has always been assumed, for instance, that little girls want to play with dolls. This led to an early form of synergy between advertisers of dolls and social trends with regard to femininity. Since the 1950s, in fact, the association of lifelike dolls with female childhood has been entrenched by both the quantity of doll types produced and their promotion in the media. Since their launch in 1959, "Barbie" dolls, for example, have become part of the experience of growing up for many little girls in North America. Incidentally, Barbies also started the trend of fashionable clothing and accessories for dolls, thus enhancing their humanoid nature even more. Barbie has also been designed to reflect many varied occupations over her history—astronaut, athlete, ballerina, businesswoman, dancer, dentist, doctor, firefighter, paleontologist, police officer, lead singer of a rock band (Barbie and the Rockets), and even UNICEF volunteer. Each of her occupational phases reflected a changing perception of American womanhood. Barbie continues to be faddish because she keeps in step with the times.

Interestingly, Barbie's faddishness started sagging in 2001 with the debut of the Bratz dolls, which have a new brassy feminine look, with bare midriffs, sequins, fur, and eye shadow. The sexual suggestiveness of the dolls is transparent, emphasized especially by "trashy clothing" (halter tops, faux-fur armlets, and ankle-laced stiletto sandals) and cosmetics (eye shadow and dark lip liner). Bratz dolls have become fads because they are perfect for the times. They have tapped into the knack of young girls to assume a "sassy" "Lolita-like" look, in synch with the look of current female celebrities. School boards across America have prohibited them. Simply put, they do not meet school dress codes.

Fetishism

Dolls (and toys generally) are fetishes, objects perceived to possess a life force. In traditional tribal cultures, the **fetish** is typically a figure modeled or carved from clay, stone, wood, or some other material, resembling a deified animal or some sacred thing. Sometimes it is the animal itself or a tree, river, rock, or place associated with it. In some societies, belief in the powers of the fetish is so strong that it becomes an idol. This is perhaps why the term fetishism is often applied in our society to describe sexual fantasies that involve the use of objects (such as shoes, stockings, and so on) that stand erotically for some part of the human body.

Fads are evidence that fetishism is not limited to tribal or premodern cultures. On the contrary, it is alive and well in consumerist cultures. In the 1970s, for example, American society went mad for "pet rocks." Many considered the fad a ploy foisted on a gullible public spoiled by consumerism by a crafty manufacturer and thus simply a quick way for that manufacturer to make money. But the fad could not have been perpetrated in the first place unless some psychic force was at work—and that force was fetishism. The same tendencies can be seen in the common view held by people that some objects are unexplainably magical. This is why, if they are lost, then impending danger is feared. If, however, they are found serendipitously—as, for instance, when one finds a "lucky penny"—then it is believed that the gods or fortune will look auspiciously on the finder.

Advertising culture is a fetishistic culture—one in which objects of consumption are revered in the same way that religious icons and sexual fetishes are. It is a result of the advertising–culture synergy that has been operative since at least the 1920s. Fads such as pet rocks could have come about only as a result of the "fetishizing" effects that this synergy has produced. The fetishism of commercial products has even spawned its own art forms and movements. One of these, called *pop art* (short for *populist art*), emerged shortly after World War II. It was inspired directly by the mass production and consumption of objects. For pop artists, the factory, supermarket, and garbage can became their art school. But despite its apparent absurdity, many people loved pop art no matter how controversial or crass it appeared to be. In a certain sense, the pop art movement bestowed on common people the assurance that art was for mass consumption, not just for an elite class of cognoscenti. Some artists duplicated beer bottles, soup cans, comic strips, road signs, and similar objects in paintings, collages, and sculptures; others simply incorporated the objects themselves into their works. Using images and sounds that reflected the materialism and vulgarity of modern consumerist culture, the first pop artists sought to provide a view of reality that was more immediate and relevant than that of past art. They wanted the observer to respond directly to the object rather than to the skill and viewpoint of the artist. In a phrase, they put the advertising-induced fetishism on display and on a critical platform for people to recognize and discuss. As Hoffman (2002: 8) insightfully muses,

Pop art made advertising its subject. Pop's critics saw that as the essential problem. "Pop's social effect," Hilton Kramer said, "is simply to reconcile us to a world of commodities, banalities, and vulgarities" — which is to say, an effect indistinguishable from advertising art." Pop art did take its spirit from the bold, bald clarity of the advertising aesthetic. It sang the praises of commercial art with tunes of irony and respect.

The pop art movement surfaced in the 1940s and 1950s, when painters like Robert Rauschenberg (1925–) and Jasper Johns (1930–) strove to close the gap between traditional art and mass culture. Rauschenberg constructed collages from household objects such as quilts and pillows, Johns from American flags and bull's-eye targets. The first full-fledged pop art work was *Just What Is It That Makes Today's Home So Different, So Appealing?* (1956, private collection) by the British artist Richard Hamilton. In this satiric collage of two ludicrous figures in a living room, the pop art hallmarks of crudeness and irony are emphasized.

Pop art developed rapidly during the 1960s as painters started to focus their attention on brand-name commercial products, producing garish sculptures of hamburgers and other fast-food items, blown-up frames of comic strips, or theatrical events staged as art objects. Pop artists also appropriated the techniques of mass production. Rauschenberg and Johns had already abandoned individual, titled paintings in favor of large series of works, all depicting the same objects. In the early 1960s, the American Andy Warhol (1928–1987) carried the idea a step further by adopting the mass-production technique of silk screening, turning out hundreds of identical prints of Coca-Cola bottles, Campbell's soup cans, and other familiar subjects, including identical three-dimensional Brillo boxes.

STUDYING ADVERTISING

Given the obvious influence of advertising on the development of modern culture, the French semiotician Roland Barthes (mentioned previously) drew attention in the 1950s to the value of studying its techniques with the theoretical tools of **semiotics**. After the publication of his pivotal book *Mythologies* in 1957, a new branch of research sprang up not only in semiotics but in other disciplines as well, focusing on how advertising generates its meanings, animating, at the same time, a society-wide debate on the broader questions raised by the entrenchment of advertising in contemporary society. Particularly worrisome to Barthes was the fact that the constant change in advertising styles, techniques, and modes of delivery tended to create an incessant craving for new goods. He called this culturally induced state of mind "neomania," which he defined simply as an obsessive desire for new objects of consumption. Barthes also criticized caustically the fact that advertising proposes marketplace solutions to social problems, elevating shopping to much more than just acquiring the essentials required for daily living.

The Semiotic Approach

Modern-day semiotic method is based on the writings of the American logician Charles S. Peirce (1839–1914) and the French linguist Ferdinand de Saussure (1857–1913). The reason why semiotics lends itself well not only to the critique of advertising but also as a source of insight into the making of advertisements and commercials is because it provides the theoretical tools, developed largely by Saussure and Peirce, for understanding how we encode and decode meaning from the **representations** we make. It explains, in other words, why something sells.

For the sake of historical accuracy, it should be mentioned that semiotics grew out of the study by the ancient physicians of the Western world of the physiological symptoms produced by particular diseases. The term *semiotics* (spelled originally *semeiotics*), from Greek *semeion* "mark, sign," was coined by the founder of Western medical science, Hippocrates (460–377 B.C.E.). A *symptom* is, in fact, a perfect example of what a *semeion* is. It is a noticeable sign—such as a dark bruise, a rash, or a sore throat—that stands for some physical condition—such as a broken finger, a skin allergy, or a cold. Medical science is, in effect, basic semiotic science since it is grounded on the principle that the symptom is a trace to an inner state, condition, and so on. The fundamental thing to notice about the *semeion* is that it consists of two parts—the discernible symptom itself and the probable condition it indicates. The two are inseparable: that is, there is no symptom that is not caused by some bodily condition, and, vice versa, there is no condition that does not produce symptoms (detectable or not). The *semeion* is a *natural sign*, that is, a sign produced by nature. But humans have also produced their own signs—words, gestures, and symbols—that can stand for all kinds of things. These are called *conventional signs* since they are invented by human beings in cultural settings for conventionalized purposes. Like natural signs, they also consist of two parts: 1) a physical part—the sounds or letters that make up a word such as *cat*—and 2) the entity, object, being, event, and so on that the physical part has been designed to stand for, whether it be real or imagined. The former is called the **signifier**. The term **representamen** is sometimes used in semiotic theory in lieu of *signifier*. Only *signifier* will be used in this book. The latter is called *signified*. This is, in effect, the meaning captured by the sign.

The method of inquiry used in semiotics is a dialectic one: that is, it consists of a series of question designed to flesh out the meaning of something. Some of these are the following:

- Who or what created the sign?
- What does it mean?
- How does it deliver its meaning?
- What medium (verbal, nonverbal, and so on) was employed?
- For whom was it intended, or how did it come about?
- In what context does it occur?
- To what system of meaning does it belong?
- How many interpretations are possible under the circumstances?

For the sake of historical accuracy, it should be mentioned that it was St. Augustine (354–430 C.E.), the philosopher and religious thinker, who distinguished between the signs found in nature as *natural*—the colors of leaves, the shape of plants, the physiology of symptoms, and so on—and those made by humans as *conventional*. St. Augustine also proposed that in every human sign there exists an implicit *interpretive* dimension that constrains its meaning. This was consistent with the so-called *hermeneutic* tradition established earlier by Clement of Alexandria (ca. 150–215 C.E.), the Greek theologian and early Father of the Church. **Hermeneutics** is the study and interpretation of ancient texts, especially those of a religious or mythical nature. Today, it is a branch of semiotics aiming to study how all texts generate meaning. The idea is to establish, as far as possible, the meaning that a text entails on the basis of symbolic considerations, relevant sources, and historical background.

The premise that guides semiotic analysis is that the recurring patterns that characterize sign systems are reflective of innate *structures* in the sensory, emotional, and intellectual composition of the human body and the human psyche—hence the term *structuralism* in the literature to refer to semiotic method. This would explain why the forms of expression that humans create and to which they respond instinctively the world over are so meaningful and so easily understandable across cultures. In recent years, a *poststructuralist* school of thought has emerged within semiotics, receiving some attention, especially among the users of semiotic theory. The leading figure of this school is the late French semiotician and philosopher Jacques Derrida (1930–2004). The main premise in poststructuralism is that signs and texts have a constantly changing meaning. But poststructuralism has produced very few usable results in reforming basic semiotic method. Its most beneficial effect on semiotics has been to make analysts more aware of the subjectivity that interpretation invariably entails.

In the study of advertising, semiotics has shown itself to be a useful general dialectic framework for decoding meanings. It will be used here as well in a general way. To grasp how this framework can be used, consider the Playboy logo, a cartoon-like icon of a rabbit head with a bow tie.

Using the previously listed questions as guides, we can start by asking ourselves, What does a rabbit mean in our culture? The rabbit is a pet, an animal kept for companionship, interest, or amusement. In a figurative sense, it also means somebody who is indulged or loved. In verb form (*to pet*), it means to stroke indulgently or to touch in a way that causes sexual pleasure. No doubt, this set of meanings is latent in the logo, given its pet symbolism. As a bunny, moreover, the pet represented by the logo also imparts a feeling of intimacy and childlike pleasure. Petting a bunny evokes this feeling.

As a symbol of the Playboy bunny, there is little doubt that all these associations are evoked, at least subconsciously, and their sexual designations become rather clear when considered in this light. Rabbits, moreover, are sexually active (promiscuous?). The rabbit ears of the logo, in the shape of a "V," also suggest a female sexual pose (the spreading of the legs?), and the round, facial part of the logo (without a mouth) is suggestive of another part of female anatomy (the woman's behind?). The bow tie is what Playboy bunnies wear, but it is also suggestive of male clothing, especially the type worn in elegant nightclubs. All these *signifiers* complement each other perfectly in delivering the meanings of the Playboy business—based on a mixture of fantasy sex and nightclub elegance rather than on a hard sexuality associated with strip joints and other such locales. Rabbits evoke archetypal notions of femininity and fertility, which come to consciousness only through reflection. But such symbolism inhabits many other archetypal regions of the unconscious. This is why it surfaces in all kinds of stories and fables, from the Easter Bunny and Brère Rabbit to the ever-satirical Bugs Bunny. The appeal and staying power of this logo is due, arguably, to its inbuilt ambiguity. Ambiguity, as a matter of fact, is what makes logos psychologically powerful. By not being able to pin down what they mean exactly but only through suggestion, we start experiencing them holistically and, thus, sensing great significance to them (unconsciously).

Logos are visual signs, created to represent products or services in ways that vary from simple illustrations of the product's design to highly symbolic forms that connect the product to unconscious fantasies and mythic themes. Logos are everywhere. Until the 1970s, logos on clothes, for instance, were concealed discretely inside a collar or on a pocket. But since then, they can be seen conspicuously, indicating, not surprisingly, that our society has become "logo conscious." Ralph Lauren's polo horseman, Lacoste's alligator, and Nike's "swoosh" symbol, to mention but three, are now shown prominently on clothing items, evoking images of heraldry and, thus, nobility. They constitute symbols of "cool" (Klein 2000: 69) that legions of people are seemingly eager to put on view in order to convey an aura of high-class "blue-blooded" fashionableness.

If there is one theme that stands out from the semiotic approach to advertising, it is that many brand names, logos, package designs, ads, and commercials are interpretable at two levels—a surface level and an underlying one. The surface level is, as mentioned, the signifier level, and the underlying one is that of the signified—where the concealed or unconscious meaning lies. More often than not, this is mythic, or archetypal, in nature, as we saw previously, and thus works psychologically at a subthreshold level of mind. Signs literally represent the world of beings, objects, ideas, and events; that is, they "present them again" within the confines of mental space. The signifier or signifiers used to make signs vary widely. A sign can be a physical object (a traffic sign), a word, a kind of sound, and even an entire story. Signs are the elements of such common **codes**, or systems of signs, as hand gestures, facial expressions, language, music, paintings, religious ceremonies, architectural styles, car designs, body image, sports clothing fashions—in a nutshell, anything that has been made (invented, constructed, thought up, or devised) by humans. Signs can be thought of as the "materials" we need and employ to create our world, from words to social institutions. By turning a product into a sign, the advertiser inserts it into that world where it becomes interconnected to the whole network of meanings in it.

In a fundamental way, advertising is itself a semiotic science since it is all about *meaning*. As Bell (1990: 1) has aptly put it,

> Advertising is all about meaning. In marketing terminology, much advertising research has been concerned with the "message take out" from the commercial. In other words, what did the consumer understand from the commercial? What did it mean? More important than that, *how* it means.

The term *meaning* is obviously crucial. But there is a problem with it. Its broad dictionary definition is "anything that is intended" or "anything of some value to human beings." The latter designation is how it will be used in this book. In their 1923 work, titled appropriately *The Meaning of Meaning*, Ogden and Richards found twenty-three common meanings of the word *meaning*, showing how important a term it is to human beings. They also made a key distinction between *reference* and *sense*. The former is what something stands for. The Playboy bunny logo stands, or *refers*, to the animal known as a rabbit. However, the **referent** of the animal (as it is called) has many *senses* in specific cultural contexts (such as ours), including that of femininity, fertility, and others (as discussed). The *meaning* of the logo, there-

Table 1.1. Meanings of the Playboy Logo

Reference/denotation	The animal known as "rabbit"
Senses/connotations	Friendliness (pet), sexuality, night club elegance, . . .
Signification	The Playboy business, as symbolized by the "bunny," provides fun, "petlike" sexual satisfaction in an elegant way

fore, involves both reference and the senses that this entails in a specific cultural context. Semioticians often use the terms **denotation** in place of *reference* and **connotation** instead of *sense*. Finally, they use **signification** to designate the system of referents and senses that are associated with a sign. The semiotic study of advertising can be defined, more specifically, as the study of *advertising signification*, that is, of the system of referents and senses (the signification system) that it taps into (see table 1.1).

Note that this assessment of the meaning of the logo is not a fact in any empirically testable or scientific sense. It is an *interpretation* based on cultural-symbolic reasoning. It is, in other words, an informed inference. Semiotics is, in effect, the science of interpretation. It is obvious that the use of signs to create messages and meanings entails an interpretation. Charles Peirce, mentioned previously, knew that the range of interpretation always varies from individual to individual, from place to place, and from time period to time period. Peirce referred to this aspect of the sign as the **interpretant**. Each sign or sign system evokes interpretants—specific interpretations that vary across time, space, and communities and that are largely unconscious. There is no one meaning to a human-made form. There are many, and these are typically automatic rather than witting. One of the purposes of this book is to show how advertising taps into the interpretant to create a series of meanings that are just below the threshold of consciousness. My goal is not to impose a specific interpretation on the reader of any specific advertising artifact (brand name, ad campaigning, and so on) but rather to illustrate the methodology of interpretation as practiced within semiotics.

So how do we flesh out the meanings (sense or connotations) in advertising artifacts? One method used by semioticians is that of **opposition**. What keeps two words, such as *cat* and *rat*, recognizably distinct? It is, in part, the fact that the phonetic difference between initial *c* and *r* is perceived as distinctive. Similarly, a major and minor chord of the same key are perceived as distinct on account of a half-tone difference in the middle note of the chord, the left and right shoes of a pair are perceived as distinct because of their different orientations, and so on. As such examples bring out, forms are recognizable as meaning-bearing structures in part through a perceivable difference built into some aspect of their physical constitution, such as a minimal difference in sound, a minimal difference in tone, or a minimal difference in orientation.

The psychological importance of this structural feature was noticed first by the psychologists Wilhelm Wundt (1832–1920) and Edward B. Titchener (1867–1927), who termed it *opposition*. Saussure saw opposition as an intrinsic property of linguistic structure, and his insight remains a basic one to this day, guiding a large part of semiotic and linguistic analysis. The linguist determines the meaning and grammatical function of a form such as *cat* by opposing it to another word such as *rat*. This will show, among other things, that the initial consonants are important in English for differentiating the meaning of words. From such oppositions the linguist establishes, one or two features at a time, what makes the word *cat* unique, pinpointing what *cat* means by virtue of how it is different from other words such as *rat*, *hat*, and so on.

Traditionally, the technique of opposition has been carried out in a *binary* fashion—that is, it was performed on two forms (for example, *cat* vs. *rat*) at a time. Because binary opposition was used extensively and unreflectively both within semiotics and linguistics in the first part of the twentieth century, to the virtual exclusion of any other kind of analytical technique, it was bound to come under criticism. According to anthropologist Claude Lévi-Strauss, moreover, pairs of oppositions seem to cohere into sets forming recognizable units. In analyzing kinship systems, for instance, Lévi-Strauss (1958) found that the elementary unit of kinship is made up of a set of four oppositions: *brother* vs. *sister*, *husband* vs. *wife*, *father* vs. *son*, and *mother's brother* vs. *sister's son*. Lévi-Strauss suspected that similar sets underlay units in other cultural systems and, thus, that their study would provide fundamental insights into the overall nature of human social organization.

Generally speaking, the notion of opposition emphasizes the fact that signs have value only in relation to other signs. The relation can be binary, as are phonemic oppositions in language (*cat* vs. *rat*); it can be "graduated," as the semantic differential technique to be discussed later has shown with respect to connotative meaning; or it can be cohesive (set based) as anthropologists such as Lévi-Strauss have discovered. These types of opposition are not mutually exclusive, as some have argued in the past. They are, in effect, complementary. The type of opposition that applies in advertising analysis, therefore, depends on what system or subsystem is involved.

As a first practical example of how the technique of binary opposition can be employed fruitfully to the analysis of an ad campaign, consider the 2006–2007 Apple Company campaign involving the "Mac guy" versus the "PC guy," which was popularized through television commercials, print advertising, and websites of all kinds. The Mac guy dressed and behaved in the style of young, urban guys who have computer and lifestyle savvy and the attendant "slacker look" to go along with it. The PC guy looked instead like a leftover from the rigid and stodgy 1950s—a lifestyle dinosaur who had ab-

Table 1.2. Oppositional Structure of the Mac Guy vs. PC Guy Campaign

Categories	PC Guy	Mac Guy
Profession	(dreary) probably an accountant	(creative) probably a designer
Musical preferences	(dull) probably music styles exemplified by Céline Dion and others like her	(trendy) probably music styles such as rap, alternative, or urban
Political preferences	(conservative) probably Republican	(liberal) probably Democrat or even Green
Fashion preferences	(conservative) as actually shown in the commercial	(trendy) as actually shown in the commercial
Movie preferences	(probably) bland Hollywood violent adventure movies, like those starring Steven Seagal	(probably) indie movies, such as those shown at festivals such as the Sundance Film Festival

solutely no savvy when it comes to the modern-day world. One way to flesh out the inbuilt meanings associated with the two individuals in the campaign is to set up an opposition grid using categories such as *profession, musical preferences, political preferences, fashion preferences, movie preferences,* and so on (see table 1.2).

These interpretations are variable, of course. But they tend to fall within ranges that are not vastly different from those given here, as I found out by testing the grid with my own students in several large classes. The fact that people provide similar interpretations indicates that the meanings are *there,* not concocted by the subjects. The opposition technique always seems to work in this way. In this case, it fleshes out the lifestyle and ideological connotations built into the two characters so as to bring out the desirable qualities that can be garnered by using a Mac computer instead of a PC computer. The target audience is, obviously, made up of young urban Generation Y individuals, who see lifestyle issues as important in the work world and who typically refuse to be slaves to the workplace in the same way that preceding generations (represented by the PC guy) were. Incidentally, generational marketing is a basic strategy in advertising. This will be taken up in the next chapter.

The foregoing discussion implies two caveats that must be stated clearly from the very outset with regard to the use of semiotics to study advertising. First, an analysis of some advertising artifact from the semiotic angle in no way can establish firmly why something sells at a psychological or sociological level. It can only suggest this. Second, the interpretation of any brand name, logo, ad, and the like (sometimes called *decoding*) is just that—one possible interpretation. Indeed, disagreement about what something means is not only unavoidable but also part of the fun of studying advertising. Differences of opinion fill the pages of the research journals and lead, as in all disciplines, to a furthering of knowledge in the field. The point of this book is simply to display the techniques of semiotic analysis in tandem with other disciplines, not to provide a series of critical and inflexible interpretations of brands, logos, ads, and commercials.

To summarize, semiotics offers a method that can be easily applied to the deciphering of the messages that advertisers weave into their artifacts. It is based on interpreting the connotative meanings of signs and the cultural codes on which they are based—systems of meanings associated with such variables as age, gender, lifestyle, and the like. These meanings are powerful psychologically because they are generally beyond consciousness. For this reason, they evoke sense and feeling. The philosopher Susanne Langer (1948) convincingly argued half a century ago that, at a primary level of mind, we apprehend the world through feeling; that is, we "feel" that the world has a structure. She called this the *presentational* form of thinking. When we attempt to explain our feeling states in terms of some event or representation (such as a work of art), we are forced to organize it in terms of language and its linear semiotic structures. She called this the *discursive* form of cognition. This is a *re-presentational* form of thinking that will never be able to cover the entire range of presentational effects produced by a meaningful stimulus or text. Advertising is effective because it works at a presentational level of mind. We react to its artifacts in terms of feeling. It is when we attempt an explanation of the artifacts that we enter into a discursive mode of thinking, subject to the constraints of the particular language being used. But this is inevitable in any interpretive venture, be it in literary criticism, musicology, or art aesthetics. Advertising, like art, works on a presentational level; semiotic interpretation is a discursive act and, thus, can never be objective and absolute. Indeed, in my view, the interesting and significant aspect of semiotics is that it allows ample space for differences in the interpretation, opening up a potentially fertile dialectic on the meaning of advertising.

Other Approaches

Psychology, sociology, culture studies, linguistics, and anthropology have also made advertising a target of interest. Using different but complementary techniques to those of semiotics, these sciences have made it possible to explore advertising from various complementary angles. Although the main orientation of this book will be on meaning and thus semiotics, it will also look to these other fields, when necessary, to complement any analysis or discussion.

For example, a technique developed by three psychologists in 1957, C. E. Osgood, G. J. Suci, and P. H. Tannenbaum, is of great interest to the study of meaning in advertising because it allows us to flesh out inbuilt or unconscious meanings in a statistical fashion. It is called the **semantic differential**. The technique consists in posing a series of questions about a specific concept— *Is it good or bad? Weak or strong?* and so on—as seven-point scales, with the opposing adjectives at each end. The answers are then analyzed statistically in order to sift out any general pattern from them. Consider the hypothetical example presented in the following section.

Suppose that various subjects are asked to evaluate the concept *President* in terms of scales such as those shown in table 1.3. An informant who feels that the *President* should be modern would place a mark toward the *modern* end of the *modern–traditional* scale. One who feels that a *President* should not be too young or old would place a mark near the middle of the *young–old* scale. An informant who feels that a *President* should be bland would place a mark toward the *bland* end of the *attractive–bland* scale and so on. If a large number of informants were asked to rate the term *President* in this way, then it would be possible to draw an ideal profile of the *presidency* in terms of the statistically significant variations in connotation that the term evokes. Interestingly, research utilizing the semantic differential has shown that, while the meanings of most concepts are subject to personal interpretation and subjective feelings, the range of variation in interpretation is not random but forms a socially based pattern. In other words, the use of this technique has shown that connotation is constrained by culture; for example, the word *noise* turns out to be a highly emotional concept for the Japanese, who rate it consistently at the ends of the scales presented to them, whereas it is a

Table 1.3.   The Semantic Differential

young	1	2	3	4	5	6	7	old
practical	1	2	3	4	5	6	7	idealistic
modern	1	2	3	4	5	6	7	traditional
attractive	1	2	3	4	5	6	7	bland-looking
friendly	1	2	3	4	5	6	7	stern

fairly neutral concept for Americans, who place it in the midrange of the scales. This same technique can, clearly, be used to flesh out the meanings of any ad text presented to subjects; for example, by using scales such as *sexy–unsexy, friendly–unfriendly, aggressive–unaggressive*, and so on, one can flesh out the connotations that a text will elicit.

Psychologists have always been extremely interested in the persuasion techniques used by advertisers. The main contribution of this field has been, in my view, that it has exposed how the persuasion techniques used by advertisers are directed to the unconscious region of the human mind. Psychoanalysts claim that it is this region that contains our hidden wishes, memories, fears, feelings, and images that are prevented from gaining expression by the conscious part of the mind. The Swiss psychologist Carl Jung (1875–1961) divided the unconscious into two regions: a *personal unconscious*, containing the feelings and thoughts developed by an individual that are directive of his or her particular life schemes, and a *collective unconscious*, containing the feelings and thoughts developed cumulatively by the species that are directive of its overall life pattern. Jung described the latter as a "receptacle" of primordial images shared by all humanity that have become such an intrinsic part of the mind as to be beyond reflection. So they gain expression instead in the symbols and forms that constitute the myths, tales, tunes, rituals, and the like that are found in cultures across the world. He called these universal images *archetypes*. For instance, the phallic symbols that advertising incorporates typically into its lifestyle ads appeal instinctively in approximately the same ways in all humans, virtually regardless of age, because they constitute archetypes of male sexuality buried deeply in the collective unconscious of the species.

Such notions are of extreme utility in any study of advertising since they help guide the search for the meaning patterns it generates or taps into. As an applied interdisciplinary science, semiotics enlists such notions only if they are useful for understanding specific signifying phenomena. Any serious study of advertising, therefore, involves an interweaving and blending of ideas, findings, and scientific discourses from various disciplinary domains. It is, more specifically, an *interdisciplinary* study.

Particularly relevant to its objectives are the findings of the *Gestalt* school (German for "configuration"). Gestalt psychology traces its roots to the early work on the relationship between form and content in representational processes, started by psychologists Max Wertheimer (1880–1943), Wolfgang Köhler (1887–1967), and Kurt Koffka (1886–1941). The two primary objectives of using Gestalt psychology in the study of advertising are the following:

1. To unravel how the perception and interpretation of advertising forms (names, logos, and the like) occur

2. To investigate how such forms interrelate with culturally relevant meanings

However, the social debate that the research in psychology has engendered is, as will be discussed in the final chapter, something that one should shy away from (to my mind at least) when investigating advertising forms. Psychologists ask the following critical question: Does advertising influence attitudes and behavior? Logically, this question has led to a spate of studies that have examined advertising from the broader behavioral perspective that such a question presupposes. The implicit premise that most of the studies have entertained, without answering it in any definitive fashion, is whether advertising has become a force molding cultural mores and individual behaviors or whether it constitutes no more than a "mirror" of deeper cultural tendencies within urbanized, contemporary societies. Without going into the debate here, suffice it to say that there is one thing with which virtually everyone agrees—advertising has become one of the most recognizable and appealing forms of social communication to which virtually everyone is exposed. The images and messages that advertisers promulgate on a daily basis delineate the contemporary social landscape.

There is no doubt advertising plays a definitive role in shaping some behaviors in some individuals. But even though people might mindlessly absorb the messages promulgated constantly by advertisements and although these may have some subliminal effects on behavior, people accept media images, by and large, only if they suit already established preferences. It is more accurate to say that advertising produces images that reinforce lifestyle models. Advertisements are not, in fact, disruptive of the value systems of the cultural mainstream; rather, they reflect shifts already present in culture.

2

General Techniques and Strategies

Advertisers are the interpreters of our dreams—Joseph interpreting for Pharaoh. Like the movies, they infect the routine futility of our days with purposeful adventure. Their weapons are our weaknesses: fear, ambition, illness, pride, selfishness, desire, ignorance. And these weapons must be kept as bright as a sword.

—E. B. White, 1899–1985

Most people do not immediately tend to buy a product that has been advertised. Indeed, they generally object to doing so. In most cases, the objection is only a way of delaying the decision to buy. The ultimate goal of advertising is to convince consumers that any doubts they have about the claims made in ad campaigns are groundless and that the buyer will, in fact, benefit from owning the product. One method of overcoming reluctance is to grant prospective buyers a trial period for using the product. Under such an arrangement, the customer can buy the product immediately. But if the buyer is not satisfied with it, he or she can return the product within a certain length of time and receive a full refund.

This is just one of the general techniques used by advertisers and manufacturers. The number of techniques has increased dramatically over the past fifty or so years. Some of these are so familiar that we hardly recognize them any longer as ploys. They range from a simple marketing ploy such as the "something-for-nothing lure" (*Buy one and get a second one free!*) to the use of such ploys as humorous ads to generate a feeling of pleasantness toward a product, endorsement advertising by celebrities to make a product appear reliable, campaigns based on the promise that a product will secure people what they want out of life, and the promotion of such goods and services as insurance, fire alarms, cosmetics, and vitamin capsules by evoking the fear of poverty, sickness, loss of social standing, and/or impending disaster.

The purpose of this chapter is to provide a classification of such general techniques as well as discussing some of their psychological underpinnings. The overall strategy in deploying such techniques is to integrate advertising with social issues and with trends in pop culture.

GENERIC STRATEGIES

In a comprehensive study of the history of advertising, Leiss, Kline, Jhally, and Botterill (2005: 5) subdivide the main techniques used in the persuasion game that advertisers have been playing since the turn of the twentieth century into *rational* and *nonrational* (see table 2.1). The former is a simple generic strategy that is based on providing information about the product; the latter is an emotion-based generic strategy that emphasizes not the product itself but what can be gained from having it (psychologically and socially).

Generic Strategies in Product Advertising

This basic dichotomy appears to capture the essence of advertising strategy, which, indeed, consists (to this day) of techniques designed to appeal to the reasoning mind (rational) and those aimed at appealing to the emotions and at evoking hidden desires (nonrational). The former type of advertising, which characterized mainly the period from 1890 to the early 1920s, focused on the utilitarian aspects of the product itself—its qualities, its price, its functions, and so on; the latter (which has typified advertising ever since) emphasizes the symbolic attributes associated with a product—status, wealth, and so

Table 2.1.   Rational vs. Nonrational Advertising

Rational	Nonrational
Utility associated with buying the product	Symbolic value of the product
Product qualities (price, look, etc.)	Lifestyle benefits derived from having the product
Objective description of the product (how the product works)	Personalization of the product (associating the product with personal benefits)
Product uses (what uses the product can be put to)	Effects gleaned by using the product (status increase, improvements in romantic life, self-transformation, gains in friendship, etc.)

on. Both, however, are still operative strategies. It all depends on the product. The nonrational approach is, however, now the default form of advertising. It can be subdivided into five basic substrategies: basic appeals, language-based techniques, testimonials, the creation of product characters, and the comparison of products.

Basic Appeals

Advertisers rely on many kinds of appeals to persuade people to buy. These can be, as mentioned, rational (informational) or nonrational (emotional and transformational). Brand names and advertisements that use a rational approach describe the demonstrable characteristics of a product. These tell what the product is all about, how it works, or how it is made. For example, the name *Easy-Off* tells us that the product (a detergent) is a user-friendly one and that it makes housework easy. Names and advertisements that use a nonrational appeal stress the ways in which a product will provide personal satisfaction or some social or psychological advantage. For example, the very name of the perfume *Miracle* (by Lancôme) promises consumers that a "miracle" in one's look and romantic life will result by using the product, thus appealing to a person's desire to be attractive. An advertisement for after-shave lotion, to cite another common example, might suggest that the product will help a man attract women.

To persuade the largest possible number of people, many advertisements combine different types of appeals. Appeals may also be aimed at a large general audience or targeted at a limited group of people. Some of these are discussed next.

The heart and soul of advertising lies in making ads and commercials that have broad appeal. A vast variety of ad-making techniques exists for this very reason. These fall, generally, into several main formats: 1) techniques designed to provide information about the qualities of the product; 2) techniques designed to link the product with subtle images—for example, a perfume bottle at the center of a print ad with light cast on it; 3) techniques designed to link use of the product with human personality; 4) techniques designed to associate the product with a particular lifestyle; 5) techniques designed to make the product appealing to people through emotional pitches and/or associations with meaningful aspects of their lives; and 6) techniques designed to convince people that they should acquire the product for some personal or social reason (to avoid social ostracism, to not miss out on some new and exciting trend, and so on). Most of these formats come under the rubric of the "iceberg principle," which claims that advertising should aim its messages at the strong needs and desires that lie hidden deeply in the psyche, in analogy to an iceberg, which is only 10 percent visible, with the remainder hidden below the water.

These formats are the basis for specific ad-making techniques. The main ones—in no particular order of utilization or importance—include the following:

- The "bandwagon" strategy, which consists of exaggerated claims that everyone is using a particular product, inviting the viewer to jump on the bandwagon
- The "educational" strategy, which is designed to educate or inform consumers about a product, especially if it has only recently been introduced into the market
- The "nostalgia" technique, which consists in using images from previous times when, purportedly, life was more serene and less dangerous
- The "plain-folks" pitch, whereby a product is associated with common people using it for practical purposes
- The "something-for-nothing" lure, also known as "incentive marketing," which consists in the giving away of free gifts, designed to provide a favorable image of the product or company (*Buy one and get a second one free! Send for free sample! Trial offer at half price! No money down!* and so on)
- The "help your child" ploy, whereby parents are induced into believing that giving their children certain products will secure them a better life and future
- The "ask mummy or daddy" tactic, whereby children are exhorted to ask their parents to purchase some product for them
- The "scare copy" or "hidden fear" technique, which is designed to promote such goods and services as insurance, fire alarms, cosmetics, and vitamin capsules by evoking the fear of poverty, sickness, loss of social standing, impending disaster, and so on
- The "history" technique, whereby a significant historical event is incorporated into the ad, either by allusion or by direct reference
- The use of humor to make a product appealing and friendly
- The use of the "infomercial format," which constitutes an extended television commercial presented in the form of a television program, often featuring celebrities who advertise a product in a format that is imitative of a talk show
- The use of an "advertorial format" that has the appearance of a news article or editorial in a print publication
- The "benefits" ploy emphasizing the advantages that may accrue from purchasing a product, such as the nutritional value of some food, the gas economy of some car, and so on

- The "mystery ingredient" technique, whereby a mystery ingredient in a drink, detergent, and so on is identified as being the source behind the product's appeal
- The "positive appeal" strategy, intended to demonstrate why a product is attractive or important to possess
- The "prestige" advertising strategy, whereby a product is placed and advertised in high-quality magazines or media programs so as to enhance the company's reputation
- The "rational appeal" technique consisting of logical arguments that demonstrate how the product might fulfill some need
- The "reminder" technique, whereby an ad or commercial is designed to recall an advertisement that viewers are familiar with
- The "secretive statement" technique consisting of the use of statements designed to create the effect that something secretive is being communicated, thus capturing people's attention by stimulating curiosity ("Don't tell your friends about . . ."; "Do you know what she's wearing?"; and so on)
- The "snob-appeal" technique, which aims to convince consumers that using a product will enable them to maintain or elevate their social status
- The "soft sell" method, which uses subtle forms of persuasion rather than blatant ones
- The "teaser" ploy, whereby little information about a product is given, thus making people curious to know more about it
- The "viral advertising" approach, which consists of statements that attempt to capture people's attention by encouraging them to "pass it on" (like a virus) to others
- The "absence-of-language" technique consisting of the intentional omission of language, suggesting, by implication, that the product "speaks for itself"
- The "retro-advertising" technique, whereby a previous ad campaign or the style of a previous ad campaign is recalled to promote the same product or something similar to it

Language-Based Techniques

Choosing the appropriate brand name for a product is perhaps the most fundamental and critical of all language-based techniques (LBTs). A name that does not grab attention will diminish recognition of the product and, in some cases, even damage the identity and salability of the product. A classic example of this in the annals of advertising history is the Edsel car, brought out by Ford in 1957 to satisfy a high demand for a relatively expensive model. But during the time it took to bring the Edsel into production, economic conditions and public taste changed. The vehicle was a financial failure and was discontinued after 1959. But it was not only the conditions that affected the failure, as other companies brought out similarly expensive cars with success, but also its name. The name simply did not resonate with people. The car was named after Edsel Ford, a former president of the company and son of Henry Ford. Surveys showed that people associated the name either with the name of a tractor (Edson) or with the word "weasel." Ever since, naming has become a critical strategy in brand identity, with word association games playing a prominent role in that strategy, as we shall see in the next chapter.

Another LBT is the coinage of an appropriate descriptive phrase that will encapsulate what the brand's signification system (system of inbuilt meanings) is all about (at least in part). For example, in print advertisements, headlines are crucial, attracting interest or attention by promising the reader a personal benefit, such as a savings in money or an improvement in physical appearance. Others are cleverly worded to arouse a person's curiosity. Still others carry news, such as an announcement of a new product, or attract attention by directly addressing a specific group. For example, a headline might read, "For the Young Single Woman." The opening lines in a radio or television commercial serve the same purpose as headlines in printed ads.

Yet another LBT is the use of slogans. These are short phrases that are used over and over to drive home a message, such as Campbell Soup's "Mmm, Mmm good" or McDonald's "I'm lovin' it." Given the vital role that this technique, among others, plays in advertising, LBTs will be discussed in more detail in chapters 3 and 7.

Testimonials

Testimonials are advertisements in which a person is shown endorsing a product. The person may be someone who looks like an average user of the product, or it may be some celebrity (a movie star or a popular athlete) who endorses it. Incidentally, under U.S. government regulations, endorsers must use the advertised product if they claim they do so. The use of celebrities has grown considerably since the 1920s, coinciding with the rise of a celebrity culture brought about by the growth of media and mass communications. The late Andy Warhol (1930–1987) was among the first artists to realize the intrinsic connection between celebrity culture and advertising. He also realized that a celebrity need not necessarily be a real person; it could also be a product or a fictional character (e.g., a cartoon character such as Mickey Mouse or Bugs Bunny or a comic book superhero like Superman or Spiderman).

Warhol's most famous artistic subjects were, in fact, both commercial products, such as soup cans and soft-drink bottles, and celebrities, such as Elizabeth Taylor and Marilyn Monroe.

A celebrity is a person, fictional character, or commercial product (adopting Warhol's categories) who gains fame by virtue of the fact that he or she (or it) is on the media stage. There is a difference between *fame* and *celebrity*. Politicians or scientists may be famous, but they are not necessarily celebrities, unless the interest of the general public and the mass media are piqued in tandem. The classic example is that of Albert Einstein, who was famous, of course, as a scientist but who also became a celebrity through the attention paid by the media not only to his work but also to his personal life. Like a movie star, Einstein has been represented in comic strips, on T-shirts and greeting cards, and by many other paraphernalia associated with pop culture. But Einstein was an exception. It is mass entertainment personalities, such as soap opera actors or pop music stars, who are the ones most likely to become celebrities, even if they deliberately avoid media attention. That became obvious already in the radio era, when a radio celebrity would get everyone's attention if found shopping or simply walking down a street.

Testimonials from sports celebrities are particularly effective for products that involve health, physical prowess, and other attributes associated with sports. The Wheaties brand of cereal, for example, has always used sports celebrities, such as basketball star Michael Jordan, in ads, commercials, and even on its boxes.

A few years ago, I conducted an informal survey of more than 200 first-year students at the Universities of Toronto and Lugano to assuage the effectiveness of celebrity testimonials. I discovered that they did indeed increase the strength of association between product and celebrity culture, since most indicated that they connected certain products with certain celebrities (Wheaties being a case in point). Overall, the survey suggested that consumers like celebrities because they are attractive in the ads (or on boxes) as opposed to a noncelebrity, even if around half of those surveyed did not believe that the celebrity actually endorsed or even used the product.

The crucial thing that the survey brought out is that the celebrity must match the product. It would be irrelevant to have, say, Tom Cruise endorse the Wheaties product in the same way that it would be useless to have Michael Jordan (or any sports star) endorse a skin product. It is more believable that a superstar like Michael Jordan would in fact sit down to have a bowl of Wheaties, the "breakfast of champions," as the product's slogan implies, than it would be for humorist Woody Allen to do so.

Sometimes a brand signs up a pop music icon and his or her song as its signature **jingle**. For example, David Bowie's *Rebel, Rebel* has been used to pitch Audi cars, Cyndi Lauper's *Girls Just Wanna Have Fun* to promote Carnival Cruises, and Bob Seger's *Like a Rock* to sell Chevy trucks. The jingle, like the name and **logo**, is a device that creates a strategic image for a brand. Essentially, the jingle is a musical slogan—a memorable melody married perfectly to its lyrics. This use of music to create brand image can be seen throughout contemporary advertising. For example, classic rock and roll is often used to accompany commercials of expensive automobiles. The classic example of this is General Motors' adoption of Led Zeppelin's 1971 anthem *Rock and Roll* for its Cadillac campaign in the early 2000s.

Product Characters

Product characters are fictional people, cartoon characters (known as mascots), and the like that are associated with a product. The characters become highly familiar to people and so provide lasting identification with a company's products. Product characters are often used in advertising aimed at children because such characters delight many young people. Table 2.2 shows a few well-known product characters.

These often add a touch of friendliness to the perception of the product. Indeed, since they are mainly cartoon characters, they tap into pop culture's love affair with comic books and animated films. Many of these have become cultural celebrities themselves, independently of the products they represent. In America, Mr. Clean, Uncle Ben, Charlie the Tuna, and Hostess's Twinkie the Kid have become such an intrinsic part of cultural lore that they were even featured in cameo roles in a 2001 animated film called *Foodfight*. Pillsbury's Poppin' Fresh doughboy character has made appearances on the *Family Guy*

Table 2.2.   Well-known Product Characters

Character	*Product, Company, or Service*
Mr. Clean	Mr. Clean household products
Ronald McDonald	The McDonald's Corporation
Tony the Tiger	Kellogg's Frosted Flakes
Betty Crocker	Betty Crocker products (General Mills)
Speedy	Alka Seltzer Tablets
Snap, Crackle, Pop	Rice Krispies
Cap'n Crunch	Captain Crunch cereal
Energizer Bunny	Energizer batteries
Gerber baby	Gerber baby food
Pillsbury Doughboy	Pillsbury products
Charlie the Tuna	Starkist Tuna
Leo the Lion	MGM
Michelin Man	Michelin tires

and *The Simpsons* sitcoms, and the Energizer Bunny has been on *Cheers*, *ABC Wide World of Sports*, the *Emmy Awards*, and the *Tonight Show*.

The range of meanings associated with the name of a product character is quite interesting. Mr. Clean's name suggests what the product does at the same time that his muscular body and bald head suggest heroic strength. The Aunt Jemima name (for a pancake mix) is actually a nickname. It was promoted at the Chicago fair in 1910 by a miller named R. T. Davis, who engaged former Kentucky slave Nancy Green, age fifty-nine, to demonstrate the mix at a griddle outside the barrel. Green was nicknamed "Aunt Jemima" by Davis in order to take advantage of the prejudicial views of the era, which saw older female slaves as "great cooks" with a friendly "aunt-like" disposition. Needless to say, the Aunt Jemima brand has been the target of many debates and justified indignation on the part of concerned African Americans.

The success of the Aunt Jemima brand spawned a number of imitators, among which one of the most successful is that of Betty Crocker, invented in 1921 by Gold Medal flour to serve as the logo of the company. As Marks (2005: 12) points out, according to a 1945 issue of *Fortune* magazine, this fictitious lady was the second most popular woman in America after Eleanor Roosevelt. As surely as young children buy into fantasy worlds, adults of the era seemed to buy into the Betty Crocker myth—an expert cook, a friend, and a friendly mother figure. Played by various actresses on radio and television, Betty became a true icon of "ideal American womanhood." She appeared in movies and on television. Her physical image was established in 1936 when her first "portrait" was put out by the company. Her countenance was shaped to have a combination of Caucasian features designed to present the perfect composite of the stay-at-home American woman. Twenty years later, a new portrait produced a new image—older and friendlier. Currently, her image has been updated to reflect yet a new image of American womanhood. She now resembles a Latina female and a soccer mom at once. The Betty Crocker "makeover" is a perfect example of how brands must constantly be reshaped to keep in step with the times. Through revision and updating, a brand can retain its popularity.

Another example of "character revision" is that of Mr. Peanut, the brand icon of the Planters Company, who has been refashioned in 2004 campaigns to be an active participant in basketball games, dance floors, and other trendy cultural venues so as to portray him as a fun character in step with the times. Mr. Peanut was born in 1916 as a "little peanut person." Although he still wears a top hat and monocle and carries a cane (suggesting the glitz, sophistication, and allure of the dance club scene of the 1920s), his demeanor has been modified to promote a different kind of lifestyle scene.

Comparison of Products

The technique of comparing products is used most frequently to sell products that compete heavily with other brands. Advertisers compare their product with similar brands and point out the advantages of using their brand. A competitor's product may be named, or it may be referred to as "Brand X" or "the leading brand." Often, the advertiser is overtly critical of another company's products or campaigns so as to bring out that the competitor is involved in various forms of "mass appeal" because its product lacks the qualities of the advertised brand. This is known as the "disparaging" technique.

CREATING A BRAND IMAGE

The technique of giving a product a name is part of the broader strategy of creating a **brand image** or *brand identity* for the product. The image-making strategy is bolstered by other techniques, as we shall see in due course in more detail. For the present purposes, it is sufficient to define brand imagery as a particular configuration of signs (and their meanings) built into a product that renders it appealing to specific types of consumers. Budweiser beer, for instance, evokes the image of "young guys hanging out together," whereas Heineken evokes an image of a "party atmosphere." This is why commercials for Budweiser are seen next to sports events on television and why those for Heineken are found primarily in magazines and programs with a distinct social flavor to them.

An **image** is, clearly, a sign system or, more specifically, a **signification system**. What does this mean? Take the State Farm Insurance Company as a case in point. The company has constructed such a system for itself through the use of four main techniques: 1) a brand name (State Farm) that can be associated with "down-to-earth" (agrarian, country, rural) values, especially friendliness and trustworthiness; 2) a logo (a box around three intersecting ovals, labeled "auto," "life," and "fire," with "State Farm" at the top and "Insurance" at the bottom) that communicates the same meaning through a sense of visual pleasantness and interconnection; 3) a jingle (*Like a good neighbor, State Farm is there*) that reiterates and reinforces the system of meanings; and 4) ads and commercials portraying State Farm employees as wholesome, neighborly individuals ready to help out in time of need. From this signification system, an image of the State Farm company as a "friendly" and "trustworthy" institution has crystallized over the years, becoming fixed in the social mind-set through repeated advertising campaigns.

These are just a few of the techniques that are used to create brand image. Others will be discussed in due course. However, two generic ones merit attention here initially. One of these is called repetition and the other positioning.

Repetition

Repetition is a basic marketing technique. As its name suggests, it implies giving exposure to an ad campaign by repeating the same type of ads in various media. A typical national advertiser will seek to gain the attention of prospective customers by repeated appeals through radio and television commercials, print ads for the same product in newspapers and magazines, poster displays in stores, Internet pop-ups, and so on. The main advantages associated with each of the main media can be synthesized in point form as follows:

- Network television is still the chief medium used by national advertisers, spending an average of 65 percent (as of the mid-2000s) of their advertising budgets on television. Television brings a product directly into people's lives (homes, hotel rooms, and so on). And network television reaches a vast audience at a low cost per viewer. The majority of television commercials consist of short spot announcements, most of which last thirty seconds.
- Advertisers also buy spot time on cable television, thus expanding their reach into specialized audience markets. Special cable entertainment programs, sports events, and certain motion pictures are often sponsored by one or two advertisers. In this way, the advertiser hopes to gain added recognition by being identified with the program, event, or movie.
- National advertisers use newspapers especially when they want to concentrate their sales pitch in particular regions. Most adults read a daily newspaper, and many of them specifically check the ads for information about products or services. Newspaper ads can be placed on certain pages, such as those devoted to travel, home life, or sports.
- Direct mail includes leaflets, brochures, catalogs, and other printed advertisements that are delivered by a postal service. Direct-mail advertising costs more per person reached than do other ways of advertising. But some products or services are too complicated to be promoted in any other medium.
- Radio advertising is highly popular because people can listen to programs while doing other things. Another advantage is that radio audiences are more highly selected by the type of programming than are television audiences. For example, stations that feature classical music attract different kinds of listeners than do those that play rock. By selecting the station, advertisers can reach the people most likely to buy their products. Radio commercials include direct sales announcements, dramatized stories, and jingles. Most last 30 to 60 seconds.
- Magazine advertising has several advantages over other print media advertising, such as newspapers. First, magazines are usually read in a

leisurely manner and are often kept for weeks or months before being discarded. Second, magazines offer better printing and color reproduction than newspapers do. Advertisers can thus show off their products with greater efficacy in magazines.

- Most advertising on outdoor signs—posters, painted posters, electric spectaculars—is placed by national advertisers. One of the advantages of such advertising is that people pass by the signs repeatedly. In addition, large, colorful signs easily attract attention. Posters (also called billboards) are the most widely used form of outdoor advertising. They can be put in or on public transit vehicles (trains, subways, buses, and taxicabs). Painted bulletins are signs painted on buildings. And electric spectaculars are large illuminated displays, many featuring changing messages and moving pictures.
- Window displays are designed to draw customers into a store. They encourage impulse buying—that is, buying without previous thought or planning.
- Novelties advertising consists of giving away inexpensive items (calendars, key rings, and so on) that carry a brand name, logo, or message.
- Internet advertising is the newest and fastest-growing type of advertising (as will be discussed later in this chapter). Many companies maintain websites on the Internet. The site may contain information about the company and its products, along with pictures or other artwork.

Positioning

Positioning is the targeting of a product through appropriate advertising for the right audience of consumers. For example, Chanel products are positioned for a female audience of a certain social class and thus are placed in media such as glamorous fashion magazines. Nike shoes, on the other hand, are positioned for a trendy adolescent and young adult audience and are thus placed in media such as popular sports magazines and placed as spot announcements during television programs dealing with issues of interest to the target audience (sitcoms, sports events, and so on).

Positioning is all about how potential buyers will perceive brand image. The term was coined in 1969 by Jack Trout in a technical paper (Trout 1969). In marketing, positioning has come to mean the process by which marketers try to create an image or identity in the minds of their target market for its product, brand, or organization. This means finding the right kind of magazine, television program, website, and the like that caters to the relevant target market. In a phrase, creating an image for a product inheres in fashioning a "personality" for it so that it can be positioned for specific market populations. The image, as discussed, is an amalgam of the product's name, packaging, logo, price, and overall presentation that creates a recognizable personality for it. The idea is, clearly, to speak directly to particular types of individuals, not to everyone, so that these individuals can see their own personalities represented in the images created by the relevant advertisements.

USES OF TECHNOLOGY

Already at the turn of the twentieth century, advertisers realized that a single ad would hardly be capable of spreading product recognition into general consciousness. To do so, they devised a truly ingenious strategy known as the ad campaign, or the spread of the same message though diverse media and through various versions of the same ad. Some campaigns were so well designed that they are still around today or else are still remembered by many. The slogans of many of these campaigns have even penetrated the common vernacular—"Mmm, Mmm, Good" (Campbell's Soup), "Think small" (Volkswagen), "Just do it" (Nike), "A diamond is forever" (De Beers), "You deserve a break today" (McDonald's), "This Bud's for you" (Budweiser), "It's the real thing" (Coca-Cola), and so on. The campaign strategy has proven to be a pivotal one in literally getting the message out there. It has been effective because of the advertising industry's utilization of new technologies the instant they came into being.

Traditional Advertising

By "traditional" technologies, I am referring to "off-line" media, such as traditional print newspapers and magazines, radio, and television. Ingenious ads, clever names, mythic logos, text layouts, and the like would have virtually no effect in ensconcing brand image if they "did not get out there," to put it figuratively. The survival of brands in today's marketplace depends largely on the use of different media to spread the word (the signification systems). This, in itself, creates a just-so effect for the brands, producing the perception that they have a necessary role to play in society.

As mentioned in the opening chapter, information about the availability, quality, and price of goods and services was spread by word of mouth (criers) and poster signs in the ancient and medieval worlds. The information thus reached very few people. But this situation changed drastically with the invention of the movable-type printing press in Europe in the mid-fifteenth century. This gave merchants the means to reach many more people through direct mail. As a consequence, it led to the rise of a whole new business, typography, which made possible the mass production of leaflets, brochures, catalogs, and other printed materials that could be delivered by a postal service or hand delivered. It also gave more importance to the outdoor sign-making business. Enhanced technology allowed merchants to print posters cheaply. In the nineteenth century, the large-scale industrialization of cities created a need for extensive advertising, leading to the invention of lithography, a printing method that made it easier to include colored illustrations on print materials. Beginning in 1867, the artist Jules Chéret revolutionized the look of posters, using illustrations as dominant features while reducing the verbal text to a minor explanatory role. Chéret's method gave rise to the practice of printing visually charming commercial posters that would appeal instantly to people (literate or not). His techniques continue to be used to this day. In the 1890s, several art nouveau artists introduced other important innovations in the craft of print advertising—namely, the use of large areas of flat color and the replacement of the idealized figures of human beings with naturalistic or caricatured figures depicted in vignettes. The art nouveau artists also introduced flowing lines and elegant, elongated forms to create exotic, stylized illustrations. Their techniques are also being used to this very day.

The radio medium became a dominant one for advertising starting in the 1920s, introducing the commercial to the field, reaching the pinnacle of its popularity and influence during World War II. The radio brought news, information, the arts, and (most significantly) brand advertising directly into homes. The parallel growth of network radio and Hollywood cinema, both of which were launched as commercial enterprises in the 1920s, created an unprecedented mass culture for people of all social classes and educational backgrounds. Only after the advent of television in the 1950s did radio's hegemony begin to erode as its audiences split into smaller, distinct segments. Today, people listen to radio mainly in their cars as they drive from location to location or in their offices (or other places of work) as they do something else. Aware of this, radio stations typically present traffic information in a regular interspersed fashion throughout their broadcasts or else present uninterrupted stretches of music during certain periods of the working day. Another advantage is that radio audiences, in general, are more highly selectable by program genre and thus allow for a brand to be more effectively positioned.

Early radio programs were integrated with brand advertising, being sponsored by brands and thus positioned for specific audiences. The soap opera genre was even named for the type of advertiser—soap companies—that sponsored them. In the United States, advertising agencies produced almost all network radio shows before the development of network television. Stations often sold agencies full sponsorship, which included placing the product name in a program's title, as with *Palmolive Beauty Box Theater* (1927–1937) or the *Texaco Star Theatre* (1948–1953). Entire radio programs became associated with specific brands. The ratings system arose, in fact, from the sponsors' desire to know how many people they were reaching with their advertising. In 1929, Archibald Crossley launched *Crossley's Cooperative Analysis of Broadcasting*, using telephone surveys to project daily estimates of audience size for the national radio networks. The A. C. Nielsen Company, which had been surveying audience size in radio since the mid-1930s, eventually became the dominant ratings service. The ratings helped set the price of advertisements and, ultimately, whether the program would stay on the air or be canceled. Only public radio stations are exempt from the "ratings game" for the reason that they are financed by government subsidies, individual donations, and corporate grants.

Starting in the early 1950s, television became a very powerful medium for delivering brand image, bringing sight, sound, and action directly to consumers in their homes. The majority of television commercials consist of short spot announcements, most of which last 30 seconds to a minute. They are usually run in groups of three to six or nine. Television networks and stations generally limit commercial time to about 10 minutes per hour during prime time and 16 minutes per hour during most other broadcast times. Television continues to be a major player in the creation and entrenchment of brand image. In a nutshell, television advertising took over the radio commercial and turned it into a more visual form, thus enhancing its multimodality. As mentioned previously, television continues to be the most popular technology for advertisers.

New Advertising Media

Today, satellite technologies and the Internet make it possible for brands to spread the word about themselves all over the globe regardless of time zone or political boundary. This is why the commercial use of the Internet has grown dramatically since the mid-1990s. Virtually any product or service can now be ordered from Internet sites. In 2002, the Nielsen/Net Ratings firm counted nearly 70,000 commercials on the Internet during the single month of May.

It is little wonder that the major brands have taken to the Web with great enthusiasm. For example, in 2001, the carmaker BMW hired several famous directors to make short "digital films" featuring its cars. The movies were viewable only on the Web but were also promoted through television spots. Those digital commercials clearly blurred the line between art and advertising, showing how a continuity had emerged between the larger cultural order and brand-based marketing. Each film was about six minutes long, each featured a prominent actor, and each portrayed BMWs used in a reckless, adventure-oriented fashion.

The blurring of lines between long-standing representational activities within the larger cultural order and those generated by advertising can be called, simply, *convergence*, a course of action designed to create a sense of continuity between the products advertised and the various artistic and social activities of the culture. Convergence can be seen both across media and within a specific medium. It can be seen clearly in ad campaigns for high-tech products, such as iPods, cell phones, digital cameras, and Palm Pilots, which are constantly related to youth lifestyles in all kinds of magazine and electronic media.

Technology is what makes (and has always made) ad campaigns effective. The complementary use of print (ads in newspapers, magazines, posters, and so on), radio, and television increases exposure to a campaign and thus enhances product recognition. More recently, advertising has joined the cinema and Internet worlds, coming up with new forms of advertising adapted to these worlds. Some of these are the following:

- Banner advertising, which involves the use of ads that stretch across the top of a Web page
- Cinema ads, which are shown on cinema screens before the featured film
- Click-through advertising, whereby a user can click on a banner ad or other on-screen ad to get through to the manufacturer of a product
- Contextual advertising, by which ads automatically intrude into a Web session, whether wanted or not
- E-mail advertising, by which e-mails are used to deliver pitches for a product or service
- Pop-up ads that pop up on the screen when a user visits a particular website
- Run-of-network banner advertising, whereby ads are placed across a network of websites
- "Run-of-site" banner advertising, whereby ads are placed on a specific website
- Extramercial advertising, which consists of the use of ads that slide down a Web page
- Impact advertising, whereby ads for the same product are run close together (on radio or television) so as to make a strong impact on a target audience
- Interactive advertising, whereby input from the audience through the Internet is sought

- Direct-response advertising, whereby an immediate response to a television commercial is requested by providing an on-screen phone number, e-mail address, or website
- Saturation advertising, whereby the same ad is dispersed through all media, from traditional print to the Internet, so as to garner for it a broad audience
- Interstitial advertising, whereby images appear and disappear mysteriously on a screen as users click from one Web page to the next
- Shoshkeles, or floating ads, whereby animated objects, such as a car, are projected across the screen

In sum, multimedia and convergent styles of advertising have extended the reach of brands into virtually all domains of society. Ads appear in movie theaters and on DVDs prior to the featured movie. They appear on ski-lift towers, and in high school classroom news programming. In supermarkets, shoppers may be exposed to in-store radio, grocery carts with miniature billboards or video screens, and television sets with programs or commercials in the checkout line. In fact, it is no exaggeration to say that vast portions of cultural space—physical and mental—have become branded. No wonder, then, that the same techniques used by manufacturers are now used by virtually anyone seeking to gain attention within that space. Already in 1952, politics got into the "advertising game," when Dwight D. Eisenhower successfully ran for the U.S. presidency with the help of advertising executives who directed his campaign. Since then, advertising has played an increasingly important role in political campaigns, with television spot announcements having become a major strategy of campaigns for public offices at all levels of government. "It pays to advertise" has become the salient aphorism of the contemporary world.

Interactivity

One innovative technique that merits separate commentary can be called simply *interactivity*. This consists of companies interacting with (potential) consumers through the new interactive technologies in various new ways. For example, in early 2007, Elizabeth Arden invited customers to go to a website to enter their personal information (name, phone, e-mail, and so on) so that a tailor-made (prerecorded) message by Britney Spears could be sent to a loved one (on Valentine's Day) by phone or e-mail. Similarly, NBC used Alec Baldwin's voice in 2006 in holiday messages to promote *30 Rock*. Baldwin appears on the show. He recorded around 500 common first names that were used in the "mix-and-match" technique.

Perhaps the best-known use of interactivity is Dove's Self-Esteem, or Real Women, campaign, where real women, with "real curves," were enlisted to be the models in print ads and television and Internet commercials. The interactivity here is between the company and actual (real) consumers. The simulation of the ad campaign with reality television style was unmistakable. Real people are more interesting than actors because they are perceived to represent the actual consumer. In contrast to professional models who are attractive, sexy, and ultrathin and have a flawless complexion, the Dove models were women of average size and appearance, which hit closer to home with female consumers.

The campaign claimed that Dove wants "real women to have real curves." But the ploy was transparent. It was really the manufacturer who told women how to celebrate their curves, not the women themselves. In the Dove Evolution commercial for the Dove Self-Esteem Fund, which was found in 2006 on websites, television, and other media, an average-looking woman gets a makeover analogous to the kind of makeover that is showcased on television programs such as TLC's *What Not to Wear*. The "Cinderella subtext" in the programs and the campaign is unmistakable. Like Cinderella, common women can be transformed into "beauty princesses" with the right clothes or the right soap and cosmetics.

MYTHOLOGIZATION

Product image is further entrenched by the use of **myth**. For instance, mythic themes such as the quest for beauty and the conquest of death, among others, are constantly being worked surreptitiously into the specific images that advertisers create for beauty products. The people who appear in beauty ads and commercials are, moreover, attractive people with an "unreal," almost deified, quality about the way they look. In a phrase, the modern advertiser stresses not the product but the social or mythic meanings that may be expected to materialize from its purchase. The advertiser is, clearly, quite adept at setting foot into the same subconscious regions of psychic experience that are explored by philosophers, artists, and religious thinkers. Like surrealist art, the connection between an ad and the psyche is symbolic and imaginary rather than realistic, turning the ad into a symbolic text.

What Is a Myth?

The word *myth* derives from the Greek *mythos*, meaning "word," "speech," or "tale of the gods." A myth is a narrative in which the main characters are gods, heroes, and mystical beings; the plot revolves around the origin of things or around the meaning of things; and the setting is a metaphysical world juxtaposed against the real world. In the beginning stages of human cultures, myths functioned as genuine theories of the world. All cultures have created them to explain their origins. And we instinctively resort to myth even today for imparting knowledge of values and morals initially to children. Stories about the tooth fairy, for instance, are residues of this mythic instinct. It also manifests itself latently in other ways. Climatologists, for example, refer to the warming of the ocean surface off the western coast of South America that occurs every 4 to 12 years as a person, El Niño ("the little one" in Spanish). Although modern people do not believe El Niño to be a person, they nonetheless find it somehow more intuitively correct to blame an imaginary being for bringing about a climate change in the world. El Niño is, ipso facto, a mythic character.

By studying myths, we can learn how different societies have answered basic questions about the world and the human being's place in it. We can study myths to learn how a people developed a particular social system with its many customs and ways of life and thus better understand the values that bind members of society into one group. Myths can be compared in order to discover how cultures differ and how they resemble one another and why people behave as they do. We can also study myths as the referential frames underlying not only masterpieces of architecture, literature, music, painting, and sculpture but also such contemporary things as advertising and television programs (as we shall see in due course).

Myths are the sources of early symbolism. The Greeks symbolized the sun as the god Helios driving a flaming chariot across the sky. The Egyptians represented the sun as a boat. Animals, human beings, and plants have all stood as symbols for ideas and events in myths of all kinds, many of which are around to this day. The Greeks portrayed Asclepius, the god of healing, holding a staff with a serpent coiled around it. The staff is often confused with the caduceus of the god Mercury, which has two snakes coiled around it. Today, both symbols are used as emblems of the medical profession. In Babylonian mythology, the hero Gilgamesh searched for a special herb that made anyone who ate it immortal. To this day, herbs are considered to have healing powers. Rarely, in fact, do we realize how much of the symbolism used by modern cultures is cut from the fabric of early myths. From the Germanic and Roman myths we have inherited, for instance, the names of most of the days of the week and months of the year; for example, Tuesday is the day dedicated to the Germanic war god Tiu, Wednesday to the chief god Wotan, Thursday to Thor, Friday to the goddess of beauty Frigga, Saturday to the Roman god Saturn, January to Janus, and so on. Our planets bear a similar pattern of

Table 2.3. Basic Oppositions

Concept	Its Opposite
Good	Evil
Right	Wrong
Mother	Father
God	Devil
Female	Male
Day	Night
Life	Death
Oneness/unity	Nothingness
Heaven (paradise)	Hell (inferno)

nomenclature: Mars is named after the Roman god of war, Venus after the Roman god of love, and so on. The residues of mythic thinking can also be seen in the fact that we read horoscopes, implore the gods to help us, and cry out against fortune.

The French anthropologist Claude Lévi-Strauss (1978) even saw myth as the original source for the development of conceptual thinking, which continues to reverberate with the oppositions constituting all myths—life versus death, maternal versus paternal, good versus evil, raw versus cooked, and so on. The nature of myth and conceptualization, Lévi-Strauss suggested, lies in the endless combination and recombination of such oppositions (see table 2.3).

Mythic Oppositions

Lévi-Strauss's notion seems to work at a practical level. If one were to ask you what evil is, you would tend to explain it in terms of its opposite (good) and vice versa. Similarly, if one wanted to explain the concept of right to someone, one is bound to bring up the opposite concept of wrong at some point.

The Italian philosopher Giambattista Vico (1688–1744) claimed that the original mythic stories led to the foundation of the first institutions. The gradual increase of control humans had over their environment and the increasing complexity of human institutions were then reflected in the functions that new gods assumed. For Vico, myth was not constructed on the basis of a rational logic but of what he called a *poetic logic*, a form of thinking based on and guided by conscious bodily experiences that are transformed into generalized ideas by the human imagination. The course that humanity runs, according to Vico, goes from an early mythical age, through a heroic one, ending at a rational one (before it starts over). Each age has its own kind of culture, language, social institutions, and narratives—the poetic mentality, for instance, generated myths; the heroic one, legends; and the rational one, narrative history.

In myth, psychoanalysts find traces to the motivations and complexes of individuals. Sigmund Freud (1856–1939), for instance, saw the conflicts recounted in myths as attempts to come to grips with unconscious psychic life. In the myth of Oedipus—the king who was abandoned at birth and unwittingly killed his father and then married his mother—he found a narrative paradigm for explaining a subconscious sexual desire in a child for the parent of the opposite sex, usually accompanied by hostility to the parent of the same sex. Carl Jung, as mentioned in the previous chapter, saw in such stories evidence for a collective unconscious in the human species constituted by primordial images, which he termed *archetypes*, that continue to seek expression through symbolism and various forms of expression.

The most popularized studies of myths in the twentieth century were those of the American scholar Joseph Campbell (1904–1987). In his best-selling books, Campbell combined insights from Jungian psychology and linguistics to formulate a general theory of the origin, development, and unity of all human cultures. If there is thunder in the sky and one lacks the notion of "thunder," then it can be explained as the angry voice of a god; if there is rain, then it can be explained as the weeping of the gods; and so on. A myth is a telling of such events.

Among the first to discern the use of mythic themes and characters in advertising (and pop culture generally) was Roland Barthes (mentioned in the previous chapter). To distinguish between the original myths and their modern-day versions, Barthes designated the latter *mythologies*, defining them as modern-day reflexes of mythic themes, plots, and characters. They come about through a blend of *mythos* (true mythical thinking) and *logos* (rational-scientific thinking). In early Hollywood westerns, for instance, the mythic conceptual opposition of good versus evil manifested itself in various symbolic and expressive ways; for example, heroes wore white hats and villains black ones, heroes were honest and truthful, villains were dishonest and cowardly, and so on. Sports events, too, are felt to be mythological dramas juxtaposing good (the home team) versus evil (the visiting team). The whole fanfare associated with preparing for the "big event," like the Super Bowl of American football, has a ritualistic quality to it similar to the pomp and circumstance that ancient armies engaged in before going out to battle and war. Indeed, the whole event is perceived to be a battle of mythic proportions. The symbolism of the team's (army's) uniform, the valor and strength of the players (the heroic warriors), and the skill and tactics of the coach (the army general) have a powerful effect on the fans (the warring nations). The game is, as television and radio announcers constantly blurt out, "real life, real drama!"

Much of advertising has mythological structure or suggestiveness. This is a theme that will be emphasized throughout the remaining chapters of this book. The images of beautiful models, male and female, that adorn lifestyle ads are not unlike ancient statues of gods and goddesses, such as Apollo and Aphrodite. Indeed, *mythologization*, as it can be called, is a major technique in advertising practice, especially in the domain of lifestyle brands. This can be defined generally as the technique of imbuing brand names, logos, product design, ads, and commercials with some mythic meaning.

Myth in Advertising

As a case in point, consider the Nike "swoosh" logo in its bare outline form (without name and other information sometimes added to it). As a visual symbol suggesting speed, it works on several levels, from the iconic to the mythical. At the iconic level, it implies the activity of running at top speed with the Nike shoe; at the mythic level, it taps into the idea of speed as symbolic of power and conquest (such as in the Olympic races). After all, Nike was the goddess of victory. The combination of these two levels creates a perception of the logo and thus the product as having a connection to both reality and narrative history. The Nike logo is a classic case of a company gradually mythologizing its corporate identity as its fame increases. The company's first logo appeared in 1972, when the word "Nike" was printed in orange over the outline of a check mark, the sign of a positive mark. Used as a motif on sports shoes since the 1970s, this check mark is now so recognizable that the company name itself has became superfluous. The solid corporate logo design was registered as a trademark in 1995.

Ads and ad campaigns based on mythic subtexts can be found everywhere. Without going into detail, a perusal of several ad campaigns of recent years reveals images such as the following. For example, ads showing purses and other products hanging over a puddle of water seem to be used frequently. These evoke the myth of Narcissus, a beautiful youth beloved by the wood nymph Echo, who refused her and anyone else who pursued him amorously. The goddess of vengeance, Nemesis, caused Narcissus to fall in love with his own reflection in a pond. Narcissus became disembodied, dissolving into the water image of himself on the pond's surface until nothing was left of him but a flower bearing his name. Ads designed to suggest that the owner of a purse can, like Narcissus, become as elegant and beautiful as a flower constitute a clever retelling of the Narcissus story. In a 1990s ad for Rémy Martin cognac, an attractive female model is shown staring seductively at someone or something beyond the visual perimeter of the ad text. She is holding a lit cigar. The whole ad is in black and white, but the smoke billowing from the cigar is cognac colored, matching the color of the bottle and two glasses containing the cognac on the bottom part of the ad. The logo of the Rémy Martin company is that of a satyr, which in Greek mythology was a minor woodland deity, attendant on Bacchus and usually represented as having pointed ears, short horns, the head and body of a man, and the legs of a goat and as being fond of riotous merriment and lechery. The female suggests a modern-day embodiment of a satyr—a subtext reinforced by the fact that her bottom half is not shown. A satyr was half human in the top part of its body and half animal in the lower part. Her glance is clearly indicative of mischief, slyness, artfulness, and lustfulness all at once—all satyr traits. Her satyr look is further reinforced by the fact that she has pointed ears—another unmistakable feature of the satyr. The implications that this mythic narrative has for imbibing Rémy Martin are self-explanatory.

A consideration of mythologization techniques leads to a consideration of two other related techniques, which can be called *aesthetic* and *subliminal*. The former inheres in the use of the same methods of artists to enhance the aesthetic appeal of ads and brand image generally. Perfume ads that show women surrounded by a dark void or that appear mysteriously "out of nothingness," as in a dream, are created according to the principles of surrealist art—the art form that expresses the workings of the subconscious through fantastic imagery and the incongruous juxtaposition of subject matter. Many ads for perfumes, such as the many Chanel ones, are essentially "surrealist puzzles." Aesthetic techniques will be discussed in various parts of subsequent chapters. The latter (subliminal advertising) involves the use of any technique designed to communicate a hidden meaning below the threshold of consciousness or apprehension (Key 1972, 1976, 1980, 1989). The most common type of subliminal technique is embedding images in an advertisement. Subtle sexual images, for instance, can be worked into the shape of spaghetti on a plate or into the puff of exhaled cigarette smoke. The theory behind such a technique is that the unconscious mind will pick up the image and make an association between eating the spaghetti or smoking a cigarette and sexuality, hence creating a false need for the product. However, no evidence has ever emerged to show that subliminal advertising is effective.

3

Brand Names

> To become a celebrity is to become a brand name.
>
> —Philip Roth, b. 1933

The names of products are known by virtually everyone. They are as recognizable as the names of celebrities. Who doesn't recognize names such as Coca-Cola, Kleenex, Scotch Tape, or Ivory Soap? They have become veritably (and literally) household names. No wonder, then, that product names, known as **brand names**, are so fiercely protected by corporations and manufacturers. In each industrialized country, anyone who uses a trademark or brand name acquires the legal right to prevent others from subsequently using a similar one. Anyone who uses one that it is likely to cause customer confusion is considered generally to be an infringer and can be sued. Unlike patent or copyright infringement, trademark infringement is defined solely by the likely confusion of customers. The usual remedy after a court trial finding trademark infringement is an injunction prohibiting the infringer from using its mark. All this bears witness to the power of brand names as primary constituents in the product's signification system.

The name is what allows consumers to identify their goods and distinguish them from those made or sold by others. The brand name identifies the source of a product and fixes responsibility for its quality. So powerful is the brand name as an identifier of the product that, on several occasions, it has instead been used by consumers as metonyms to name the product type. Such names then lost their legal status as trademarks. Examples include *aspirin*, *scotch tape*, *cellophane*, *escalator*, and, more recently, *iPod*. This chapter looks at the naming strategies used to create brand image. A product without a name simply will not sell in today's world. The reasons for this will be woven into the ensuing discussion.

WHAT'S IN A NAME?

In Shakespeare's *Romeo and Juliet*, Romeo Montague and Juliet Capulet meet and fall in love. But they are doomed from the start since they belong to warring families. In the second act, Juliet tells Romeo that a name is an artificial and meaningless symbol and that she loves the person who is called "Montague," not the Montague name and not the Montague family. She states, "What's in a name? That which we call a rose by any other word would smell as sweet." This short line certainly encapsulates the central struggle and tragedy of the play. But it is not a statement that a manufacturer or advertiser would ever entertain as constituting good advice.

As we saw in the previous chapter, there are many sophisticated strategies and techniques that advertisers can use to create persuasive messages and anchor brand image firmly into social consciousness. But without naming the product first, all these would be ineffectual. People perceive the image or personality communicated by a product as being imprinted into the name it bears. Indeed, the term *brand* is really the word for product name. Branding was, originally, the searing of flesh with a hot iron to produce a scar or mark with an easily recognizable pattern for identification or other purposes. The Egyptians branded livestock as early as 2000 B.C.E. In the late medieval period, trades people and guild members posted characteristic marks outside their shops, leading to the notion of trademark. Medieval swords and ancient Chinese pottery, for instance, were also marked with identifiable symbols so that buyers could trace their origin and determine their quality. Among the best-known trademarks surviving from early modern times are the striped pole of the barbershop and the three-ball sign of the pawnbroker shop. The practice of branding was brought to North America in the sixteenth century by the Spanish conqueror Hernán Cortés (1485–1547). Used primarily as proof of ownership, it developed over time into a practice for keeping records on quality. In most American cattle states, the law requires to this day the registration of brands, and altering a brand is a criminal offense. Branding has also been used on human beings—the branding of prisoners, for instance, was a form of punishment used by the ancient Greeks and Romans and later adopted by the Anglo-Saxons. Criminals, slaves, army deserters, and "sinners" (such as women alleged to be witches) have been branded in the past. The practice declined around the middle of the nineteenth century.

Names

A *name* is a special kind of sign. It is particularly interesting semiotically because of the fact that it links the possessor of the name to the culture in which he or she is born. Across cultures, a neonate is not considered a full-fledged member of the culture until he or she is given a name. The act of naming a newborn infant is his or her first rite of passage in society, becoming identified as a separate individual with a unique personality. If a person is not given a name by his or her family, then society will step in to do so. A person taken into a family—by marriage, adoption, or for some other reason—is also typically assigned the family's name. Throughout the world, the name is perceived as identical to the person. In Inuit culture, an individual is perceived to have a body, a soul, and a name; a person is not seen as complete without all three. A few years ago, a British television program called *The Prisoner* played on this very same latent perception in our own culture. It portrayed a totalitarian world in which people were assigned numbers instead of traditional names—*Number 1*, *Number 2*, and so on. The idea was, obviously, that a person could be made to conform to the will of the state and could be more easily controlled by state officials if he or she did not have a name. The whole series was, in a sense, a portrayal of the struggle that humans feel to discover the meaning of self. The use of numerical identification of prisoners and slaves is, in effect, a negation of their humanity and, ultimately, their existence.

All names have historical and culture-specific meanings, even though today we may no longer be aware of them. Documents reveal that early peoples gave someone a name with a definite knowledge of the meaning of the name. In the Bible, for example, a widow exclaims, "Call me not Naomi (*pleasant*), call me Mara (*bitter*): for the Almighty hath dealt very bitterly with me" (Ruth 1:20). Most of the common given names in Western culture come from Hebrew, Greek, Latin, or Teutonic languages. Hebrew names taken from the Bible have traditionally provided the most important source of Western names—for example, *John* (gracious gift of God), *Mary* (wished for), *Michael* (who is like God), *David* (beloved), *Elizabeth* (oath of God), *James* (may God protect, or one who takes the place of another), *Joseph* (the Lord shall add), *Hannah* (God has favored me), and *Samuel* (God has heard). Greek and Latin names often refer to abstract qualities—for example, *Alexander* (helper of humanity), *Barbara* (stranger), *George* (farmer), *Helen* (light), *Margaret* (pearl), *Philip* (lover of horses), *Stephen* (crown or garland), *Clarence* (famous), *Emily* (flattering), *Patricia* (of noble birth), *Victor* (conqueror), and *Virginia* (maidenly). Teutonic names usually consist of two elements joined together without regard to their relationship. For example, *William* is composed of two name elements, *Wille* (will or resolution) and *helm* (helmet). Some of these name elements are found at the beginning, such as *ead* (rich) in *Edwin* and *Edmund*, or at the end, such as *weard* (guardian) in *Howard* and *Edward*.

Name giving is extended across cultures to inanimate referents. When this is done, the objects somehow take on, as if by magic, an animate quality of their own. Throughout the world, naming objects and artifacts is felt to bestow on them a mysterious life force. When a child names a teddy bear, that toy comes to life in the child's imagination. Similarly, when we name storms or commercial products, they too seem to come to life. Things with names have a personality; those without names do not. In effect, when a product is named, it enters into the human cultural sphere, becoming identified as a separate entity with a unique personality.

Brand Names

Names were first used toward the end of the nineteenth century. Previously, everyday household products were sold in neighborhood stores from large bulk containers. Around 1880, soap manufacturers started naming their products so that they could be identified—Ivory, Pears', Sapolio, Colgate, and so on—because the market was starting to be flooded by uniform mass-produced and, thus, indistinguishable products. It is not known which product was named first, but the 1882 naming by Harley Proctor of his generically named "White Soap" as "Ivory Soap"—an idea that apparently came to him while reading a psalm in church—is considered to be the most likely candidate by most historians of advertising. In December of that year, Proctor also introduced the slogan into advertising, referring to Ivory Soap in all his promotional literature as "99 and 44/100% pure." As Proctor realized, a slogan is effective as a memory-aiding device because it is an elaboration of the brand name—a kind of self-styled definition of it. The concept of brand was thus born. By simply labeling products in grocery, dry goods, and department stores with descriptive or colorful names, manufacturers soon found that sales of the products increased significantly. In some cases, the trademark was used as the brand name for the product. Such was the case with the Parker Pen Company—one of the first trademarks to be converted into a brand name in 1888 in Janesville, Wisconsin, by George Safford Parker. Parker simply named each pen produced by his company a "Parker pen." The strategy worked brilliantly—the Parker Pen Company became the world's largest producer of fountain pens in the latter part of the nineteenth century.

By the early 1920s, it became obvious that branding was not just a simple strategy for product differentiation but also the very fuel that propelled corporate identity and product recognition. As Naomi Klein (2000: 6) aptly observes, brand naming became the general practice among manufacturers of products because the market was starting to be flooded by indistinguishable products: "Competitive branding became a necessity of the machine age." By the early 1950s, it became obvious that branding was not just a simple strategy for product differentiation but also the very semiotic fuel that propelled corporate identity. Even the advent of no-name products, designed to cut down the cost of buying them to the consumer, have had little effect on the semiotic power that brand naming has on the consciousness of people. Names such as Nike, Apple, Body Shop, Calvin Klein, and Levi's have become cultural symbols recognized by virtually anyone living in a modern consumerist society. As Klein (2000: 16) goes on to remark, for such firms the brand name constitutes "the very fabric of their companies."

Above all else, the names assigned to products are intended at a rudimentary level of perception to convey a specific type of meaning. For example, products bearing the names of the actual manufacturers evoke images of tradition, reliability, artistry, sophistication, and so on, such as Armani, Benetton, Folger's, Calvin Klein, and Gucci. Products named after fictitious characters elicit specific colorful and appealing images; for example, Mr. Clean evokes the image of a strong toiler and Betty Crocker of a modern woman with cooking savvy. And products named with combinations of words are intended to elicit composite meanings, such as Fruitopia (Fruit + Utopia) and Yogourt (Yogurt + Gourmet).

The list of brand-naming strategies is an extensive one. More will be said about these in the remaining parts of this chapter. Suffice it to say at this point that throughout the history of modern advertising, the coinage of an appropriate brand name has always been perceived to be the first crucial step in getting a product into social consciousness. Often this implies keeping in step with the times. In early 2000, some carmakers, for instance, started looking at newer naming trends that were designed to appeal to a generation of customers accustomed to an Internet style of communication. Cadillac, for instance, announced a new model with the monogram name CTS in 2001. Acura also transformed its line of models with names such as TL, RL, MDX, and RSX. Such names are now proliferating, as will be discussed later.

FROM PRODUCT TO BRAND

Brand names, clearly, do much more than just identify a product. As the previous examples show, they are constructed to create signification systems for the product. As Alina Wheeler (2003: 2) has observed, "Products are created in the factory; brands are created in the mind." Names are "life givers," as we have seen. By naming a product, the manufacturer is, in effect, bestowing on it the same kinds of meanings that are reserved for people. In a basic semiotic sense, a product that is named is "humanized."

At a practical informational level, naming a product has, of course, a denotative function; that is, it allows consumers to identify what product they desire to purchase (or not). But at a connotative level, the product's name generates images that go well beyond this simple identifier function. Consider Armani shoes as a specific case in point. Denotatively, the name allows us to identify the shoes should we desire to buy them rather than, say, Nike shoes. However, this is not all it does. The use of the manufacturer's name, rather than some invented name, assigns an aura of craftsmanship and superior quality to the product. The shoes are thus perceived to be the "work" of an artist (Giorgio Armani). They constitute, in effect, a "work of shoe art," not just an assembly-line product for everyone to wear.

Naming the Product

Naming a product makes it possible to refer to it as if it had a distinctive character or quality. And it is easier to remember things as words than to remember the things themselves. A word classifies something, keeps it distinct from other things, and, above all else, bestows socially relevant meanings to it. The name Ivory, for example, evokes an image of something "ultrawhite," Royal Baking Powder of something "regal" and "splendid," Bon Ami of "a good friend," and so on. Such suggestive images stick to the mind in the same way that the meanings of ordinary words do. They become a part of our semantic memory system. Because of this semantic and cultural dimension of naming, it comes as little surprise to find that the term *brand* is used today to refer not just to a specific product line but also to the company that manufactures it and to the social image that the company wishes to impart of itself and of its products. Thus, the name Coca-Cola now refers not only to the actual soft drink but also to the company itself, the social meanings that drinking Coke entails, and so on. Coca-Cola was one of the first brands to carve out for itself a brand image.

So how are product and services named? As was implicitly suggested earlier, the name must fit the product and can range from the name of the manufacturer to simple descriptive names, telling the consumer what the product will do. Thus, for instance, in the world of fashion, designer names such as Gucci, Armani, and Calvin Klein are highly effective because they evoke images of objets d'art rather than images of mere clothes, shoes, or jewelry; so too do names such as Ferrari, Lamborghini, and Maserati in the world of automobiles. The manufacturer's name, in such cases, extends the meaning of the product considerably. When people buy an Armani or a Gucci product, they feel that they are buying a work of art to be displayed on the body; when they buy Poison, by Christian Dior, they sense that they are buying a dangerous but alluring love potion; when they buy Moondrops, Natural Wonder, Rainflower, Sunsilk, or Skin Dew cosmetics, they feel that they are acquiring some of nature's beauty resources; and when they buy Eterna 27, Clinique, Endocil, or Equalia beauty products, they sense that they are getting products made with scientific precision. No-name products do not engender such arrays of connotations.

Manufacturer brand names are, in effect, eponyms of a particular kind since they refer to a person whose name is on the product and is thus perceived as being the source of the product itself. This is why they must have an appropriate "phonetic quality," so to speak; otherwise, they will likely fail in the marketplace. This is why a company will change its name or else use an acronymic name derived from the actual name. For example, the New York designer Ralph Lifshitz chose to change his "unpleasant-sounding" name to Ralph Lauren, creating a multi-billion-dollar clothing enterprise as a result. Similarly, Pietro Cardino of France modified his Italian name to Pierre Cardin so as to give it a more appropriate "French sound." The Ikea furniture company was one of the first to use acronymy—the first two letters are taken from the initial letters of the name of its founder *I*ngvar *K*amprad, the third letter comes from the initial letter of Kamprad's family farm called *E*lmtaryd, and the final letter comes from the first letter of the Swedish village of *A*gunnaryd (where the farm is located).

Marketing research shows that luxury items named after the manufacturer has produced a cult of connoisseurship whereby ordinary products, such as Calvin Klein jeans, have become the symbolic means by which consumers convey individuality. Consumer discernment is now a subtle form of social status climbing. Brands like Calvin Klein have become the symbolic means through which people can distinguish themselves, replacing membership in organizations (such as religions).

Iconic brand names are also effective because they are memorable. An **icon**, in semiotic theory, is a sign that resembles its referent. Photographs, portraits, maps, and roman numerals such as I, II, and III are iconic forms designed or created to resemble their referents in a visual way. The Apple computer logo is an example of a visual icon because it portrays its referent (an "apple") visually. Onomatopoeic words such as *drip*, *plop*, *bang*, and *screech* are vocal icons simulating the sounds that certain things, actions, or movements are perceived to make. A name such as Ritz Crackers, for example, assigns an iconic sonority to the product that is simulative of sounds that crackers make as they are being eaten. Another example is the name Drakkar Noir, chosen by the Guy Laroche company for one of its cologne products. The dark bottle conveys an imagery of "fear," the "forbidden," and the "unknown." Forbidden things take place under the cloak of the night, hence the name *noir* (French for "black"). The sepulchral name of the cologne is clearly iconic with the bottle's design at a connotative level, reinforcing the idea that something desirous in the "dark" will happen by splashing on the cologne. The name Drakkar is also obviously suggestive of Dracula, the deadly vampire who mesmerized his sexual prey with a mere glance.

A classic case in the annals of marketing history shows how audio-oral iconicity can be a brand's greatest asset. The case I am referring to is that of Smuckers jam (named after the manufacturer), which appears to be a bad name but actually turns out to be a highly effective one. The slogan of the company plays cleverly on this initial perception: "a name like Smuckers, it has to be good." But the name is a good one because, as Neumeier (2006: 83) aptly puts it, it is "distinctive, short, spellable, pronounceable, likable, portable, and protectable." And, more important, it is onomatopoeic: "Smuckers" sounds like smacking lips, which as Neumeier (2006: 83) goes on to point out, is the preverbal "testament to a yummy jam."

INSIDE THE NAME

The creativity displayed by advertisers to name products seems to know no limits. However, as already intimated, they seem to fall into several generic categories, such as the use of *manufacturer names*, *fictitious character names*, *descriptors*, and *suggestive names*. The first two have already been discussed in some detail and thus will not be taken up as a separate section in this chapter. Essentially, the manufacturer, or *heritage*, name (Armani, Gucci, Benetton, Calvin Klein, Gillette, Folger's, Kraft) imbues the product with connotations of tradition and artistry, whereas products named for a fictitious character (Mr. Clean, Barbie, Betty Crocker) suggest qualities that the name itself is designed to emphasize, such as cleanliness or idealized models of American femininity.

The other two strategies are rhetorical ones. As such, therefore, the line between them is a fine one. They are separated here for the sake of convenience. From ancient times, the use of figures of speech, or *tropes*, has been seen primarily as an essential part of persuasion—a form of discourse employed by orators and writers to strengthen and embellish their speeches and compositions. Aristotle—the one who coined the term **metaphor**—itself a metaphor (*meta* "beyond" + *pherein* "to carry")—saw the power of figurative reasoning in its ability to shed light on abstract concepts. However, he affirmed that, as conceptually powerful as it was, its primary function was stylistic, a device for sprucing up more prosaic and literal ways of communicating. Remarkably, this latter position became the rule by which figurative language came to be judged in Western philosophy ever since. But as a seminal study by Pollio, Barlow, Fine, and Pollio (1977) showed, Aristotle's original view was in effect the correct one. Those researchers found that speakers of English uttered, on average, 3,000 novel verbal metaphors and 7,000 idioms per week. Shortly thereafter, it became clear to language scientists that metaphor was hardly an optional flourish on literal language. On the contrary, they started discovering that it dominated everyday communication and was the source of many symbolic practices. Certainly, advertisers, marketers, and manufacturers have always known about the power of metaphor and verbal suggestion generally.

Descriptors

At the lowest end of the rhetorical scale, as it may be called, is the descriptor name. This is simply a word or phrase, such as Easy Off, that describes the product in some way. Descriptors are called weak in the profession, in opposition to a strong brand, which is a product name that has no recognizable meaning, such as Kodak. These receive broad protection from being used by other companies who might play on the name in order to cause confusion among consumers. Weak brands, on the other hand, are product names created with common descriptor words, such as Wet 'N Wash. These receive less protection, unless the public identifies them with a certain manufacturer as a result of extensive advertising and long, continuous use.

A common type of descriptor name is the toponymic brand name, or the name identifying the geographical location of a product or of a company: American Bell, Bank of America, Western Union, and so on. Another one is the coinage of a word or expression that indicates something about the product. For example, some combinations of words describe product makeup: Frogurt (Frozen + Yogurt). Some descriptors indicate what a product can do or allow the user to accomplish:

Air Fresh
Bug Off
Close-Up Toothpaste
Drip-Dry
Easy On
Easy Wipe
Easy-Clean

Kleenex
Lestoil
Light 'N Easy
No Sweat
One Wipe
Quick Flow
Wash 'N Wear

Even in relaying seemingly straightforward information, such as identifying the manufacturer, indicating the geographical location of the company, or
describing what the product can do, descriptor brand names nevertheless create signification. They identify the product not as a simple product but as
something that belongs somewhere, is created by someone, or can do various
things. And often it is linked subconsciously to significant areas of lifestyle.
For example, in 1998, General Mills introduced a yogurt category called Go-
Gurt. The name was perfect for the tween market for which it was intended.
It applied perfectly to the tween's world and lifestyle. With alliterative and
fun flavor names such as Berry Blue Blast and Rad Raspberry, the brand was
a hit. To quote Siegel, Coffey, and Livingston (2004: 185),

> The name, Go-Gurt, focuses on the idea that this is yogurt you can eat "on the
> go," and "on the go" is expressed as tween activities—playing sports, skate-
> boarding, and playing music. The characters used on the packaging are obviously
> tweens, not kids, not teens, and not adults.

In effect, the brand name entails an unconscious signification system that
can be used and reused for various advertising purposes. The more relevant
meanings a name evokes for a target audience, the more powerful it is and, as
a consequence, the more possibilities it offers to the advertiser for creating
truly effective ads and commercials directed at that audience. The higher the
"connotative index" of a signification system, as it can be called (Beasley and
Danesi 2002), the greater its market appeal.

Suggestive Naming

Names that go far beyond descriptive value can be called, simply, *suggestive
names*. These are constructed rhetorically to make suggestions about product
use that reach into lifestyle, myth, and other domains of human life. Suggestive names raise the connotative index considerably.

Take, for example, the name of the Acura automobile, a name that suggests
both Italian and Japanese words. Italian feminine nouns end in -*a* and certain
Japanese words end in the suffix -*ura* (*tempura*). The brand name is thus

linked iconically to Italian and Japanese words and, by extension, the perceived qualities of the respective cultures at once. Carmakers have used the same strategy of creating car names ending in the vowel *-a*, which, given the inbuilt melodious quality of such words, makes them not only easier to remember but also suggestive of specific qualities. Here are a few examples:

Achieva
Altima
Asuna
Aurora
Corsica
Elantra
Festiva
Integra
Lumina
Maxima
Precidia
Samara
Sentra
Serenia
Sonata

Coining names ending with the vowel *-a* are certainly easier to remember. Moreover, each name contains a lexical part that suggests a specific meaning. For example, Altima suggests reaching the "ultimate heights," Achieva "achievement," Festiva a "festive lifestyle," and so on. The same type of "metaphorical suggestiveness" is noticeable in a host of brands with names consisting of two or more parts, each one suggestive of a specific concept. The following are examples of such names as given to Viagra-type products:

Androgel = suggests androgen (a steroid hormone, such as testosterone or androsterone, that controls the development and maintenance of masculine characteristics)
Viramax = suggests maximum virility

Some names are designed to refer to some aspect of nature, bestowing on the product the meanings that the particular aspect evokes:

Aqua Velva
Cascade
Irish Spring

Mountain Dew
Surf
Tide

Names indicating the kinds of things, such as a vehicle, or the kinds of places that can be visited with it evoke connotations of lifestyle such as "country living," "back-to-nature living," "wild west lifestyle," and so on. The names of car models such as those here (past and present) are fashioned in this way:

Dodge Durango
Ford Escape
Ford Expedition
Ford Explorer
Hyundai Santa Fe
Jeep Grand Cherokee
Jeep Renegade
Jeep Wrangler
Mercury Mountaineer

These names convey the sense that the vehicles will allow city residents to escape and explore the outdoors, to be "renegades," or to live the "cowboy dream" of freedom from the constraints of civilization. Names of products, services, and companies constructed as hyperboles, on the other hand, suggest superiority, excellence, the big picture, a forward-looking attitude, strength, and power:

Future Now
MaxiLight
Multicorp
PowerAde
SuperFresh
Superpower
UltraLite

Some names suggest political ideologies (such as egalitarianism), social attitudes (such as free-spiritedness), potential benefits, and the like:

Advantage Plus
General Electric
General Foods

General Mills
Okay Plus
People's Choice
Viewer's Choice

Various kinds of names are designed to evoke scientific connotations (such as accuracy, precision, or reliability). This is accomplished by the use of word parts (affixes, word endings, and so on) and expressions that come out of the science lexicon:

Anusol
Biogenical
Panasonic
Proof Positive
Technics
Timex
Vagisil

Actually, the technique of combining morphemes (parts of words) strategically abounds in naming practices. For example, the endings -*tastic* (suggestive of words such as *fantastic*), -*tacular* (suggestive of *spectacular*), -*licious* (suggestive of *delicious*), -*rama* (suggestive of *panorama*), and others are found throughout the brand-naming landscape. Here are a few examples (Cook 2004: 68):

Kid-Tastic
Snack-Tastic
Pet-tacular
Sports-tacular
Ice-A-Licious
Carb-O-licious
Beef-a-rama
Stretch-O-Rama

The discussion of the actual types and tokens of suggestive names could go on and on. In addition to those just illustrated, the range goes from suggestive nobility and majesty (Coronation, Morning Glory, Burger King, Monarch's Flour) to common emotions, affective states, and desires (Cheer, Joy, Pledge, Promise). Suggestive names stick to the mind in the same way that colorful words do. They tend to become part of our unconscious semantic memory system because they link the actual product to some referent that is ideally associated with it by means of suggestion. For example, many detergents have names referring to some aspect of nature so as to reinforce the connection between the product and nature's own cleaning resources. Other detergent brand names specify the emotional effects that ensue from using them or else guarantee some positive outcome.

Metaphorical Games

Suggestive names go, clearly, beyond mere description to suggest meanings that reach into specific domains of cultural symbolism. Automobiles named after animals—Mustang, Jaguar, Cougar, and so on—are part of a long-standing perception of the automobile as a replacement of animals as transporters of people. This is why we still refer to the energy associated with motor vehicle engines in terms of "horsepower." This rhetorical linkage reaches as well into other domains of meaning. Animal car names also suggest the qualities of the actual animals after which they are named—a Jaguar suggests a large and powerful creature, a Cougar a fast and exotic animal, and so on. Such naming strategies can be called, generally, metaphorical games (MGs). A car model named Breeze, for instance, suggests metaphorically that the driver will feel a breeze by driving the vehicle and that driving the vehicle is "a breeze." A model named Pathfinder suggests instead that the vehicle will allow its driver to discover a new path or way into unexplored regions. And a model named after a zodiac sign (Aries, Taurus) suggests character traits associated with that sign. In a phrase, MGs allow carmakers to link automobiles with aspects of psychological and social life, such as the following:

- Upscaleness (Park Avenue, Fifth Avenue, Catalina, Monte Carlo, Capri)
- Various lifestyles (Outback, Towncar, New Yorker, Villager)
- Social rank (Viscount, Marquis, Diplomat, Monarch, Ambassador)
- Animal personality characteristics (Beetle, Colt, Cougar, Viper, Mustang, Cobra)
- Exploration or escape from city life (Dakota, Montana, Yukon, Sierra)
- Various social advantages, such as protection, friendship, or security (Protegé, Sidekick, Escort, Cavalier)
- The artistry and elitism associated with classical music (Sonata, Tempo, Prelude)
- World travel, car racing, and the alluring qualities of foreign worlds (Seville, Grand Prix)

MGs reveal the essence of what advertising is all about—creating sense through what Vico called poetic logic (see chapter 2). For example, the per-

Table 3.1.   Video Game Names

Name	*Suggested Associations*
Xbox Final Fantasy X	X-Files, X-rated movies, etc. (= forbidden pleasures, intrigue, mystery, etc.)
GameCube PlayStation	Rubik's Cube, video game parlors, etc. (= intelligence, technology, etc.)
Gran Turismo Grand Theft Auto	Gran Prix (= speed, power, coolness, etc.)
James Bond 007 Agent Under Fire	Intrigue, life on the margins, excitement, cool, James Bond, etc.
Melee Metal Gear Solid	Car racing, adolescent-type clashes, free-for-alls, etc.
Wii	Internet style and savvy (iPod, iMac, etc.) and a play on the sound of the name (Wii = We) and (Wiki, as in "Wikipedia")

fume named Poison, by Christian Dior, is a pure metaphor because, as Wolfe (1989: 3) observes, it evokes a sense of "mystery, alchemy and the archetype of the sorceress." The metaphorical meanings of *poison* are thus transferred to the product, greatly enhancing its allure.

MGs abound in the names given to video games. Names such as PacMan, Pitfall, and Pong that were common in 1970s and 1980s (when video games came onto the social scene) have been replaced with new, trendy names, such as those shown in table 3.1.

One may ask why MGs are used so frequently to name products. The simple answer seems to be that they work. Let me suggest that they work because modern-day society is willing to embrace consumerism with its implicit promise of a world based on pleasure for the masses. And metaphor is a mental link to that world. The term "brand logic" is now used in marketing to explain the logic behind naming products in ways such as those described here. This is indeed the correct term—itself suggestive of Vico's term *poetic logic* (mentioned a few times in this book). The word *logic* derives from the Greek *logos* meaning both "word" and the "thought" it evokes. A product is something made in factories, in shops, and so on. A brand, on the other hand, is a logical construct—a name evoking an unconscious system of thought. But the "logical reasoning" used is hardly deductive or rational; it is, rather, based on a poetic sense of the meaning nuances built into words. The underlying hypothesis I have woven throughout this chapter has been, in fact, that the whole brand-naming process is essentially a "poetic act."

Vico defined poetic logic as the faculty of the mind that guides our attempts to make sense of things in his landmark treatise of 1725 *The New Science* (Bergin and Fisch 1984). It is an imaginative form of reasoning that allows us to understand the world on our own human terms by endowing us with the ability to make connections within the world. These connections result in metaphors. Brand names are, essentially, metaphors in the Vichian sense. As such, they become themselves constructs for further rhetorical processes. This can be seen in a fairly concrete way in the tendency of brands themselves to become part of what can be called "social logic," an unconscious system of reasoning and inference that is tied to the rhetorical values of the brand names. In a phrase, brands make poetic sense.

SYMBOLIC BRANDS

Brands named with symbols such as letters of the alphabet or with acronyms abound in the marketplace today. These can be called, simply, *symbolic brands*. Brands such as X-Factor drinks, BVD underwear, CNN, V-8 vegetable juice, the Toyota XR Matrix, and so on are all symbolic brands. Abbreviated writing and name giving was used by the Greeks as early as the fourth century B.C.E., gradually evolving into a true shorthand code known as *tachygraphy*. It was the slave Tyro who probably invented the first true shorthand system around 60 B.C.E. (after alphabets had become the norm), apparently for recording the speeches of Cicero.

The use of all forms of symbolism in advertising links it directly to the world of human meaning. The twentieth-century German philosopher Ernst Cassirer (1874–1945) characterized the human being as a "symbolic animal," which was his way of emphasizing that symbols are to the human psyche what food is to the body. This is an implicit truism that the world of modern-day persuasive marketing has always known. In fact, what is marketing if not the science of symbolism? The current practice of coining symbolic names brings this out rather conspicuously.

Zipf's Law and Symbolic Names

Symbolic naming strategies are of great interest to semioticians not only because they reveal our symbolic nature but also because they fall under the rubric of what is known as Zipf's law, after the late Harvard linguistics professor George Kingsley Zipf (1929, 1932, 1935, 1949). In a series of statistical studies during the late 1920s and early 1930s, Zipf noticed that the shortest words (in number of alphabet characters) were the most frequently used ones in all kinds of written texts—in English, these would include words such as *a*, *the*, and *and*. Zipf then went on to generalize his discovery with the notion that languages tend to evolve economically, making progressively greater use of such "compression strategies" as abbreviation, acronymy, and the like: ad = advertisement, NATO = North Atlantic Treaty Organization, laser = light amplification by stimulated emission of radiation, and so on. This derived "principle of economy" can also be seen in the use of tables, technical and scientific notation systems, indexes, footnotes, and bibliographic traditions. All such phenomena validate the underlying implication in Zipf's law that compression saves effort. The operation of Zipf's law is particularly evident in how languages have been changing in cyberspace, where coinages such as *b4* = *before*, *f2f* = *face-to-face*, *gr8* = *great*, *h2cus* = *hope to see you soon*, *g2g* = *gotta go*, and so on have become the norm.

There are five types of compression or miniaturization forces that are generally at work in Netlingo, as the language used on the Internet has been called (Crystal 2006): abbreviation, acronymy, phonetic replacement, compounding, and symbol replacement. Abbreviations are shortened words: *ppl* for *people* and *b/c* for *because*. Acronyms are forms composed of the first letter of every word within a phrase: *OMG* for *oh my God* and *LOL* for *laugh out loud*. Phonetic replacements are words in which certain letters and numbers replace entire words because they represent the pronunciation more compactly, such as *cu* for *see you* and *l8r* for *later*. Compounding involves the combination of separate words or parts of words to make a new one (i.e., shorter than the forms taken separately): *mousepad*, *webonomics*, *netlag*, *netizen*, *hackitude*, and *geekitude*. Symbol replacement, as its name implies, is the use of symbols or letters with symbol value (such as *e-*) in place of letters and words: *e-zine*, *e-commerce*, and so on.

Coining brand names using similar miniaturization techniques fits in nicely with the times. But it does much more than that. Consider the letter X, which seems to be used all over the brand-naming landscape. Table 3.2 shows some examples.

Table 3.2. Names Constructed with an *X*

Clothing and Footwear	Electronic Products	Household Products, Foods, Drinks	Miscellaneous
X-treme	X-cam	Xanath	XactValue
3xdry	Xybernaut	Xellent Vodka	X-Tend (pen)
MaxX	Amtex	Xuxu	X-Acto (knives)
X-tech	NeXT	Xyience	Xcite (herbal Viagra)
Xcess	XM Satellite Radio	X-Stick	X-Lite (bicycles)
X-Girl	Xbox	Xzude	X-Factor (TV show)
X-Cape	Xobile	Xtreme 3 Razor	X-Terra (vehicle)
XOXO	Xincom	Xantax (prescription)	X-Trail (vehicle)

These seem to have a mysterious, occult quality to them. In a fascinating book titled *Sign after the X* (2000), Marina Roy has traced the history of this sign, showing that it has had very little to do with phonetics at any period of its history but everything to do with symbolism. Here are a few of its traditional meanings:

- Any unknown or unnamed factor, thing, or person
- The signature of any illiterate person
- The sign for mistake
- Cancellation
- The unknown, especially in mathematics
- The multiplication symbol
- The roman numeral 10
- A mechanical defect
- A location on a map
- A choice on a ballot
- A motion picture rating
- A symbol for Christ
- The symbol for a kiss
- The symbol for Chronos, the Greek god of time
- The symbol for the planet Saturn in Greek and Roman mythology

Today it seems to stands for youth culture (Xbox), adventure comic heroes (X-Men), and erotic movies (X-rated). It is little wonder to find that this very symbol is now found throughout the advertising and brand-naming world, reverberating with its many meanings latently. Single-letter symbolism does not stop at X. Here are other examples of similarly constructed symbolic brand names:

Names with *i*
iCaps (eye care products)
iCom (computer software)
iMac
iMark (eye shadow)
iPod
iTunes
iZod (shoes)

Such names reverberate with Internet savvy and technological chic. The lowercase *i* suggests "imagination," "Internet," "ingenuity," and "intelligence," among many other things. And, above all else, it suggests a "Net-savvy strategy," as it can be called. This will be discussed more generally later in the final section of this chapter. At this point, I would like to suggest that symbolic brand names are powerful because they produce a kind of magic spell on the product that is not unlike the sense of magic that the ancients associated with names in general. From the beginning of time, names have been thought to have special magical powers. This perception is woven into the prayers, formulas, incantations, and litanies of all religions, which are seen as capable (potentially at least) of curing disease, warding off evil, bringing good to oneself, and so on. In many early cultures, even knowing the name of a deity was purported to give the knower great power—in Egyptian mythology, the sorceress Isis tricked the sun god, Ra, into revealing his name and thus allowing her to gain power over him and all other gods. In some cultures, the name given to the newborn child is thought to bring with it all the qualities of the previous individuals who shared that name, weaving a sort of magical protective aura on the individual named after them. The brand name also seems to work an unconscious magic on modern-day humans, making them see, for example, products as necessary for success, beauty, adventure, and so on or creating distinctions between better or worse—be it in body, hairstyle, or general lifestyle. Symbolic brand names create belief in products in the same way that certain words create belief in magic.

Net-Savvy Symbolic Names

In effect, the names discussed in the foregoing section are, as mentioned, Net-savvy symbolic names. They tap into general cultural trends, indicating that naming practices in the advertising/marketing world are constantly attempting to keep in step with the times. Car model names based on single letters now seems to be the rule, not the exception, with names such as X-Terra, X-Trail, TL, RL, MDX, RSX, Aero X (Saab), and so on. Mobile phones, predictably, are also named in a similar way, with alphanumeric forms such as Sony's W810i and Motorola's RZAR V3T abounding; so too are video games, with names such as XBox, PS3, and Wii. This naming strategy also taps into an emerging pop culture style of writing words as they sound, not as they are spelled. Products named with trendy spelling styles, with combinations of words and parts of words, or with uppercase letters in the middle of compound words, now abound. Here is an illustrative list (Frankel 2004: 106–7):

AvantGuide
FedEx
GoVantage
Mentium

Oriens
PlainSight
Revelist
Solutionary
Verizon
Vonage
WorldWise

The integration between advertising style and pop culture involves not just products but services, stores, and entire corporations as well. It has become a veritable fad. Here are the names of a selection of businesses, products, services, and so on that have adopted this style (Cook 2004):

Alphanumeric Brands
2BFree (clothes)
2CE (computer software)
4 Ever Nails
4 Runners Only
Cabs 4 Kids
H2Optix (eyewear)
XM4Home (radio system)

Letter-Name Brands
C-Thru-U Beautifying Sheer Tint
E Z Taxi
Fax-U-Back Services
Skin-Eze
Spex Appeal
Xpert Stationers
Xpressair
Xylocaine

Brand Names Using Letter Substitutions or Symbols
Afrique Fabriks
Bratz dolls
DataViz
Glam Gurlz
Graphic M*I*S (computer software)
Hotpak
Kidz Karz
Krispie Kreams

Minds@Work (digital equipment)
Playskool

In fact, some of these tendencies existed long before the Internet age. Products such as Cheez Whiz, Spic 'N Span, Wheetabix, Kool cigarettes, and others were so named in an early manifestation of symbolic savvy. The Toys R Us model, with *R* constituting a letter-name technique, has been copied by brands, stores, and companies extensively: Babies R Us, Ratz R Us, Cats R Us, and Vans R Us. The letters *N* and *U* were also used in this way in the pre-Internet age. Here are some examples:

Spic 'N' Span
Wet 'N' Wild
Free N Cool
U-Haul
Nails U Love

Brand names such as Pret-O-Lite, U All Kno After Dinner Mints, Phiteezi Shoes, and U-Rub-IN go back to the 1920s (Cook 2004: 44). It seems that this play on the letter–number–sound pattern has always been a brand-naming strategy for the simple reason that it is iconic and thus highly memorable. Moreover, it is a pattern within pop culture and, thus, shows synergy with it. Rock and hip-hop artists use this pattern consistently, adopting names such as Guns N Roses, Snoop Dogg, Salt N Pepa, and so on, and so do video game players who assume avatar names such as Mysticc, Xiryc, Zaxh, and Zidex (Cook 2004: 58). And, of course, the same pattern and overall style characterizes the language of chat rooms, online newsgroups, and social sites such as YouTube and MySpace.

Above all else, such spelling patterns suggest coolness. For example, many businesses have used the letter *K* for *C* to name products since the 1920s, when this practice was adopted by young people to set themselves apart from the adult mainstream. The hippies of the 1960s used the same letter to spell "Amerika," indicating that they were different from the "establishment" and thus claimed the country on their own terms. The spelling symbolized this. Here are examples of businesses who spell themselves in this ersatz subversive way, thus imprinting a sense of youth coolness into the name as a subtext:

Kid Krazy
Krazy Kapers
Kool (cigarettes)

Krustee's Pizza
Kwik Kopy

As the stage for pop culture shifts to cyberspace, or at least converges with it, Zipf's law will guide the future course of brand naming more and more, showing how extensive has been the integration between technology, culture, marketing, and advertising since the advent of the latter as a social force in the early part of the twentieth century. And as technology leads to new forms of communication and symbolism, the synergy between advertising and culture will become even more inevitable. It will extend the *simulacrum*; the late French semiotician and philosopher Jean Baudrillard (1929–2007) called this synergy. Baudrillard claimed that the borderline between our symbols and reality has utterly vanished in today's mediated world, collapsing into a universal simulacrum, a mind-set where the distinction between texts and reality has merged completely.

The Power of Numbers

Alphanumeric names were also used in the past to great effect. As Altman (2006: 70) points out, numbers are magical given their various connotations:

> Think about the difference between a "blended vegetable drink" and "V8." From the name, you know that there are eight kinds of vegetables in every container. Heinz 57 explains on its Web site that in 1896 H. J. Heinz arbitrarily turned "more than 60 products into 57 varieties." The magic number became world renowned and now is virtually synonymous with the H. J. Heinz Company.

The link to numerological symbolism is obvious in many brand names and marketing ploys. Letters and numbers were once the same thing. Indeed, alphabetical order is the way it is because each letter once represented a number—alphabetical order is numerical order. Using numbers in marketing products has become a veritable trend—for example, Mercedes Benz's E3-20, the Saab line of cars that all start with the number 9, the Mazda RX-7, the Pontiac G6, the Corvette C6, the Audi A4, and so on. At one level, these alphanumeric trends are clearly designed to appeal to a new generation of Net-savvy customers as mentioned. But at a different level, they conjure up the same images of occultism evoked by ancient numerological practices. And these have hardly disappeared from modern-day cultures.

Just think of the number 13 and how many high-rises in large cities acknowledge its numerological value by simply avoiding to use it. So widespread is the "fear" of this number that it has even been assigned a clinical name: *triskaidekaphobia*. And, needless to say, the satanic number 666 is recognized by virtually everyone as indicating something malevolent, even by skeptics, given its cultural history. In the book of Revelations the number 666 is mentioned as the "number of the beast." It has been surmised that this referred to Nero the Roman emperor, whose name has this numerological value if written with the Hebrew alphabet. The interpretation of this number as referring to the Antichrist is due to Martin Luther (1483–1546), the German leader of the Reformation. Luther claimed that 666 years was the duration of the papal regime.

Numerology is the belief that numbers possess mystical meanings. And it is this belief that, in my view, is worked into many alphanumeric names. Consider two numbers, 5 and 7, which have made their way into a vast array of products. I mention just two cases in point—Chanel No. 5 and the Mazda RX-7. There are, of course, practical reasons for naming products this way—Chanel No. 5 was the fifth perfume created by Coco Chanel (so the story goes). But the instant a product is named in this way, our reaction to it is hardly rational. Imagine naming a perfume product with the number 666 no matter what practical reason this may have. The number 5 was associated in ancient numerological systems to the pentagon and its mystical derivative the pentagram. The Pythagoreans ascribed the power of womanhood to this five-sided figure—a symbol that blended the profane and sacred elements of life. Have you ever wondered why the most powerful nation in the world has named and designed the headquarters of its defense system as the Pentagon? Mysticism reaches clearly beyond the commercial domain. There is little doubt that Chanel No. 5 unconsciously evokes the symbolism of the sacred feminine. The number 7 has a long tradition of mysticism and occultism. There are seven days and seven nights, seven wonders of the world, seven dwarfs, seven deadly sins, and seven gods of good fortune in Japanese lore. The list of the mystical meanings associated with the number 7 is a truly mind-boggling one. No wonder that so many products now incorporate the number 7 as part of their identity.

Belief in the magical powers of symbols is clearly not limited to tribal cultures. The marketer's occultism works its unconscious magic on modern-day humans, making them see, for example, products as necessary for success or creating distinctions between better or worse—be it body shape, hairstyle, or brand of blue jeans. It is the symbolism of products that creates allegiances to them.

A recent example of numerological branding, as it can be called, is Camel No. 9 cigarettes. Eager to increase sales of the Camel brand among women, the R. J. Reynolds Tobacco Company named the brand with the number 9 not only to suggest women's fragrances like Chanel's numbered perfumes and songs like *Love Potion No. 9* (from the 1950s) but also to link the brand to the occult and mythic senses that this number probably elicits unconsciously. For one thing, 9 is a product of 3 × 3, and this number has a long-standing connection to myth, legend, and religion—I mention simply the Triune God of Christianity as a case in point. Together with a package design with colors such as hot-pink fuchsia and mint-green teal and the slogan "Light and Luscious," the brand name is clearly directed at a female audience, trying to eclipse the Virginia Slims brand that has always been popular with women smokers. In effect, the new brand is a text in the semiotic sense—a signifying form that leads suggestively in many directions, from the occult to the trendy female market of today. It shows, yet again, that signs and symbols are more powerful than physical stimuli in human life.

4

Logos

If we could pull out our brain and use only our eyes.

—Pablo Picasso, 1881–1973

In chapter 2, the topic of the Nike logo came up—a logo representing the wing of the Nike, the Greek goddess of victory. It was designed in 1972 by a graduate student who was paid, so the story goes, a mere $35. The check mark, or "swoosh," has gone on since then to become one of the most recognizable global symbols. Together with its "Just Do It" advertising slogan, the check mark is now perceived to be shorthand for winning, achievement, and excellence. How could a simple visual sign accomplish so much? As mentioned in the previous chapter, a sign does so because we are, as the German philosopher Ernst Cassirer so aptly put it, a symbolic species—a species that responds to symbolism emotionally, aesthetically, and intellectually. As mentioned, as a visual sign suggesting speed, the Nike logo works on several levels, from the iconic to the mythical. At the iconic level, it implies the activity of running at top speed with the Nike shoe; at the mythic level, it taps into the idea of speed as symbolic of power and conquest (such as in the Olympic races). The combination of these two signifying levels creates a perception of the logo—and thus the product—as having a connection to both reality and narrative history.

Visual symbolism in particular is powerful because it is more ancient and, arguably, more essential than its verbal counterpart. This basic truth has not gone unnoticed by the marketplace. Wherever one looks in that marketplace, there are visual advertising symbols, known as logos, designed to enhance recognition of products, from jeans and automobiles to toothpaste and running shoes. Companies and products like NBC, Bell, United Air Lines, Warner Communications, Macintosh, IBM, the United Way, and Playboy are equivalent to the logos that represent them—the NBC peacock, the Mac apple with a bite taken out of it, and so on. Until the 1970s, logos on clothes were concealed discretely inside a collar or on a pocket. But today, logos such as Ralph Lauren's polo horseman and Lacoste's alligator are shown prominently on clothing items. They constitute symbols of "ersatz nobility" that legions of people are eager to wear. They also have implicit narrative meaning. The stagecoach logo of the Wells Fargo Company, for instance, tells a condensed story of early America since the stagecoach was not only the means by which mail and various goods were once transported in the United States but also a symbol of the Wild West and all the Hollywood adventure that it elicits.

In a sense, such visual signs are the modern-day counterparts of the carvings of animals on roofs and walls, along with sculptures of animals and human figures, that go back tens of thousands of years. According to some estimates, the earliest known visual symbol might even be 135,000 years old! It is an animal bone with 70 arcs, bands, and chevrons etched in it. Whether for decorative reasons, to record something, or for some mystical rite, the bone was undoubtedly created to identify something to the eyes long before the invention of alphabets around 1000 B.C.E. (Davenport 1984). Contemporary logos are not much different from that bone. The technique of promoting products by identifying them with logos has become a primary marketing strategy since the turn of the twentieth century. It was (and continues to be) based on the premise that the appeal of a product increases if it can be literally associated to some distinguishing visual mark. And, it would seem, the more the mark evokes the same kinds of meanings that early tribal carvings, sculptures, and etched bones evoked, the more psychologically effective it is. As the modern marketer has come to realize, the world of modern human beings is a de facto world of mystical archetypal images manifesting themselves in many forms and disguises.

The objective of this chapter is to discuss the semiotic role that logos play in advertising. As visual signs, they reveal that we literally read meaning into the things we see, and, like names, we link these meanings to cultural systems and history.

WHAT IS A LOGO?

As straightforward as the meaning of the term *logo* appears, it is actually rather complex, as Neumeier (2006: 1) points out:

The term *logo* is short for *logotype*, design-speak for a trademark made from a custom-letter word (*logos* is Greek for *word*). The term *logo* caught on with people because it sounds cool, but what people really mean is a trademark, whether the trademark is a logo, symbol, monogram, emblem, or other graphic device. IBM uses a monogram, for example, while Nike uses a symbol. Both are trademarks, but neither are logos. Clear? What really matters here is that a logo, or any other kind of trademark, is not the brand itself. It is merely a symbol for it.

While Neumeier may be technically correct in discerning differences between different types of visual forms, it is also true that they really fall under the same semiotic rubric and thus can all be considered to be types of logos—visual signs that stand for a brand in some way. Neumeier is partly right in pointing out that a logo is really a "cool name" for trademark. The trademark is any symbol that distinguishes the products of one company from those of another. Most trademarks appear on the product, on its container, or in advertisements for the product. A service mark identifies the source of a service rather than a product. For example, an electric company may use a lightbulb as a symbol of the service it offers to its customers.

A modern-day logo does much more than identify products or differentiate them from others. What possible identifier connection to the hamburger-selling business do the McDonald's golden arches have? They are certainly a trademark for the company, but as a symbol arches tell a story that goes beyond the food offered for sale. Of course, at a primary level the arches form the letter *M*, the first letter in the McDonald's brand name. But at a secondary level, arches are mythic structures that seem to beckon people to march through them triumphantly into a paradise of cleanliness, friendliness, hospitality, and family values. Like the arches of ancient cities, they symbolize tradition and allegiance. Few families today have the time to eat meals together within the household, let alone the energy to prepare elaborate dinners. In modern-day households, meals are routinely consumed separately by the members. The home, ironically, has become a place where people now tend to eat apart. Enter McDonald's to the rescue! In the cheery atmosphere of a McDonald's restaurant, family members can be brought together, at the same table, under the same roof. All you have to do is walk through the arches, and McDonald's "will do it all for you," as one of its past slogans so aptly put it.

There are three basic kinds of logos—portrait, descriptive, and symbolic. Portrait logos correspond to the strategy of using the name of a real or fictitious person (chapter 2). For example, Betty Crocker products show the figure of the fictitious Betty Crocker person, Wendy's restaurants display a portrait of Wendy, and so on. Descriptive logos correspond to descriptor brand names (chapter 2). For example, the logo of a phone company that uses the icon of a phone is a descriptive logo. A symbolic logo is the counterpart to a suggestive, metaphorical, or symbolic name (chapter 2). The logo of the Jaguar automobile is the jaguar animal, the logo of Wells Fargo is a stagecoach, and the logo of the McDonald's eatery is the golden arches. Such logos do more than identify or describe the product or service to which they are associated.

Logos and Cultural Symbolism

Symbolic logos are particularly powerful because they evoke mythic stories or symbols unconsciously (latently). Consider the simple version of the apple logo adopted by the Apple Computer Company for its Mac brand: the outline of an apple with a tiny leaf on top and a bite taken out of the side. There is little doubt that this logo brings to mind latent religious narrative symbolism, suggesting the story of Adam and Eve in the Western Bible, which revolves around the eating of an apple that was supposed to contain secret forbidden knowledge. In fact, the Hebrew account of the Genesis story tells of a "forbidden" fruit, not specifically of an apple. The representation of this fruit as an apple came about in medieval depictions of the Eden scene, when painters and sculptors became interested in the Genesis story artistically. Now the biblical symbolism of the apple as "forbidden knowledge" continues to resonate in our culture. This is why the Apple Computer Company has not only named itself with the word *Apple* but also chosen the picture of this fruit as its trademark, symbolizing the fact that it, too, provides forbidden knowledge to those who buy and use its products. The bite taken from the apple, thus additionally reinforces the biblical connotations and associates the use of Apple computers and products with Eve, the mother of humanity.

Does this imply that Apple users will have access to forbidden knowledge? Does it link them with Eve, the mother of humanity? By the way, the creator of the Apple logo, a man named Rob Janoff of Regis McKenna Advertising, has consistently denied any intent to connect the logo to the Genesis story, claiming instead that he put the bite there in order to ensure that the figure not be confused as a tomato. Whatever the truth, the bite in the apple evokes the Genesis story nonetheless because we cannot help but sense culturally based symbolism in visual signs.

Aside from the fact that Mac computers are easy to use and computationally versatile, they are also perceived generally as trendy, sexy, and cool. Why? There are a variety of reasons for this—from the aesthetically pleasing design of the computers to the use of a symbolic marketing strategy as can be seen in the iMac name itself, written with a lowercase *i*, a letter that is suggestive of lowercase Internet style and of words beginning with it, such as *intelligence*, *imagination*, *illumination*, and *I* (chapter 2). The design of the computers is

Table 4.1.   IBM vs. Mac Oppositions

Category	IBM	Mac
Gender	masculine	feminine (or trendy cool male)
Religion	Protestant	Catholic
Neurology	left-hemisphered	right-hemisphered
Aesthetics	virile, macho	effeminate, beautiful (or male cool)
Intellect	rational, linear	imaginative, associative
Politics	right-wing, conservative	left-wing, liberal
Look	traditional, bland	cool, trendy
Career	business, science	arts, design

sleek and attractive. It makes them stand out on the market and sets them into an anthropomorphic opposition with PC (IBM) computers, as discussed already with regard to the Mac guy versus the PC guy ad campaign. In an informal 2001 survey, I asked 50 University of Toronto students (25 males and 25 females) to write down their views of IBM computers versus Mac ones in terms of a series of anthropomorphic categories that I provided (see table 4.1). The student responses were collected and classified. I then repeated the same survey with an identical group in early 2007 (six years later). There was no significant difference in the results. By and large, the students provided the following oppositions to the categories (with only minor exceptions).

This was not a scientific study, of course, but it does seem to flesh out the fact that symbolic meanings are built into products in ways that are suggested by logo design. Is the IBM logo, with its rigid linearity, a symbol of the corporate business world, where flair and style are discouraged? Is Mac the way of the future for that business world, with women (Eve?) starting to penetrate it more and more? Does the Mac logo suggest an "Eve code" and the coming of an "age of womanhood"?

This very code was evident in Apple's brilliant 1984 television commercial, which was shown on January 22, 1984, during the third quarter of Super Bowl XVIII. Obviously evocative of George Orwell's (1903–1950) novel *1984* (published in 1949) and directed by Ridley Scott, whose 1982 movie *Blade Runner* was already a cult classic at the time, the commercial won countless advertising awards and was characterized by culture historians as "the commercial that outplayed the game." Following is a synopsis of the commercial:

- The number 1984 appears at the start of the commercial.
- Marching like automatons through a tunnel are a horde of shaved-head, expressionless men, in prisonlike uniforms and boots marching mindlessly

toward a gigantic television screen and then sitting in front of it as a chief-executive-officer-type, Orwellian Big Brother figure shouts meaningless platitudes at them. The men stare at the screen as if in a zombielike state.

- Then, out of nowhere, a blonde, beautiful, athletic woman appears in a white jersey and red shorts running.
- The woman is pursued by a group of stormtroopers.
- She enters the room where the men (inmates) are, and she hurls a sledge-hammer at the televisions screen, which, as a consequence, explodes.
- The inmates remain seated, open mouthed and dazed.
- A message then appears on the screen, announcing that Apple will be introducing its new Macintosh computer shortly: "On January 24th, Apple Computers will introduce Macintosh, and you will see why 1984 won't be like *1984*.

The symbolism of the commercial is unmistakable—we are in a new age of womanhood (the Eve code), and Mac is leading the way into the future. Berger (2000: 126–27) describes the woman in the commercial insightfully as follows:

> Who is she? We do not know, but the fact that she exists tells us there must be forces of resistance in this totalitarian society, that not all are enslaved. We see shortly that she is being pursued by a troop of burly policemen who look terribly menacing in their helmets with glass face masks. Her color, her animation, her freedom, even her sexuality serve to make the situation of the inmates even more obvious and pathetic. Her image functions as a polar opposite to the enslaved men, and even though we only see her the first time for a second or two, her existence creates drama and excitement.

The subtext of the Mac computer as liberating, like female leadership will be in the future, has penetrated the mind-set of consumers and explains why results such as those presented in table 4.1 are obtained to this day. The logo of the Apple now makes even more sense. It is women who will liberate men from the dreary Orwellian world they have created. And the way out of 1984 is through feminine symbolism, starting with the symbolism of the Eve code. Berger (2000: 131) puts it eloquently as follows:

> The blonde heroine, then, is an Eve figure who brings knowledge of good and evil, and by implication, knowledge of reality, to the inmates. We do not see their transformation after the destruction of the Big Brother figure—indeed, their immediate reaction is awe and stupefaction—but ultimately we cannot help but assume that something will happen and they will be liberated.

It is not coincidence, to my mind, that the emphasis on conformity in the workplace started to decline shortly after the airing of the commercial. Today, computer geeks and chief executive officers of computer companies and Internet businesses are conforming to a different model—that of the Eve code, even if the actual embodiment of that code is a male (as in the Mac guy). It is also little wonder that Orwellian themes have found their way into a host of commercial campaigns, including the one by Zenith in the early 2000s that showed automatonic, depersonalized human robots walking all in tandem, without eyes, and a little girl who, with bright eyes, sees a new Zenith television set sitting on a column in the midst of an arid, spiritless, totalitarian world. The apparition and her childlike discovery of the apparition instantly humanize the mindless throng as their eyes emerge as if by metamorphosis from a cocoon. The little girl is a clear textual descendant of the Mac woman.

Given their obvious psychological power, it is little wonder to find that logos (or the logo concept) are used as well by noncommercial enterprises and organizations. One of the most widely known ones is the peace sign, often worn on chains and necklaces (see figure 4.1). Derived from an ancient runic symbol of despair and grief, it became the logo for philosopher Bertrand Russell's (1872–1970) campaign for nuclear disarmament in the 1950s. The logo's first widespread exposure came when it surfaced in the 1962 sci-fi film *The Day the Earth Caught Fire*, leading to its adoption by the counterculture youth of the era.

Visual Thinking

Visual thinking is a fundamental cognitive state and is, in all likelihood, preverbal and unconscious. It is thus very powerful. In a widely respected book, psychologist and art critic Rudolf Arnheim (1969) even goes so far as to claim that visual thinking is the primordial, or "default," mode of conceptualizing the world.

This was also the belief of ancient philosophers such as Plato, who went even further and claimed that certain visual forms are innate. And, indeed, it was claimed that the science of geometry was all about "ideal visual forms," such as triangles, circles, and squares. Amazingly, such forms have allowed

Figure 4.1

us to draw inferences about reality and about ourselves. This is perhaps why the basic geometric figures are imbued with symbolism in cultures across the world. Here are a few examples:

Figure 4.2

• The square symbolized the earth's surface in antiquity, indicating the four points of the earth's compass or the outermost points of the earth.

Figure 4.3

• The triangle has acquired many symbolic meanings throughout the world, of which the idea of "trinity" comes instantly to mind.

Figure 4.4

• The circle has been a symbol of perfection and infinity since antiquity. This is probably because it suggests eternal recurrence.

Figure 4.5

• The cross has been used to represent everything from Christianity to the plus sign. If tilted it becomes an X, which can stand for a signature, something wrong, something forbidden, and so on.

The use of geometric shapes in logo design is discussed later in this chapter. Suffice it to say here that they seem to function as a type of archetype based on patterns and symmetries that are unique to human cognition.

VISUAL BRANDS

Given the power of the logo, it is little wonder that some brands have transformed their very names into logos. Recall from the previous discussion the use of the arches figure to stand for the first letter in the McDonald's brand name. Such a logo can be called a *letter logo*. Sometimes, a product character is both the brand name and the logo for the brand. Mr. Clean is a case in point. The product character "Mr. Clean" both bears the brand name and is the trademark logo of the detergent brand. This type of logo can be called a *portrait logo*. Both brands can thus be called *visual* and defined as brands that mesh their name or identity with their logo in one of these two ways.

Letter Logos

The classic example of a letter logo is the one used by Coca-Cola. In this case, the name written in a distinctive style (a stylized, cursive font) is its logo. The logo is, in effect, a simple but attractive calligraphic rendering of the brand name. It is probably the most recognizable visual symbol in the entire world today, bringing out the power of visual branding.

Coca-Cola was one of the first brands to spread its image throughout society, integrating with it in various ways—a technique known as *placement* (chapter 9). It did this at first by imprinting its logo on drinking glasses, providing them to diners and other eateries that featured foods meant to be eaten quickly and cheaply. Since then, Coca-Cola has used a simple yet effective strategy—adapt its image to shifting trends in lifestyle. It has thus co-opted themes, from the one of brotherly love and peace espoused during the counterculture era of the late 1960s and early 1970s with its "I'd like to teach the world to sing in perfect harmony" campaign to its "Coke is the real thing" campaigns shortly thereafter to current ones showing coke as the drink of athletes and cool people. The Coca-Cola type of letter logo can be called, simply, *letter brand logo* and defined as a logo that stylizes the letters of the brand name. Another famous letter brand logo is the one for Campbell's soup, featuring a white cursive font on a red background.

In the case of McDonald's, the arches, as mentioned, are shaped in such a way that they represent the first letter of the eatery's name. The letter logo in this case can be called *alphabetic* since it is designed to represent the initial letter of its brand name, not the whole name. Another example of this subtype of letter logo is the Volkswagen one, where the V and W of the two parts of the name—Volks (people) and Wagen (vehicle)—constitute the basis of its distinctive logo. The logo was designed around 1937 by F. X. Rempeiss, engineer of the car's engine. It is a perfect example of what makes a geometrically designed logo effective. The uncomplicated geometry of this logo involves the integration of similar angles of the V (Volks) and W (Wagen) into a single composite whole, within a circle. It is simple and eye-catching. A third subtype of letter logo is an *acronymic* one, that is, one formed from the initial letters of the brand name. A perfect example of this is the IBM logo, the letters of which stand for International Business Machines. The design, with each letter made up of stacked, horizontal parallel lines, conveys a sense of something precise, methodical, and systematic. Other well-known letter logos are described in box 4.1.

Letter logos constitute a large category. Kellogg's, Heinz, Kraft, Illy, Tide, Ajax, Bounty, Nestle, UPS, and Perrier are other well-known examples. It seems that the blending of the linguistic (the brand name) with the visual (the stylized representation of the name or parts of the name) is highly effective since it taps into two forms of memory—the verbal and the eidetic.

Box 4.1. Companies with Letter Logos

Here are descriptions of some famous letter logos. The logos themselves can be found easily in simple searches on the Internet.

Hyundai Motor Company: The Hyundai logo has a stylized "H" appearing in an oval figure, standing for the first letter of the car name. It is also suggestive of two people shaking hands. It is an example of an alphabetic letter logo.

FedEx: The Federal Express logo—the brand name "FedEx"—is not only a letter logo but also has space in between the *E* and the *X* forming a right- or forward-pointing arrow. It is an example of a quasicomplete letter brand logo.

Adidas: The Adidas logo is a pyramid shape made up of three solid bars, with "adidas" below it in a round, sans-serif font. Although various interpretations are possible for the logo (such as the possibility that the three slices in the logo represent the three sons of the founder of the brand), it clearly represents both the letter *A* (the first letter of the brand name) and the shape of a running shoe. It is an example of an alphabetic letter logo.

FIAT: The FIAT logo is a simple letter logo encased in a circular shape, rendering it pleasing yet effective. The FIAT name is an acronym for *Fabbrica Italiana Automobili Torino* (Italian Car Factory of Turin). It is an example of an acronymic letter logo.

Dell: The Dell logo is the brand name "DELL" in capital letters, with the "E" tilted to the left, making it look like a diamond shape. The "tipsy E" both alphabetically and visually suggests electric power.

Portrait Logos

A perfect example of a portrait logo (sometimes called a mascot) is the cartoon character Mickey Mouse, which became the Disney logo in 1929, when the corporation allowed Mickey Mouse to be reproduced on school slates. A year later Mickey Mouse dolls went into production, and throughout the 1930s the Mickey Mouse logo was licensed with huge success. In 1955, the Mickey Mouse Club premiered on U.S. network television, further entrenching the Disney brand into the cultural mainstream. Today, Disney toys, television programs, movies, DVDs, theme parks, and the like have become part of the experience of childhood.

Mickey Mouse is, more specifically, a *cartoon* logo. Like a mascot in sports, it is something that brings good luck. Other well-known cartoon portrait logos are described in box 4.2.

Box 4.2.   Cartoon Portrait Logos

Here are descriptions of some famous character portrait logos. The logos themselves can be found easily in simple searches on the Internet.

The Michelin Man: The idea for the Michelin Man logo came to Edouard Michelin at an exhibition in 1889, when he saw a pile of tires which looked lifelike. The Michelin Man (named Monsieur Bibendum) was thus created. In 2000, the Michelin logo was chosen "Logo of the Century" by an international jury of advertisers and advertising agencies.

Mr. Clean: Mr. Clean is both the product character and the brand name of the household cleaning product. He has become a true emblem of the "dirt fighting superhero" with his powerful body, crossed muscular arms, and bald head—reminiscent of the late Hollywood actor Yul Brynner, who often played mythical or heroic roles in blockbuster movies.

Speedy: The logo for Alka Seltzer is a toy called Speedy, whose torso is an actual Alka Seltzer tablet. The character's childlike appearance and conspicuous smile communicates friendliness and assurance that the product will work perfectly.

Tony the Tiger: Cartoon character Tony the Tiger, with his blue nose and red bandana, is the logo for Kellogg's Frosted Flakes. His humorous demeanor and friendly ways impart a feeling of happiness and joy associated with the product.

Charlie the Tuna: Charlie, a cartoon tuna with a red beret and chunky-rimmed glasses, is the product logo for Star-Kist tuna. His friendly and humorous appearance also impart joyfulness and sociability.

Another subtype of portrait logo is that of a *human effigy* (real or fictitious). The Betty Crocker products, for instance, bear the effigy or portrait of a fictitious female, and Wendy's restaurants display a portrait of Wendy. Betty Crocker is particularly interesting as a portrait logo. The logo was invented in 1921 by Gold Medal flour to serve as the face logo of the company. Her physical image was fixed in 1936 when her first "portrait" was put out by the company. Her countenance was shaped to have a combination of Caucasian features designed to present the perfect composite of the stay-at-home American woman—an expert cook, a friend, and a friendly mother figure. By the mid-1940s, the fictitious lady was the second most popular woman in America after Eleanor Roosevelt (as mentioned previously). She was even portrayed by various actresses on radio and television. Twenty years later, a new portrait produced a new image—older and friendlier. Currently, her image has been updated to reflect yet a new image of American womanhood. She is beautiful and independant. The Betty Crocker "makeover" is a perfect example of how brands must constantly be reshaped to keep in step with the times.

Some seemingly fictional portrait logos are based on real people. For example, Duncan Hines is a character seen on boxes of cake and brownie mix. Most people assume he is a fictitious character. In actual fact, there really existed a Duncan Hines, who was born in Bowling Green, Kentucky, in 1880, becoming widely known for his newspaper columns. Around 1950, Hines agreed to let his name be used for food and kitchen products. Another example is the Wendy character of the Wendy's restaurant chain. Dave Thomas, the founder of the chain, actually named it after his daughter, even though the image on the logo is not a photo or portrait of his daughter but rather a stylized version.

INSIDE THE LOGO

Letter and portrait logos constitute a part of the typology of logo-making strategies. Essentially, the logo that a brand adopts is the visual counterpart of the brand name (chapter 3). For example, *descriptor logos* are visual equivalents of the brand name (the Bell telephone company uses the figure of a bell for its logo). *Suggestive logos* are visual signs that represent the product as something other than itself, such as arches standing for an eatery, and *symbolic logos* are visual symbols that often merge with letter logos (e.g., the Xbox video game system uses the X itself as its logo). This iconic relation between brand name and logo constitutes a semiotic isomorphism whereby one type of sign system (the verbal) is made to mirror or reflect another (the nonverbal).

Descriptor Logos

Descriptor logos require little commentary here. They put into visual form the brand name, company image, the company's country, and the like. A simple example of the descriptor logo is that used by Maple Leaf Food Company. This logo resembles a waving flag, with red and white stripes and a red maple leaf on the top third of the flag and a blue field with "Maple Leaf" in white letters on the bottom two-thirds. Research by the Canadian Company in the 1990s indicated that consumers associated it with the flag symbol for Canada. The logo, with its leaf figure, was well received by consumers when it was introduced in 1999 who said it conveyed a strong sense of Canadian identity. Well-known descriptor logos include the bell logo used by Bell telephone (as mentioned), animal figures such as the jaguar and the cougar that stand for cars called Jaguar and Cougar, and the yellow tail kangaroo logo for Yellow Tail wine. The latter brings out the fact that, even though descriptor logos are iconic with their brand names, they nonetheless add meaning to the product.

Yellow Tail is owned by Casella Wines, an Australian family business. The name comes from the yellow-footed rock wallaby, a small, colorful breed of kangaroo. The name is run in square brackets and lowercase letters, which associates it with technological or Internet savvy. The logo is a distinctive kangaroo figure that is eye-catching because it appears to be similar to the type found on ancient caves and walls. Thus, while the logo links the wine to Australia and its emblematic kangaroo species, it also suggests notions of prehistoricity and, thus, tribalism. The wine is, in fact, marketed at young tribes of people (young urban professionals), so to speak, who appear to have responded favorably to its Internet-style name and prehistoric tribal logo, given that it is one of the fastest-growing wine labels in the world today.

As a final word on animal logos, it should be noted that they connect products to an important part of cultural symbolism. In our own culture, for example, we use the names of animals for sports teams (Chicago Bears, Detroit Tigers, Toronto Blue Jays, Denver Broncos, and so on) so as to impart character to the team in terms of animal qualities, we name cartoon characters (Bugs Bunny, Daffy Duck, and so on) to represent human personality types, and we tell our children animal stories in order to impart morals to them. The gods of many early cultures were conceived as animal figures—Egyptian gods had animal heads, the principal god of the Hindus is Ganesha the elephant, the godhead of the Aztecs was the green-plumed serpent Quetzalcoatl, and the list could go on and on. Animals are used in astrology to symbolize human character and to predict destiny in tandem with the movement of celestial objects. Even though we may not believe outright in the power of astrological signs to predict our future, we nevertheless keep an open mind about them, as evidenced by the ubiquity of horoscopes in modern culture.

Animal metaphors constitute the central idea behind *totemism*, an Ojibway word (Great Lakes region of North America). Totems are spiritual entities represented by animal species. A particular totem symbolizes a specific clan. People who share the same totems cannot marry. An individual may have a totem—a personal guardian spirit—but then can never eat the animal that represents his or her totem.

Suggestive Logos

An example of a suggestive logo is the apple logo for the Mac computer discussed previously, which suggests an "Eve code." Another example of a suggestive logo that has already been discussed is the Playboy bunny logo (chapter 1). This suggests an "animal code" based on metaphor. A similar type of code can be found with the animal names and logos given to some cars. For example, the Ferrari logo is a powerful black horse, which suggests all the metaphorical qualities associated with such a horse—nobility, status, power, and beauty. These are emphasized by the technique of inserting the horse in a shield—a heraldic figure that goes back to feudal times, when it was necessary for a knight to be recognized from a distance. The Cadillac car company also uses a shieldlike crest figure as the basis of its logo. The suggestion of nobility and royalty is instantly visible in the logo, with a crown and a shield suggesting noble origins. The upper-class heraldic-style identity and distinctiveness is what sets such logos apart from others. In feudal times it was, in fact, upper-class families that passed their coats of arms down from one generation to the next. And by heraldic law, no two families could use the same coat of arms.

Symbolic Logos

Symbolic logos are essentially symbols that have a specific visual form, such as an alphabet character. For example, the lowercase *i* used by Apple in naming various brands and subbrands—iMac, iPod, iPhone, iTunes, and so on—is both a brand name and a logo. It suggests Internet style, where lowercase letters are used frequently in place of uppercase (e.g., in e-mails), and individuality ($i = I$), among other symbolic things.

Another symbolic alphabet logo is the letter X, which, again, is both an element in brand names and often a logo—for example, in the Xbox video game system. The twenty-fourth letter of the English alphabet has, as mentioned in the previous chapter, been around for centuries as a pure symbol—as a mathematical variable, as a sign of danger on bottles of alcohol and boxes of dynamite, as a symbol marking a secret treasure on a pirate's map, and so on. In a word, X has always constituted a pictography of danger, mystery, the unexplained, and other occult meanings from times that pre-date X-treme sports and *The X-Files* television program—a pictography now embedded in everything from car names to video game consoles. By imbuing products with hidden ancient symbolism, the marketer strategically re-creates our psychic past—a past in which symbols emerged as the elemental building blocks of culture. Early symbolism was inextricably intertwined with an innate sense of mystery—a sense leading to the establishment of the ancient crafts of astrology and alchemy. Incidentally, the symbols and ideas created by both of these have hardly disappeared from modern-day culture—to this day we even name days of the week and months of the year with astrological concepts, from the "day of the moon" (Monday) to the "day of Saturn" (Saturday), among many others. The principal activity of the alchemists, by the way, was to search for the "philosopher's stone"—a quest popularized by the highly popular Harry Potter movies of the early 2000s—and the production of gold by artificial means. Gold meant (and continues to mean) power, deification, and immortality.

Neumeier (2006) calls a logo that is both a name (or part thereof) and a visual symbol an icon, much like a computer iconic symbol. Icons are effective because they "respond to the new reality by jumping off the printed page and interacting with people" (Neumeier 2006: 87). He goes on to claim that the most effective visual logo is an avatar, which is a logo "that can move, morph, or otherwise operate freely as the brand's alter ego."

GEOMETRICAL LOGOS

The foregoing discussion of symbolism leads to another type of symbolic logo that can be called a *geometrically based logo* (GBL). Geometrical figures have always been perceived as beautiful and perfect symbols because, as Plato believed, they are probably innate. They come as part and parcel of having a human brain. Indeed, circles, triangles, and perfect squares are not seen in nature; they are seen only in human images and representations throughout the world and across time. The circle, for example, is a universal symbol of perfection and infinity, probably because it suggests eternal recurrence. Geometry, as the Greeks envisaged it, was all about "ideal forms," such as triangles, circles, and squares. Amazingly, it quickly developed into a science that has allowed us not only to do many practical things but also to draw inferences about reality that would not have been possible otherwise. GBLs tap into a universal form of representation.

Geometrically Based Logos

Geometrical forms have been found etched as petroglyphs on cave walls throughout the world, long before the advent of geometry. The bodies of the animals portrayed on rocks by prehistoric members of tribes are typically square, rectangular, or circular and the horns curved and angled. Like Plato imagined, there really does seem to be an innate instinct to use the same basic geometric shapes to represent the same kinds of things. Circles and squares are just as likely to be found in doodles and in logos as they are on prehistoric cave walls.

Many of today's most recognizable and memorable logos are based on geometrical forms. A well-known example is the Mercedes Benz logo—a simplistic three-pointed star. The three points purportedly represent the company's domination of the land, the sea, and the air because Daimler, the founder of Mercedes, had a strong desire to produce not only cars but also ships and aircraft. After World War I, Mercedes and Benz merged, and their logos, the three-pointed star of Mercedes and the laurel wreath of Benz, were combined to become the present logo of the star encased in a circle. The geometrical simplicity of this logo is truly magnificent, evoking a latent form of geometrical symbolism of a star inscribed in an eternal circle. Indeed, a large number of carmakers have adopted similar types of geometrical forms. Kia, for example, has designed a logo consisting of an ellipse encasing its name, and Nissan uses a circle with its name going through it diametrically.

The circle and oval (ellipse) are particularly popular as figures in GBL design among carmakers. Two other well-known GBLs that employ these figures are described in box 4.3. Such forms have always been associated with myth and the sacred. Indeed, many, if not most, of the world's religions have adopted geometric shapes as the basis for their sacred symbolism. For exam-

---

Box 4.3. Companies with Geometrically Based Logos

Audi: The Audi logo consists of a horizontal row of four interlocking rings symbolizing the 1932 merger of four independent motor vehicle manufacturers. This is a perfect visual symbol for eternal partnership and stability.

Toyota: The Toyota logo consists of three ovals: two perpendicular, overlapping center ovals surrounded by a larger oval. The perpendicular ovals represent a relationship of mutual trust between the customer and Toyota. They also combine to symbolize the letter *T* for Toyota. The space in the background implies a global expansion of Toyota's technology and unlimited potential for the future.

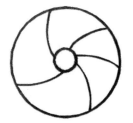 

Figure 4.6. Mayan symbol (left) and Star of David (right)

ple, the ancient Mayan symbol of faith was a circle containing spirals emanating from an inscribed smaller circle, and the mystical Star of David consists of two intertwined equilateral triangles at opposite orientations to each other (see figure 4.6).

One of the first pictographic systems to be fashioned as a sacred representational one was the one used in ancient Sumer around 3500 B.C.E. By about 3000 B.C.E., the Egyptians also started using a comparable pictographic system, known as *hieroglyphic*, to record hymns and prayers, among other things (*hieroglyphic* derives from Greek *hieros*, "holy," and *glyphein*, "to carve"). They are so pleasing and effective because they are, as Merrell (2007: 188) calls them, ancient "habits of mind." They form part of an instinctive "recognition system," so to speak, whereby forms created by the human imagination seem to have an instinctive poetic logic all their own.

Logos, Brand Names, and Marketing

The histories of brand naming, logo design, and marketing overlap considerably. The reason is a straightforward one—it is impossible to advertise and promote "nameless" and "logo-less" products with any degree of efficacy. These are signs that influence people's unconscious perception of objects as necessary accouterments of life. They "represent" the product, that is, "present it again," not as a product but as a sign standing for a panoply of meanings (obvious or otherwise). The only way to explain why logos in particular are so suggestive of ancient or archetypal meanings is to suggest, like Arnheim (mentioned previously) has, that pictorial symbolism is more fundamental to the human psyche than other types and, thus, continues to have emotional hold on the modern mind.

The objective of marketing today is, arguably, to get people to react to logos in ways that parallel how people once responded (and continue to respond) to sacred or mythical forms. Of course, not all logos are successful. Some are dull and largely ineffectual. To be appealing, it would seem that they should be interconnected visually to the name and the signification system built into the product. The best logos, however, would seem to be those that are akin to prehistoric carvings and pictographs because they echo with mysticism. Logo designers and marketers are, in a fundamental sense, our modern-day pictographers.

5

Language-Based Techniques

The human being is a creature who lives not upon bread alone, but princi-pally by catchwords.

—Robert Louis Stevenson, 1850–1894

Most people living in America today would have very little difficulty recog-nizing phrases and expressions such as the following ones: "Diamonds are for-ever," "Just do it," "I'm lovin' it," or "Mmm Mmm good." They may not nec-essarily know that they are advertising slogans or, if they do, to what products they refer, but they will recognize them nonetheless as they would statements such as aphorisms or proverbs that seem to have authority or significance of some kind. The reason is that they are virtually everywhere and have a mem-orable poetic quality to them that seems to make sense in and of itself in some indefinable way. Along with brand-naming and logo-design techniques, the coining of such phrases, known as **slogans** and **taglines**, is a central strategy in the "semiotizing" or representation of a product—that is, in the presentation of a product as something other than the product itself. The use of language-based techniques (LBTs) probably traces its origin to the nineteenth-century entrepreneur, showman, and circus operator P. T. Barnum (1810–1891), who used expressions such as the following to lure people to his circus:

Don't miss this once-in-a-lifetime opportunity!
All this at an unbelievably low price!
All items must go!
Not to be missed!

This chapter looks at Barnum's legacy by discussing LBTs and their rela-tion to advertising. The overriding pattern that can be extracted from even a cursory consideration of LBTs is that, like Barnum's hyped-up language, the advertiser never uses language literally but, rather, in a highly rhetorical and thus very persuasive fashion. The following statement by Neumeier (2006: 39) with regard to the Nike slogan "Just do it" brings out perfectly why such language is effective:

> As a weekend athlete, my two nagging doubts are that I might be congenitally lazy, and that I might have little actual ability. I'm not really worried about my shoes. But when the Nike folks say, "Just do it," they're peering into my soul. I begin to feel that, if they understand me that well, their shoes are probably good. I'm then willing to join the tribe of Nike.

GENERAL TECHNIQUES

An Iron Cologne print ad seen prominently several years ago showed a handsome, muscular man embracing a voluptuous woman. At the bottom, the ad page itself was shown as ripped, revealing just below it the bottle of Iron Cologne being sprayed. The tagline "Pump some Iron" completed the text.

At a primary level, the message of the ad seemed to be simply: "Enjoy a great sex life, as physically energetic and satisfying as pumping iron by wearing Iron Cologne." But delving a little deeper into the tagline's several layers of meaning revealed another story, complementing the visual part of the text seamlessly. First, it suggests the aggressiveness associated with the strenuous activity associated with lifting weights. The expression "pumping iron" means "working out with weights." And, of course, the word "iron" is a clever play on the brand name Iron. The passionate aggressiveness of the man's embrace and the ripped section of the page at the bottom fit in perfectly with this meaning. But the spraying bottle "underneath" the male's act of passion suggests another meaning of the tagline—one that is more congruous with the spraying action. In fact, "pumping" is a common slang metaphor for sexual intercourse and "iron" a slang metaphor for male genitalia.

The ambiguity inherent in the tagline and accompanying visual text is a result of the rhetorical structure of the words used. The tagline is, in short, a one-line poem that is layered with various levels of meaning.

Conceptual Metaphors

The use of figurative language in the construction of taglines such as the Iron Cologne one is the sum and substance of LBTs. The tagline became, in effect, the linguistic slogan for the cologne's ad campaign in the late 1990s. Indeed, an ad campaign is defined by the tagline or slogan it employs. Consider as a case in point an ad campaign for the perfume Volupté, which appeared in magazines several years ago structured around the tagline "Trust your senses." The campaign typically showed the perfume bottle in the center with the tagline just below it. The bottle had a dark, round bottle cap that was highly suggestive of an aroused nipple. The tagline tapped perfectly into the suggestion of the intuitive "sensing" involved in sexual foreplay. The background scene in the ad reinforced this interpretation since it showed a secluded, dark place where the bottle could be "sensed" voyeuristically through the beam of light that fell on it.

A few years back, a Miller beer commercial shown on television breaks during Sunday afternoon football broadcasts ended with the expression "Love is a game" appearing on the screen. The commercial would show two guys in a bar wanting to "win over" a woman in the bar, each one taking advice from his separate clique of buddies. The actions of the two cliques simulated football action play between two teams. "Winning" the game in this case was "getting to" the female prize. In order to accomplish this, the first male leader, or "quarterback," needed the support of his "team" to be effectual in carrying out the crucial play, which, of course, he was. By getting his clique to successfully block the path of the other team's quarterback to the girl, the first quarterback wins the "game." He "scores" sexually, as the expression goes. The simulation of a football play by the commercial is reinforced by the play-by-play description of an announcer whose voice and descriptive style are made to emulate those of a television football announcer as well as by the concluding statement "Love is a game." This expression complemented the action perfectly, mirroring an unconscious pattern of thinking about love that Lakoff and Johnson (1980) call a **conceptual metaphor**. "Love is a game" is a formula of thought that constitutes a metaphorical conceptualization of courtship as a "game" to be played out according to specific cultural rules. A conceptual metaphor is, thus, an unconscious habit of mind that manifests itself in everyday discourse, as the following expressions show:

She left him, because he didn't *play* by the rules.
He *lost* her to his best friend.
She attempted to *win* his affections but wasn't able to.
He didn't quite *score* with her the other night.
Their love has lasted because they have always *played* on an even field.

Each one of these manifestations is called an actual *linguistic metaphor*. A *conceptual metaphor*, on the other hand, is the overarching associative formula—"Love is a game"—from which each linguistic metaphor is derived. Conceptual metaphors are found throughout the advertising world. For example,

Table 5.1.   Conceptual Metaphors in Automobile Taglines

Conceptual Metaphor	Taglines
The car is a weapon (used in fighting)	"Let's take this outside" (Mercedes C-Class) "When it's time to go toe-to-toe" (Honda S2000) "Punches above its weight" (Hummer H3) "Pure muscle" (Porsche Cayman S) "Blows away the competition" (Chevrolet Impala)
The car is a means to an exciting life	"Whoever said life begins at 40?" (Toyota Aygo) "A vehicle with room for all parts of your life" (Chevrolet Uplander) "Always choose dare" (Toyota Matrix) "Wanna play?" (Suzuki)
The car is a means of escape from boredom	"Road grip. The most basic law of nature" (Subaru) "Open your mind" (Chrysler Smart) "Because gas stations are hard to find at 10,000 feet" (Ford Escape)
The car is a means for self-distinction	"Everything else will seem ordinary" (Nissan Altima) "Slip behind the wheel of the breathtaking Chrysler 300C and just watch your stock take off" (Chrysler 300)

the De Beers "Diamonds are forever" slogan is a specific instantiation of the "Love is a precious or long-lasting stone" conceptual metaphor that can be seen in common everyday discourse: "Their love is as solid as a rock," "Their love is a nugget," and so on. The Frosted Flakes tagline of a few years ago, "Frosted Flakes brings out the tiger in you," is a specific instantiation of the "Humans are animals" conceptual metaphor, which is an ever-present one in everyday conversations concerning human personality: "My grandson is a puppy dog," "My granddaughter is a tiger," and so on.

Conceptual metaphors are found especially in automobile taglines. Table 5.1 shows some of the conceptual metaphors I found in a survey of car ads from 2006.

Other Techniques

In addition to the use of conceptual metaphors, there are several LBTs that advertisers use effectively in creating taglines and slogans so as to generate po-

Table 5.2. Taglines Constructed with the Imperative

Brand	Tagline
Marlboro cigarettes	"Come to Marlboro Country!"
Virginia Slims	"Do the Woman Thing!"
Tango Twist (Nordstrom)	"Reinvent Seduction!"
Disaronno Originale (Amaretto)	"Light a Fire!"

etic logic for products. From a perusal of nearly 500 ads, I was able to establish the main ones as metonymy, linkages, the use of the imperative, tautologies, aphoristic style, alliteration, double entendre, absence of language, gossip, parallelism, tone of voice, register, style borrowing, and personal testimonials (see also Dyer 1982: 151–82; Tash 1979):

Metonymy, or the use of a part of something to represent something more general, creates powerful imagery for the product: "Bring a touch of Paris into your life." *Linkages* are statements linking a brand to social trends and themes: "Pepsi: The drink that is forever young." Statements constructed with the *imperative* of the verb create the illusion that advice is coming from an unseen authoritative source: "Pump some iron," "Trust your senses," "Come to where the flavor is," "Have yourself a Bud," and "Drink Coke." Such statements impel us to "obey them" because we associate them unconsciously or latently to people in authority—parents ("Don't touch that"), teachers ("Do your homework"), clerics ("Love your neighbor"), law enforcers ("Do not drive fast,"), and so on. A few imperative taglines used by brands in recent years are shown in table 5.2. The Virginia Slims tagline shown in the table is particularly interesting because it is also a linkage statement, suggesting by innuendo that women are now the smokers and, thus, in charge of things. The same innuendo can be detected in other Virginia Slims taglines:

- "I look temptation right in the eye and then I make my own decision: Virginia Slims. Find Your Voice!" (2002)
- "I know that I'm very complicated. I like it that way: Virginia Slims!" (2003–2004)

These deliver the signification system on which the Virginia Slims brand was founded effectively. The brand has always emphasized that smoking, once considered a "male thing," has empowered females, allowing them a symbolic means from which to declare their independence from social patriarchy. The history of the Virginia Slims brand constitutes, in effect, the brand's version of women's liberation. For women to smoke "their own brand" of cigarette has always been promoted by Virginia Slims as a subversive social act, thus tapping into the history of smoking itself, which shows, in fact, that smoking has always been perceived symbolically. Smoking is a symbol of sexuality, power, and self-control. Smoking is, as Virginia Slims clearly knows, both a subversive and a tantalizing activity allowing women to do their own thing.

The use of the imperative is one of the most common LBTs. I found the following imperative verbs used in hundreds of ads for a variety of products:

Be . . .
Bring . . .
Come . . .
Do . . .
Drink . . .
Eat . . .
Explore . . .
Find . . .
Give . . .
Go . . .
Have a . . .
Imagine . . .
Join . . .
Keep . . .
Let . . .
Look . . .
Make . . .
Open . . .
See . . .
Stay . . .
Take . . .
Try . . .

Tautologies are meaningless statements that sound truthful because they present something as obvious: "Triumph has a bra for the way you are" or "A Volkswagen is a Volkswagen." The tagline created to resemble an *aphorism* or proverb—a tersely phrased statement that seems self-evident and insightful or else is designed to illustrate something as a basic truth or a practical precept—is a frequently used LBT: "Somewhere inside, romance blossoms." A 2002 ad for Visa Gold was based on the aphoristic tagline "He who has the gold makes the rules!" The tagline was a clever play on the "golden rule"—

the precept that people should do to others what they would have others do to them. Aphoristic or proverbial language abounds in tagline creation. For example, in a sales pitch for its newspaper, the *New York Times* created the following headline during the early 1980s:

Clarity begins at home
with the home delivery of
the New York Times

The line "Clarity begins at home" is an obvious modified version of the proverb "Charity begins at home." This clever use of such phraseology imparts a sense that the product is itself imbued with proverbial qualities.

The **alliteration**, or repetition, of initial sounds in slogan or tagline construction increases the likelihood that a brand will be remembered: "The Superfree sensation" or "Guinness is good for you." This technique makes taglines and slogans particularly memorable and pleasing. For instance, an ad designed to attract business in the *New York Times* in 1977 begins as follows:

Franchisers
Find
Franchisees
Fast

The alliteration of four consecutive *F* sounds creates a tongue-twisting effect that is pleasurable in itself. Also, the consecutive sequence of a trisyllabic word followed by a monosyllabic one creates a catchy rhythm. In 2002, Burger King also used the alliteration of the "F" sound in its "Fiery Fries" ad campaign, reinforcing the alliteration visually by showcasing a french fry tipped with ketchup, making it look like the substance used to produce a flame on a match. Also, the sequence of a trisyllabic word ("Fiery") followed by a monosyllabic one ("Fries") creates a catchy rhythm, further enhancing the poetic force of the tagline.

The *double entendre* is also a common LBT. For example, in the 1970s, Sudden Beauty products used the following tagline in one of its ad campaigns based on the double entendre of the word *makeup*:

How to make up
Without make-up!

Such poetic license is not only appealing; it is memorable because it conveys its message aesthetically. The same kind of technique was used successfully by TWA in a 1970s ad campaign that used the following tagline:

TWA's
Spring Sale
on the Rockies

The phrase "on the Rockies" is, of course, a slight modification of "on the rocks," as in "I'll have my martini on the rocks." The pictorial part of the various ads used in the campaign showed people "on the Rockies" with their skis and poles leaning against a tree as if they were hanging out in a bar waiting for their drinks "on the rocks."

Some ads strategically avoid the use of any language whatsoever, suggesting, by implication, that the product speaks for itself. Or else they may lead us on to believe that there is some deeper reality behind the ad. As Dyer (1982: 170) puts it, the *absence of language* technique "has the effect of making us think that meaningful reality lies directly behind the signs once we have succeeded in deciphering them." This technique is a prevalent one in print ads for cosmetic products. Typically, such ads show perfume bottles, cologne bottles, and the like as if they were works of sculpture art, suggesting that the bottle is an objet d'art or a mystical icon to be revered.

This *gossip* technique is based on the fact that gossip, rumor, hearsay, and tittle-tattle are forms of communication designed to grab attention: "Does she or doesn't she?"

Parallelism is the technique of repeating linguistic patterns (such as sentences or phrases): "It's longer / It's slimmer / It's surprisingly mild" (advertisement for More cigarettes).

In commercials, the *tone of voice* is particularly crucial in conveying mood (friendliness, joy, romance, or happiness). So too is *register* (level of formality). In ads and commercials, the structure of sentences can be informal or formal, depending on product. It is informal and colloquial for brands such as Budweiser but formal and elegant for brands such as the BMW and Mercedes-Benz automobiles.

Some LBTs are based on (*borrowed* from) specific discourse styles. For example, a tagline can take the form that resembles an interview, a testimonial, an official interaction, and the like: "Name: Mary; Age: 16; Problem: Acne." Finally, *personal testimonials* are statements made by someone (and thus in the first person)—"I'd rather fight than switch" or "I'm lovin' it"—or else made about someone (and thus in the third person).

Needless to say, there are other types of LBTs used by advertisers to construct their taglines and slogans, as in the use of foreign words to convey connotations of exoticness and refinement or the use of suggestive word layouts and fonts. It is beyond the limits of the present chapter to discuss them in detail. Suffice it to say that they are part of a general rhetorical strategy that is designed to impart poetic meaning to a product and, thus, "semiotizing" it verbally.

THE TAGLINE

A tagline is a statement constructed with one or a combination of the techniques discussed previously to accompany an ad text or to characterize an entire ad campaign. As Berger (2000: 61) designates them, taglines are verbal forms with a "pseudo-poetic character" to them. In his book *Culture against Man*, anthropologist Jules Henry (1963) sees this as perhaps the most effective of all advertising strategies because of the archetypal nature of poetic language. He calls the pseudoimitative poetic style of advertising a pecuniary distortion of values, that is, a distortion of poetic value for monetary reasons: "Millions will respond to poetry as a value and feel good when they think they are responding to it, and this process of getting people to respond to pseudo-values as if they were responding to real ones is called here *pecuniary distortion of values*" (Henry 1963: 59).

In *Just So Stories for Little Children* (1902), Rudyard Kipling wrote stories for children to explain natural phenomena in fanciful yet compelling ways. The expression "just-so story" crystallized shortly thereafter as a widely used one in reference to any artfully contrived explanation or story, even if it has no basis in fact. It is certainly an apt one in reference to modern-day taglines, which are, essentially, just-so stories.

Linguistic Games

Tagline creators produce their just-so stories by playing on words, formulas, and other linguistic and rhetorical forms. A simple yet effective game is the *hyperbole game* (as it can be called), a game that originated with P. T. Barnum and is characterized by a profuse use of descriptive and colorful words or by a repetition of words and phrases to create a quasi-mesmerizing effect:

> "A wholesome, healthy, pure banana. Look for Chiquita's label" (Chiquita Banana)

"Taste the high country, taste the high country, taste the high country, taste Coors" (Coors beer)
"Come alive, come alive, you're in the Pepsi generation" (Pepsi)

Another game consists in playing on the different meanings of words, known technically as polysemy (*Shakespeare's play* vs. *He likes to play*). Here are some taglines constructed as *polysemic games*:

"You can't top the copper top" (Duracell)
"Armour hot dogs, the dogs kids love to bite" (Armour)
"I'm stuck on Band-Aid, 'cause Band-Aid's stuck on me" (Band-Aid)

Playing on the suggestive, sensory, alliterative, or imitative value of sounds; on the onomatopoeic structure of words; and on rhyming and rhythmic patterns to create catchy, poetic taglines is another common tagline-making technique. This can be called simply a *poetic game*:

"Plop, plop, fizz, fizz, oh, what a relief it is" (Alka-Seltzer)
"Snap, crackle, pop, Rice Krispies" (Rice Krispies)
"I love Bosco, it's rich and chocolatey, oh I love Bosco, that's the drink for me" (Bosco Chocolate Syrup)
"Yum, yum bumble bee, I love Bumble Bee tuna" (Bumble Bee Tuna)
"Mmm Mmm good" (Campbell's)
"See the USA in your Chevrolet" (Chevrolet)
"You can't beat Cream of Wheat" (Cream of Wheat)
"Tum, tum, tum, tum, Tums" (Tums Antacid Tablets)
"It ain't easy being cheesy" (Cheetos)

Sometimes the poetic pattern used in the tagline is one whereby the brand name itself suggests the choice of words within it. So, for example, a tagline for the Doublemint chewing gum brand was constructed with the word "double" to suggest its romantic function as a breath mint that allows people to "double up" with a romantic or sexual partner: "Double your pleasure, double your fun with Doublemint gum." So effective was it as a tagline that it became the brand's slogan.

As mentioned previously, the use of taglines that are constructed syntactically to resemble aphorisms, proverbs, or other kinds of sententious formulas is highly effective because such formulas seem to have a commonsense or "folk-wisdom" style of meaning built into them—a meaning that, however, cannot be pinned down precisely. This can be called a *formula game*. An example is GMC Truck's tagline "Like a rock, lean on me." It can also be seen in advice-giving taglines, such as "Not going anywhere for a while? Grab a Snickers (Snickers)" and "If you haven't looked at a Ford lately, look again" (Ford). Sometimes the tagline or slogan is made to resemble a well-known phrase. Take, for instance, Taco Bell's "Think outside the bun." The slogan in this case is fashioned after the well-known phrase "Think outside the box," which refers to a type of thinking (called "lateral") that is imaginative and creative rather than rigid and conservative. The Taco Bell slogan is, clearly, a clever modification of this expression, replacing "box" with "bun" and suggesting, consequently, that eating a Taco Bell product is akin to making an intelligent choice over the bun-based products available at other fast-food eateries (hamburgers and hot dogs), which are boring and mind numbing.

The type of tagline that asks the reader a rhetorical question—"Have you driven a Ford lately?" (Ford)—can be called a *rhetorical game*. The question puts the non-Ford buyer in a position of feeling left behind. It is the equivalent of someone asking us, "Haven't you heard or done something?" Answering in the negative makes us feel in the dark about whatever that something is and, thus, of missing out on something important. A second type of rhetorical game is to create questions directed at a character in an ad—"Does she or doesn't she?" (Clairol). We perceive this as "the voice of those around us," as Altman (2006: 97) puts it, dragging us into the gossip that is ongoing. A version of this game, which can be called simply a *communication game*, consists in using statements or questions designed to create the effect of an ad or brand communicating directly with consumers: "What would you do for a Klondike bar?" (Klondike). Communication games are effective, as Altman (2006: 95) notes, because they talk directly to the consumer by using the second person:

> Most taglines are written in the second person, or the "you" narrative. It's logical because we want our products and their promises to speak to our audience. The "you" narrative literally brings the person into the conversation. "You deserve a break toady," "Just do it," "You and us," "Betcha can't eat just one."

As one other linguistic game, consider the one that links the tagline to some social or cultural trend or theme. For example, the tagline for Barbie Dolls of a few years ago—"We girls can do anything. Right, Barbie?"— tapped cleverly into the rise of "girl power" in pop culture and society generally. This can be called, simply, a *sociolinguistic game*. The forever-young theme that contemporary pop culture promotes through celebrities, plastic surgery, and media-hyped messages can be seen in both the Pepsi tagline "Pepsi: The drink for those who are forever young" and the Toys R Us tagline "I don't want to grow up." A 2006 Xbox 360 ad for a wireless headset to accompany the game used the tagline "The next generation is a wireless

world." This talked directly to users of the game, young people who are totally immersed in an ever-expanding world of sophisticated technology. A
common sociolinguistic game is to use the slang or colloquial language of the
target readership. A 2006 ad for a Wii combat game used the following
tagline: "The story of your fighting is a poem of two words: You suck." The
use of the latter phrase reflects the type of language that typical users of the
game (young males) would use.

There are, of course, many other kinds of semantic games that tagline creators play, including the use of conceptual metaphors. These have already
been discussed briefly. Suffice it to say that taglines are effective because we
are fascinated by the boundless range of meanings that language has the potential to encode. By inventing new linguistic ideas, advertisers are perceived
unconsciously as filling in the gaps that we otherwise would feel exist in the
language. Tagline construction reveals, in effect, that the structures we use to
make words provide us with the means to play an endless game with reality.
As two great twentieth-century linguists, Edward Sapir (1884–1939) and
Benjamin Lee Whorf (1897–1941), showed in their groundbreaking research,
human ideas are rooted in the structure of language.

Fascinated by the relation between linguistic structure and meaning, an association called Oulipo—an acronym for *Ouvroir de littérature potentielle*
(Workshop of potential literature)—was founded in Paris in the mid-twentieth
century by a small group of writers and mathematicians in order to explore the
relation between language structure and reality. For example, Raymond Queneau, one of the founders of Oulipo, published a book of poetry titled *100 Trillion Sonnets*, consisting of 10 sonnets, one on each of 10 pages. The pages are
cut so as to allow each of the 14 lines of a sonnet to be turned separately. The
physical format of the book allows 100 trillion combination of lines—100 trillion sonnets. All of them, Queneau claimed, "make sense." Similarly, the
taglines created for brands seem to make sense, and the reason for this is that
they are couched in language forms and structures that we perceive as somehow telling us something meaningful about the world.

Symbolism

Taglines that tap into symbolic domains merit separate commentary because
they show how language and symbolism are intertwined. In a brilliant analysis of the symbolism of the peach as used in an ad for a moisturizer called
Living Proof Cream Hidracel, Berger (2000: 59–60) showed how powerful
the interconnection between language and cultural meaning is in advertising.
The ad begins with a headline (a tagline that is found at the top of an ad text)
that reads as follows:

There is a fountain of youth.
It's called water.
Nature has been telling us this forever. Water keeps a rose fresh and beautiful. A peach juicy. All living things, living. Including your skin. The millions of cells in your skin contain water. This water pillows and cushions your skin, making it soft and young-looking. But, for a lot of reasons, cells become unable to hold water. And the water escapes your skin. (If you'll forgive us, think of a prune drying up and you'll know the whole story.)

The headline itself transports us into two symbolic worlds—that of the fountain of youth and that of water. The latter is a component of the fountain, of course, and (not uncoincidentally) is an archetypal symbol of femininity. The ad text promises to help women remain young and avoid "drying up" like prunes. The phrase "A peach juicy" is an interpretive key to unlocking the ad's symbolic code. Having *peachlike* skin, by "moistening" it, has, as Berger suspects, a connection with fertility. The genital symbolism of the peach as a "moist" fruit reinforces this association rather strongly.

The same kind of symbolism was encoded into Pango Peach—a color introduced by Revlon in 1960. This is why taglines about the product invariably described its use in highly erotic ways (Berger 2000: 61). The following taglines were used in different ads in the 1960s:

"Pink with pleasure"
"A volcano of color"
"Fullripe peach"
"Succulent on your lips"
"Sizzling on your fingertips"

These were all suggestive, metaphorically, of female sexuality. At the same time, they evoked the gustatory reactions that would ensue from eating a peach. Either way, the taglines played on the symbolic value of the *peach* as a symbol of femininity, sexuality, eroticism, youth, and beauty at once.

THE SLOGAN

The *slogan* is an expression coined for a brand or ad campaign that is associated with a brand. Whereas a tagline is coined specifically for an ad or ad campaign, a slogan constitutes the linguistic moniker for a brand. For example, Campbell's "Mmm Mmm good" tagline, created in 1904 and featuring the rosy-cheeked Campbell Kids, became, from the outset, the identifying verbal formula for the company.

Table 5.3. Examples of Sloganish

Brand	Slogan
Wheaties	"The breakfast of champions"
Frosted Flakes	"They're grrrrrreat"
McDonald's	"I'm lovin' it"
Nike	"Just do it"
Allstate Insurance	"You're in good hands with Allstate"
State Farm Insurance	"Like a good neighbor, State Farm is there"

The first true slogan was, in all likelihood, the Pears Soap company's 1888 tagline "Good morning, have you used Pears' soap?" As Hoffman (2002: 17) phrases it, this was the "first brand slogan to be completely absorbed by an entire culture." To compete with Pears, the B. T. Babbit's Soap and Powder Company quickly came up with its own slogan for its Best Soap product, a slogan that played cleverly on the brand's name—"Be wise! Use the best!" The brand wars based on "sloganish" as the main weaponry—the language of slogans—had started in earnest even before the turn of the twentieth century.

Sloganish

Slogans have played an integral part in advertising and in establishing brand identity since the late 1880s, as just mentioned. This language of slogans, or "sloganish," is a highly pleasing language, characterized above all else by poetic structure, and thus highly memorable and effective. This is borne out by the fact that some of the most memorable expressions of the past 100 years are slogans (see table 5.3).

While many brands stick to a slogan throughout their existence—as is the case with Campbell's—many others change their slogans to fit the times. Two companies that have done this consistently (and continue to do so) are Coca-Cola and Pepsi-Cola. A few examples of Coke and Pepsi sloganish are shown in table 5.4.

An obvious function of such adaptive sloganish is to guarantee that the product's image keeps in step with the changing times. For example, consider the Pepsi slogans given in the table:

- "The original pure food drink" was constructed to emphasize the fact that the drink was not some chemical concoction but a "pure" one, as customers started to challenge the nutritional quality of pop drinks in the early 1900s.

Table 5.4. Examples of Coca-Cola and Pepsi-Cola Sloganish

Coca-Cola	Pepsi-Cola
"Coca-Cola satisfies" (1904)	"The original pure food drink" (1907)
"The drink of quality" (1906)	"Drink Pepsi-Cola. It will satisfy you" (1920)
"Quenches thirst as nothing else can" (1910)	"Twice as much for a nickel too" (1939)
"Ice-cold sunshine" (1932)	"Bigger drink, better taste" (1943)
"How about a coke?" (1944)	"Refreshing without filling" (1954)
"For people on the go" (1954)	"You're in the Pepsi generation" (1963)
"Relax with Coke" (1960)	"Pepsi pours it on" (1967)
"Coke adds life" (1976)	"The choice of a new generation" (1984)
"Coke is it" (1982)	"The joy of cola" (1989)
"Always Coca-Cola" (1993)	"The drink that is forever young" (2002)

- As society became more affluent in the 1920s, Pepsi changed its slogan to reflect people's demand to be satisfied: "Drink Pepsi-Cola. It will satisfy you."
- The Depression years forced Pepsi to change its slogan to "Twice as much for a nickel too" in 1939, a slogan introduced cleverly by the cartoon called *Peter & Pete.*
- The slogan "Bigger drink, better taste" was designed to tap into the new affluence of the early 1940s.
- With the growing concern over obesity, Pepsi created a new weight-conscious slogan in 1954: "Refreshing without filling."
- Aware that the new "youth generation" had financial and social clout by the early 1960s, Pepsi beckoned people to join that generation, which it named outright "the Pepsi Generation."
- With its 1967 "Taste that beats the others cold: Pepsi pours it on" slogan, Pepsi tapped into a growing competitiveness in society.
- In 1984, the "Choice of a new generation" slogan reached out to the children of baby boomers (so-called Gen-Xers), the first generation to have grown up as "TV's babies." Gen-X pop icons Michael Jackson, Tina Turner, Gloria Estefan, Lionel Ritchie, Joe Montana, Dan Marino, Teri Garr, and Billy Crystal were featured in the "New generation" commercials on television.
- Tapping again into the ever-expanding domain of pop culture, Pepsi's "Joy of cola" slogan featured Marlon Brando, Isaac Hayes, Aretha Franklin, and Jeff Gordon in commercials that, like the slogan, proclaimed that fun and entertainment were the only true ideals or pursuable objectives in today's world.

- Aware of the tendency in society to worship youth and to remain young as long as possible, Pepsi introduced its "Forever young" slogan in 2002.

McDonald's is another company that has changed its slogans consistently to reflect new social emphases and cultural trends. With its "You deserve a break today" slogan, for example, it spoke directly to busy people and to arguing families to take a break and let McDonald's "Do it all for you," thus linking its sloganish variants. With "I'm lovin' it" and, by implication, "Why don't you join me?" the eatery tapped into an unconscious *carpe diem* mindset that characterizes today's world—namely, to seize the pleasures of the moment without thought for the future.

As examples such as these bring out, the relation between advertising and culture cannot be underestimated. More often than not, slogans are guides to a culture's mind-set, articulating in a condensed yet powerful way what is really going on in the world and, thus, perceived unconsciously to be bestowing on everyday life implicit meaning and value. But they are vacuous forms of language, reducing the portrayal of the world to formulas and catchy phrases. Sloganish is not tied to a larger social, religious, or philosophical grammar. It is instantaneous, geared to encapsulating fleeting images and condensed thoughts. It constitutes a form of discourse that celebrates consumption; it is the language used in a liturgy of consumerism.

The use of language in ritual is not to create new meanings but to reinforce traditional ones and, thus, to ensure cultural cohesion. Societies are held together as a result of verbal rituals. People typically love to hear the same speeches, songs, or stories at specific times during the year (such as at Christmas or Passover) in order to feel united with the other members of the culture. These are passed on from generation to generation with little or no modification. Slogans seem to fulfill this ritualistic function in their own surreptitious way. They are part of traditions of "word magic," as they are called in anthropology. This is the belief that words have power. In early cultures, those who possessed knowledge of certain words were also thought to possess supernatural or magical powers. Even knowing the name of a deity was purported to give the knower great power. In Egyptian mythology, the sorceress Isis tricked the sun god Ra into revealing his name and, thus, gained power over him and all other gods. In some cultures, the name given to the individual is perceived as having a "life force" independent of the individual, bringing with it the spirit of the previous individuals who shared that name. Throughout the world, the names of ancestors are perceived to weave a sort of magical protective aura on the individual named after them. In some traditional Inuit tribes, for instance, an individual will not pronounce his or her name, fearing that this senseless act could break the magical spell of protection that it brings with it. As Espes

Brown (1992: 13) puts it, "The fact that when we create words we use our breath, and for these people and these traditions breath is associated with the principle of life; breath is life itself. And so if a word is born from this sacred principle of breath, this lends an added sacred dimension to the spoken word."

Belief in the mystical powers of language is not limited to tribal cultures. It abounds even in modern technological cultures. "Speak of the devil," we say in common parlance, and "he will appear." When someone sneezes, uttering "Bless you" is meant to ward off sickness. Slogans are powerful as well because they seem to tap into this latent sense of words as being magical. If one is in difficulty, then all you have to do is "Have a Coke and smile," as the beverage proclaimed in 1979, or else there is "Always Coca-Cola," as it decreed in 1993.

Jingles

The proverbial allure of slogans and other linguistic forms can be reinforced by putting them to music. The result is the *jingle*. The "Plop, plop, fizz, fizz, oh what a relief it is!" jingle for Alka-Seltzer is memorable because of the simple catchy tune with which it is delivered in commercials, imparting a friendly, humorous quality to the product's image. The following selection of slogans for Coca-Cola and Pepsi-Cola were delivered in jingle form in radio and television commercials, becoming well-known tunes throughout society in the era in which they were used. They are among the most memorable of all the slogans/jingles created by the beverage companies:

Coca-Cola
"Things go better with Coke" (1963)
"It's the real thing" (1970)
"I'd like to buy the world a Coke" (1971)
"Can't beat the real thing" (1990)
"Always Coca-Cola" (1993)

Pepsi-Cola
"Come alive! You're in the Pepsi generation" (1963)
"Taste that beats the others cold" (1967)
"Join the Pepsi people feelin' free (1973)
"Have a Pepsi day" (1975)
"Gotta have it" (1992)

Interestingly, but not surprisingly, several jingles of the beverage companies became hits on their own—for example, *Nickel, Nickel* (Pepsi-Cola,

1939) and *Girlwatchers* (Pepsi-Cola, 1966). In effect, the battle of the brands in this case has unfolded as a battle of jingles. The two beverage giants have, since at least the 1940s, been constantly creating jingles to gain leverage in the soft-drink market. The jingle rivalry started in 1939 when Pepsi-Cola made advertising history by having a jingle, *Nickel, Nickel*, broadcast nationwide on the radio. The jingle was soon after played in jukeboxes, becoming a hit record in America and many other countries. To counteract the "Pepsi challenge" (no slogan pun intended), Coca-Cola managed to get a full hour of radio programming on NBC called *The Coca-Cola Hour*. The most popular feature of the show was the opening jingle, called the "signature tune," accompanied by the sound of a Coca-Cola bottle being opened. The lyrics of the tune were simple and catchy:

> Ice cold Cola makes anyone pause.
> The pause that refreshes.
> And Coca-Cola is everywhere.

The radio was, in fact, the medium that introduced the jingle to the advertising world. Given the ability of this medium to reach households nationwide through broadcast technology, it instituted slogans and jingles into the mindset of both advertisers and society at large. It still plays a prominent role in this regard, although television has been the dominant purveyor of jingle innovations since the early 1950s. And the longer a jingle is maintained as a "signature" of the brand, the more likely it will be remembered. A few examples are the following (see also Karmen 1989):

- Mr. Clean: "Mr. Clean gets rid of dirt, grime, and grease in just a minute"
- Chevrolet: "See the USA in your Chevrolet"
- Miller Beer: "If you've got the time, we've got the beer, Miller Beer"
- Raisin Bran: "Two scoops of raisins in Kellogg's Raisin Bran"
- Juicy Fruit: "Juicy Fruit, it's gonna move ya"
- Pepsodent: "You'll wonder where the yellow went when you brush your teeth with Pepsodent"
- Oh Henry: "Oh hungry? Oh Henry!"
- Taco Bell: "Yo quiero Taco Bell" (Spanish for "I want Taco Bell")

Clearly, by adding music to the slogan or tagline, the advertiser enhances recognition and recall of the product. It can be suggested, in fact, that the very structure of human memory is musical. The anecdotal proof of this lies in the fact that a beautiful or catchy melody is something that we hardly ever forget, no matter how long ago we heard it. As the poet W. H. Auden

(1907–1973) once put it in his book *The Dyer's Hand* (1962), "A verbal art like poetry is reflective; it stops to think. Music is immediate, it goes on to become." A catchy jingle, in fact, goes on to become the trigger that brings about an association with a product. As French playwright Jean Genet (1910–1986) phrased it in his play *Prisoner of Love* (1986), "Perhaps all music, even the newest, is not so much something discovered as something that re-emerges from where it lay buried in the memory, inaudible as a melody cut in a disc of flesh. A composer lets me hear a song that has always been shut up silent within me."

HUMOR

Linguistic humor has become an important LBT in advertising, showing an understanding on the part of advertisers of the highly satirical, ironic mindset of today's sitcom-influenced world. Typically, the humor used is consistent with that used on television and in cinema and reflected in society at large. In this way, it can be used in line with what makes people laugh, thus making the product or service appear contemporary and friendly. Budweiser Beer, for instance, is constantly creating humorous commercials, allowing it to keep in step with the changing times and with changing trends within its target market—young males. Budweiser television and Internet commercials typically show males hanging out together, performing male bonding rituals (such as watching television sports programs together). The details of the scripts and the humor employed by the characters changes constantly, but the subtext remains the same: "You're one of the guys, bud."

And, of course, humor is the main vehicle through which children's advertising is delivered. This can be seen in everything from the creation of cartoon characters such as Tony the Tiger, who are intrinsically funny, to the frequent coinage of linguistic expressions such as "goooey good" that are mirthful in themselves.

Whassup?

The Budweiser ad campaigns of the 1980s and early 1990s emphasized rural ruggedness and female sexuality from a male viewpoint. The actors in the commercials were "Marlboro men" and the women their sexual partners. In the early 2000s, the beer company changed its image to keep in step with the changing sociopolitical climate, which was critical of the Marlboro man and more inclined to see men as actors in sitcoms, from *Seinfeld* to *Friends*. Its new approach consisted in putting on male-directed skits—that is, the kinds of skits that males would probably enjoy. The strategy worked beyond the company's expectation. In early 2000, for example, one of the Bud commercials showed the movie dog Rex chasing an imaginary Budweiser beer truck, leaping blindly over a hedge, and plunging face-first into a van. In 2001, a commercial shows Cedric the Entertainer's dream date go awry when his shaken-up bottles of Bud Light spewed on his date. The commercial was, clearly, imitative of the "nerdy" humor of contemporary sitcoms and movies. In 2002, we see a wife luring her husband to a bedroom with the promise of Bud Light. He dives for the beer and slides out a window on their satin sheets. In 2004, we see a yuppie's pedigree pooch fetching him a Bud Light and biting his crotch to get some of it—a skit that was clearly in line with the moronic humor of sitcoms such as *South Park*.

But perhaps Budweiser's most successful humor campaign was its "Whassup?" one. It was so appealing, in fact, that its signature catchphrase was joked about on talk shows, parodied on websites, mimicked in other media, and used by people commonly in conversations. The makers of Budweiser had clearly tapped into social trends.

The campaign showed how integrated advertising and pop culture had become. Actually, the "Whassup" campaign began not in an ad agency but as a short film by a relatively unknown director named Charles Tone. The film caught the attention of an ad agency that worked for Anheuser-Busch, the manufacturer of Budweiser, seeing in the film its potential for Budweiser's new image. The ad agency was prophetic. The phrase was, incidentally, taken from hip-hop culture. It caught on with young people everywhere who started greeting one another comically and in jest like the characters in the Bud commercials. The phrase, as mentioned, found its way also into late-night talk shows and into imitation commercials, especially on the Internet. As Frankel (2004: 165) recounts it, rather than sue other advertisers for breach of copyright, Anheuser-Busch welcomed the imitations. The brand manager for the company put it as follows: "But we said, Stop? What, are you crazy? This is great, this idea is cool, and Bud is an integral part of it."

The campaign won numerous industry awards, highlighting the degree to which advertising, pop culture, and society had become integrated facets of the modern world. By becoming part of everyday lingo, Budweiser increased recognition of its brand name. "Whassup!" became (and probably still is) a linguistic trademark of the Budweiser brand. The commercials were hilarious, the humor was perfect for the times, and the whole experience of greeting someone in imitation of the campaign was fun. And it is little wonder that the Bud commercials are always among the funniest ones on the Super Bowl television spectacle. Beer, sports, moronic humor, and young males seem to go together perfectly in today's America.

Humor, Advertising, and Contemporary Language

Humor has become a major LBT in advertising, probably reflecting the Zeitgeist of the times. Through humorous slogans, jingles, and commercials, many brands attempt not only to convey a friendly and folksy image of themselves but also to tap into current comedic styles. With its condensed style, its trendy slang form, and its ephemerality, advertising humor is thus reflective of broader trends within pop culture. This is why the Budweiser campaigns are always so funny. They are, in a phrase, au courant.

A perfect example is the 2005 TV commercial campaign by the feminine birth control product Alesse, which played on a type of wry humor that pitted women against men with the product functioning as "code" for the secret knowledge possessed by women. This commercial started with several young women of various ethnic backgrounds using the phrase "I'm on Alesse." They all wore different styles of clothing, and their personalities also seemed very different. Only those familiar with the code could relate to the phrase until the end, when a young male appears on screen yelling, "What's Alesse?" The male looked utterly confused as an "outsider" and, significantly, did not receive a response to his question, as the women just chuckled dismissively. The final frame of the commercial revealed a package of oral contraceptives, providing the visual key to the "code."

A similar example was the 2005 Tampax tampon campaign, which featured a scene in a coed upper-school classroom where a girl passes a note to another classmate. The other student tries to pass something back to her but is caught by the male teacher and asked to bring it to him. She walks to the front and hands him a small object wrapped in yellow paper. The teacher admonishes her with, "Ms. Maggie, I hope you have enough for everyone." She replies back, "Enough for the girls." The teacher looks confused, as do the boys in the classroom. The girls, on the other hand, giggle and look at each other knowingly.

Co-opting humor styles and comedic formulas is a central LBT of many brands. Even brands that once used a different style are now jumping on the humor bandwagon. Recent cases in point are Dairy Queen's commercials of a baby trying to steal his father's Cheesecake Sundae, a man who starts fires after eating a Flamethrower Burger, and the Six Flags commercials that featured a bald old man in a tuxedo who drives his vintage bus into neighborhoods and tap dances joyfully to the catchy tune "We want to party."

Has this kind of language had a negative impact on society? Some would say that it has, impoverishing our ability to use language for more important things. It has been described as the equivalent of pop music. The linguist Savan (2005) has recently suggested that such language can be called "pop language"—a language crystallizing from the pop culture–advertising partnership that has purportedly damaged true human conversation. She describes, for example, the use of slang forms, such as "like," which are used in movies and television sitcoms constantly: "She's, like, so cool." This is why conversation today, Savan claims, seems to carry with it a built-in applause sign or laugh track. Trendy phrases such as "That is so last year," "I hate it when that happens," "Don't go there," and the sneering "I don't think so" are delivered in a theatrical way, as if waiting for an audience reaction. Such language is perceived as "hip" not because it is intrinsically meritorious but because it is everywhere in pop culture and advertising. It is light, self-conscious, and highly sitcommish, replete with put-downs and exaggerated inflections. It is simulated language. Savan compares the 1953 Disney cartoon *Peter Pan* with the 2002 sequel *Return to Never Land* showing how remarkably free the former one was of packaged phrases and slang. The sequel, on the other hand, speaks in pop language, including such phrases as "In your dreams, Hook," "Put a cork in it," "Tell me about it," "You've got *that* right," and "Don't even *think* about it."

Savan's critique is very close to the heart of those who descry the advertising language discussed in this chapter that now seems to be entering everyone's discourse on a daily basis. It is true that, in the past, the primary conduits of new language were writers. But, not to defend the advertising domain, this is not unexpected. In the past, even the great writers were not averse to incorporating and, through their works, spreading slang. Shakespeare, for instance, brought into acceptable usage such slang terms as *hubbub*, to *bump*, and to *dwindle*. But not before the second half of the twentieth century did it become routine for the conduit to be the media recycling essentially adolescent words. The words *pot* and *marijuana* became common words in the 1960s after they were adopted by the counterculture youth of the era. These were spread by television sitcoms and other programs of the era to society at large. The number of such words that have entered the communal lexicon since the 1960s is truly mind boggling, constituting strong evidence that pop trends in all domains of modern-day life have become a major social force, as Savan suggests.

6

Art

Advertising is the greatest art form of the twentieth century.

—Marshall McLuhan, 1911–1980

Shopping or simply browsing in a food store, variety store, or pharmacy is an eye-pleasing experience. The different colors, shapes, and sizes of the packages entice us with their variety and ingenious mode of presentation. A modern-day store is a cornucopia of visual delights that seduce and gratify us at once. Through differential packaging, design of containers, and other such presentational techniques, advertisers and marketers not only impart identity and distinctiveness to their products but also create a spectacle of sensory stimulation within stores that is not unlike the spectacles of circuses. Brie cheese is brie cheese. The only way to distinguish one brand from the other, other than reading the brand name, is to look at the wrapping or package in which the cheese is presented. And the more attractive the packaging, the more likely it is that we will notice it. Although we should "not judge a book by its cover," as the expression goes, we actually end up doing so more often than not.

In addition to presentational style, the advertiser has become adept at using the arts and crafts more generally to make products stand apart from others and to increase their appeal. The advertiser has, in effect, tapped into one of the most unique of human instincts—the "art instinct"—an impulse for fantasy and desire that involves the entire range of feelings and emotions that differentiate humans from other life forms. Artistic traditions are preserved and passed on from generation to generation throughout the world because they are perceived universally as transcending time, as saying something true and profound about the human condition, and as being simply pleasurable and beautiful. Today, advertising is an art form. And many modern-day artists have been employed to create ads and commercials, from Ridley Scott, who was hired by the Apple Corporation (chapter 4), to Salvador Dalí by the Gap and Datsun. But even without the employment of artists, advertisers now produce ads and commercials that rival paintings and other art forms. Of course, we recognize advertising art for what it is—art with a commercial objective—but it pleases us nonetheless. The difference between so-called real art and advertising art is highlighted eloquently by Hoffman (2002: 6) as follows:

> In the hierarchy of cultural criticism the lines drawn between art and advertising started out fairly clear. Art is high. Advertising is low. Art is elite and refined. Advertising is vulgar and democratic. Art is original. Advertising is derivative. Art is a product created by people to express their personal vision. Advertising is created by people who get paid to sell a product. Art is defined by the truth of the insight it expresses. Advertising expresses the insight of truisms. Art is disturbingly honest. Advertising is only as honest as it has to be, and occasionally less. Art is eternal. Advertising is ephemeral.

But despite such differences, it is advertising art that most people are exposed to on a daily basis, not the art kept in galleries or shown in sophisticated art books. Today, the commercials shown at the Super Bowl garner as intense a reaction that any veritable work of art has ever garnered in the past. People rate their favorite commercials online and download the most popular ones to safekeep like they would a work of real art. Clearly, the topic of advertising art is a central one. This chapter looks at the clever artistic hand of the advertiser—a hand that is now involved in packaging, in the making of soundtracks in commercials, and in the style used to create ads and commercials. For the sake of convenience, I will use the term *art* in reference to any aspect of advertising that involves some aesthetic reaction on the part of people, from the visual pleasure we get from looking at product design through packaging to the diversion we get from viewing television commercials.

ADVERTISING AND ART

Defining *art* is an impossible task. Art is something that everyone recognizes because it elicits a unique kind of sensory and emotional reaction, producing a distinctive way of looking at the world. In classical and medieval times, poets were praised and recognized for their artistic endeavors, whereas musicians, painters, sculptors, and other artists who used physical skills were considered less important and, therefore, often remained anonymous. However, starting in the early Renaissance, those skilled in the visual and performing arts gradually gained greater recognition and social prestige and thus the right to authorship. By the eighteenth century, a more sophisticated public felt the need to distinguish between art that was purely aesthetic and art that was practical or ornamental. Thus, a distinction was made between the fine arts—including literature, music, dance, painting, sculpture, and architecture—and the decorative or applied arts—such as pottery, metalwork, and furniture and carpet making—which for a time were demoted to the rank of crafts. Because the prestigious École des Beaux-Arts in Paris taught only the major visual arts, the term *art* has since been reserved in the West to refer mainly to drawing, painting, architecture, and sculpture. However, since the mid-twentieth century, greater appreciation of all types of art, of non-Western art, and of folk artistic traditions has expanded the view of what constitutes art considerably and given back to the word its broader meaning. And there is no doubt in my mind that advertising art has been pivotal in reinstating this larger view of art.

But, then, are print ads and television commercials really art forms? At a rudimentary level, they are indeed since they were made by someone using a high degree of imagination and great skill. They also produce an aesthetic effect, whether we wish to admit it or not. However, one may ask, What is their message? What is their purpose? The objective of advertising art is, of course, to represent a product or service rather than some aspect of life. But because ads and commercials have all the structural and aesthetic characteristics of traditional art and because they are everywhere we turn, advertising art is becoming simply art. Because of this, advertising has profoundly influenced how we view products—not as products that allow us to accomplish something but, as mentioned several times in this book, as objets d'art. So, rather than look for a message in advertising art, we glean from it a new perception of what products represent in personal, social, and even philosophical terms. The products are then transformed in our minds into "interpretants"—messages related to happiness, youthfulness, success, status, luxury, beauty, and so on. Recall from chapter 1 that the term *interpretant* is used in semiotics to refer to any meaning that we glean from a sign in a specific personal, social, historical, and physical context. The interpretant of products is no longer a view of them as simple products but as something much larger. That, in my view, has been the most profound effect brought about by advertising art on the modern mind-set.

Pop Art

Logically, the first to pick up on the impact that advertising has had on our perception of products as meaningful objects were the so-called pop artists who emerged shortly after World War I. The practitioners of pop art started out, not surprisingly, in the world of commercial design. Andy Warhol, for example, was a designer of shoe ads before venturing into the domain of pop art. In effect, the pop art movement legitimized advertising art.

As mentioned already, the pop art movement was inspired by the mass production and consumption of objects. For pop artists, the factory, supermarket, and garbage can became their art school. But despite its apparent absurdity, many people loved pop art no matter how controversial or crass it appeared to be. In a certain sense, the pop art movement bestowed on common people the assurance that art was for mass consumption, not just for an elite class of cognoscenti. Some artists duplicated beer bottles, soup cans, comic strips, road signs, and similar objects in paintings, collages, and sculptures; others simply incorporated the objects themselves into their works. Using images and sounds that reflected the materialism and vulgarity of modern consumerist culture, the first pop artists sought to provide a view of reality that was more immediate and relevant than that of past art. They wanted the observer to respond directly to the object rather than to the skill and viewpoint of the artist. As Hoffman (2002: 101) has aptly put it,

> Pop, like advertising, is interested in the concept more than the rendering. It uses the objects that inhabit the world every individual of every class takes for granted—the mundane, mass-produced stuff that is all around us. The things you use and like. Pop artists don't use these things because there is nothing else to paint, they use them to make a point.

As already discussed, the pop art movement surfaced in the 1940s and 1950s, when painters like Robert Rauschenberg and Jasper Johns strove to close the gap between traditional art and mass culture. Rauschenberg constructed collages from household objects such as quilts and pillows and Johns from American flags and bull's-eye targets. The first full-fledged pop art work was *Just What Is It That Makes Today's Home So Different, So Appealing?* (1956, private collection) by the British artist Richard Hamilton. In this satiric collage of two ludicrous figures in a living room, the pop art hallmarks of crudeness and irony are emphasized. American pop artist Roy Lichtenstein became so interested in mass-produced commercial illustrations, especially comic strips and advertisements, that he created works portraying single products and single frames of comic strips on canvas surfaces in order to draw attention to the most common images in daily life. Lichtenstein's comic strip paintings include words simulating sounds or a portion of dialogue, as in real comic strips.

Pop art developed rapidly during the 1960s, as painters started to focus their attention on brand-name commercial products, producing sculptures of hamburgers and other fast-food items, blown-up frames of comic strips, or theatrical events staged as art objects. Pop artists also appropriated the techniques of mass production. Rauschenberg and Johns had already abandoned individual, titled paintings in favor of large series of works, all depicting the same objects. In the early 1960s, Warhol carried the idea a step further by adopting the mass-production technique of silk screening, turning out hundreds of identical prints of Coca-Cola bottles, Campbell's soup cans, and other familiar products, including identical three-dimensional Brillo boxes.

Advertising Art

To quote Hoffman (2002: 101) again, pop art and advertising art converged in the same era, one becoming indistinguishable from the other, thus signaling "the total triumph of the selling state in American culture." Advertising art—in the form of packaging, product design, and the ingenious and constant mass creation of new ads and commercials—has become a kind of cultural meta-art. The magazine ad, for instance, is really a contemporary art genre all its own. Fashion and lifestyle magazines are virtually artwork catalogs, displaying visual images that are not unlike those of the great portrait painters. No wonder, then, that advertising is being acknowledged officially as veritable art more and more, having even its own prize categories at major film festivals. Although we may superciliously be inclined to condemn its objectives, as an aesthetic-inducing experience we invariably enjoy it. Ads convince, please, and seduce. And they invariably contain a subtext—a meaning below the surface that engages us in an inner semiotic self-dialogue, not unlike the kind of self-dialogue we engage in when viewing paintings in an art gallery.

Consider a 2007 print ad for PhotoAlto, a stock photography supplier, that appeared in a lifestyle magazine. As mentioned, looking at the ad produces an interpretive effect that is not unlike that produced when we look at a painting hanging on the wall of an art gallery. It entices us to understand what is going on and what its subtext is all about. Or else, it might simply give us visual pleasure and delight, as do many paintings of the masters. Let's attempt an interpretation. In the ad, we see a young girl sitting on a wall bench in a hospital-like place. With elbows on her knees, chin on her hands, and head tilted upward, the fair-skinned blonde girl appears to be peering coyly (almost enamoredly) at something above her. Her feet are perched upward, and her toes are curled. Her clothes are white, with a blue tinge to them, and, strangely, she dons angel wings.

At a superficial level, the ad is in synch with the brand name "PhotoAlto," which means, literally, "looking at a photo on high." But there seems to be something else much more subtle going on. The girl is, in fact, looking at the tagline "Photography that dares." But, then, what does the photography dare her (us) to do? The logo of the brand has a mischievous (almost devilish) appearance. So, is she being dared by the devil? Is this a mythical fight between good and bad angels? Being shoeless certainly has a mythical quality to it— angels and other mythical creatures do not wear shoes. Is the angel/girl a messenger for the brand, telling people to take the dare of the brand? The set of questions the ad evokes could go on and on. Suffice it to say that it would not do so if it did not have the form that it has. It is a work of visual art no matter what its ultimate objective. It anticipates an interpretant, conscious or unconscious. In a phrase, it is a work of art.

In previous times, the commissioners of the arts were churchmen and aristocrats. They employed artists for their own personal desires and pleasures. Today, the commissioners are advertisers. They also employ them for their own objectives. In a way, advertising art is subversive in that it challenges canons of traditional art making and the elitist aesthetics of high culture. It costs nothing to look at it (unless, of course, it induces one to buy the product), and at the same time it imparts an aesthetic feeling. In a phrase, advertising art is the art of capitalist societies. But there is a fundamental difference between the great works of art that attempt to "say something" about life and advertising art. Not to belabor the point, advertising is the art of the trivial, dressed up in traditional aesthetic costume. And its aim is transparent. That is why ads quickly become meaningless and replaced by new ones with new simulated forms of visual representation.

Aware of the obliteration of the boundary between pop art (and art generally) and advertising art, some brands have incorporated art techniques explicitly and directly as part of their construction of identity. One of these is Absolut Vodka, which has employed some of the world's top artists to construct its ads, blurring the line between art and brands even further. On a recent website, the brand showed its "top 100 ads" proudly, as would any art catalog or technical study. Absolut Vodka even has its own art museum, accessible through the Web. Apparently, people rip out its print ads from magazines or else download them from the Internet, collecting them as they would any works of art. Since the brand enlists real artists to design its ads, they are, in fact, construable as veritable works of art. Each ad is signed by an artist as part of the taglines "Absolut Adams," "Absolut Kosolapov," and so on. Given the success of Absolut Vodka, it is little wonder to find that the major brands of alcoholic beverages have followed suit, using art explicitly in the design of their ads no matter how controversial this technique is. As Hoffman (2002: 122) aptly puts it, "The land where art and commerce meet continues to be a fertile place for marketers who are willing to take risks and court controversy."

ART TECHNIQUES

One of the distinctive features of art is that it stimulates sensory reactions. One of these is evoked indirectly, as when the hearing of a sound produces the visualization of a color. Recall the discussion of the expressions connected with peaches in the previous chapter—"Succulent on your lips," "Sizzling on your fingertips." These stimulate gustatory and tactile sensations indirectly. One can almost "taste" or "feel" the peach. This indirect, imaginary stimulation of sensation is known as **synesthesia**. Synesthesia connects the viewer to an ad text in a sensory way in the same way that paintings and other art forms do. It is a technique that is used extensively and, seemingly, protected avidly. For instance, Kellogg's patented its distinctive crunchy sound associated in commercials with eating its cornflakes—a synesthetic sound created professionally in sound labs (Lindstrom 2005). Similar cases of synesthetic patenting, as it can be called, are found throughout the advertising world.

Synesthesia is only one of the art techniques used in advertising today. Another main one is *surrealism*—an art movement that attempts to express the workings of the subconscious during dream states, characterized by fantastic imagery and incongruous juxtaposition of subject matter. In effect, the techniques used in advertising art are designed to elicit a sensory-imaginative reaction, a reaction that is intentionally built not only into ads but also into logo design and brand name. As Neumeier (2006: 88) puts it,

> Cognitive scientists estimate that more than half the brain is dedicated to the visual system, adding weight to the argument that a trademark should be strongly visual. Yet it can also involve other senses, including smell, touch, taste, or hearing. Take, for example, the auditory counterpart to an icon, sometimes called an "earcon." The experience of flying United Airlines is now inextricably linked to Gershwin's "Rhapsody in Blue," and the Intel Inside brand would be less memorable without its "bong" sound bite.

Synesthesia

I recently checked ads for all kinds of products in over 100 magazines published in North America and Europe to assay if synesthesia was, in actual fact, a widespread ad-making strategy. As it turned out, I determined that over 900 of the ads had a synesthetic quality built into them, which is a significantly high number. For example, I collected ads that showed people splashing in water with ecstatic expressions on their faces. These invariably imparted to me the sensation of actually feeling cool water on my skin. The feel of leather, satin, or silk was elicited, instead, by ads for clothing products through the vividness of the colors used, which literally brought the fabrics and materials to life (in my imagination at least). And, of course, the erotic feel of lips was elicited by pictures of young, attractive women in ads with sensuous lips (which are spotlighted in the ads). I showed the same ads to my students at both the University of Toronto and the University of Lugano and got identical assessments of the ads (without me telling them how I reacted to them).

Synesthetic ads allow viewers to indulge in an ersatz form of sensory voyeurism. They allow entrance into a multidimensional "sensorium" of the mind, as Marshall McLuhan called the sensory world. The ad text, which identifies a product and presents a situation or image, unfolds in the mind as an action sensory sequence, so to speak. The synesthetic effect occurs not from individual elements in the surface text but rather in their relationships to each other. Thus, the sensation of cold comes across not from viewing, say, an ice cube by itself but from observing its placement on a body in an ad. The level at which these relationships generate sensations and other kinds of meanings is commonly referred to as the **subtext**. Another kind of relationship occurs "outside the text." The erotic sensation derived from viewing the lips in ads discussed previously comes not from the nature of lips themselves but from their erotic symbolism as portrayed in all kinds of other texts. Allusions of this kind are considered to be elements of **intertextuality** (Allen 2000; Beard 2001).

The idea behind synesthetic advertising is an obvious one—to associate a sensory and an emotional experience with a product. The combination of visual and audio stimuli in commercials, for instance, is a powerful one, triggering at least two sensory channels at once. This is why certain brands now consistently use classical music excerpts—earcons, as Neumeier calls them—as their soundtracks. Recently, for instance, Playstation 3 (Baby Doll, 2006) featured Carl Orff's *O Fortuna* (from his *Carmina Burana*). In the commercial, a baby doll is seen sitting in a corner of a white room, with a Playstation 3 system on the opposite corner. The baby looks at the video game system and giggles. It then starts laughing maliciously. A close-up of the doll's face is seen, with its eyes welling up with tears. At the end, the name Playstation 3 is shown on the screen. The subtext is transparent—a new plaything has come into the world, replacing all previous ones, symbolized by the doll. The *Carmina Burana* is a musical setting of medieval poems discovered in 1803 in the library of the Benedictine monastery of Beuron, near Munich. The *O Fortuna* is a desperate chant, powerfully evocative of agony and loss. It matches the visual text perfectly.

Surrealism

To get a sense of how advertisers incorporate surrealism as an ad-making technique, consider a classic Coco Chanel ad campaign that started in the

1990s and continued on well into the mid-2000s. The ads show a voluptuous, young woman dressed up to resemble a bird with a tail. She has a rope tied around her ankle and is dressed in erotic clothing (sexy stockings, black gloves, and so on). The number of meanings suggested by the text is unquantifiable. The woman appears to come at us out of a dream. Who is she? Where is she? Who is holding the rope (which goes beyond the actual ad text)? One possible interpretation is suggested by the Coco name itself, which was the nickname of the late founder of Chanel, Gabrielle Bonheur Chanel. Its phonetic quality suggests onomatopoeically the sound a bird is perceived to make. Coco is also an abbreviation for "cocaine," which is not only a narcotic but also an aphrodisiacal intoxicant. Together with the visual image, the text seems to suggest that the perfume will allow females to be "sexually wild" and "uninhibited." Reinforcing this interpretation is a ravenous, "birdlike" expression on the model's face. The metaphorical association of the female figure to a bird is a deeply embedded one in our culture. In English slang, for example, a young woman is called a "chick," and the expressions "stuffing a bird" and "getting tail" mean "to have sex" with a woman. The oversized Coco bottle, with its vivid amber color, juxtaposed against the dark background, is highly suggestive of fire and flames and, thus, reinforced the sexual sense of "burning desire" communicated overall by the ad.

But this interpretation is only one of many others that are possible. Another plausible interpretation of the ad could be that of women as "pets" who are to be adored, pampered, and "maintained" (enslaved?) by men for sexual amusement and gratification. This interpretation is reinforced by the fact that the woman in the ads was tied to a rope, making her escape from the scene impossible, perhaps. Another possible interpretative line of reasoning is that of "woman as sexual slave." The rope tied around her ankle has a spermatozoid shape, although it is colored red—a symbol of female sexuality. The ambiguity of the rope's meaning is brought out further by the fact that the one who holds the rope cannot be seen—he or she is just beyond the contours of the ad space. Is the holder of the rope—the source of her enslavement—a man, the dark forces of nature, or even the woman herself?

The woman in the ads is barefoot, which is suggestive of the female's biological role as "mother" and as an "earth bearer." The woman holds a bottle of Coco next to her face and breast as she would a child. And while the woman's bare back, shoulders, and scanty attire produce erotic imagery, her slightly turned bodily orientation, concealing the front part of her body, is suggestive of modesty.

The ad is, in a phrase, a masterpiece of surrealist art. The dark void that surrounds the woman and the fact that she seems to appear mysteriously "out of nothingness" have all the qualities of a surrealist dream sequence. Like true surrealist art, there is no end to the meanings one can extract from the ad. As Judith Williamson (1996) has astutely pointed out, texts like the Coco Chanel one constitute "surrealist puzzles." In general, ads for perfume, clothes, alcoholic beverages, and other lifestyle products are designed either to produce a synesthetic reaction, to pose surrealist puzzles, or to generate mythic images. This is because the products are all about desire, and surrealist art is a perfect conduit for the conveyance of desire, especially subconscious desire. Hoffman (2002: 71) summarizes the use of surrealism in advertising eloquently as follows:

> Unlike the way they use classical painting, advertisers don't often reproduce the actual surrealist images. More often they transpose the visual rhetoric of surreal paintings with a glib indifference to the deeper issues and ideas that spawned the movement in the first place. Part of the comfort art directors felt when they presented surreal images to their clients must have sprung from the fact that surrealism, like advertising, is at its heart about desire.

Some advertisers allude directly to surrealist texts in their ad. Salvador Dalí's (1904–1989) *Persistence of Memory* (1931), which shows a desolate landscape inhabited by limp, melting watches and which is now emblematic of the whole surrealist movement, has been used in ads by the Gap and Datsun. Major brands have even employed surrealist painters to create their ad texts. Dalí himself was hired to paint timescapes for both the Gap and Datsun, whose ads featured the taglines "Salvador Dalí wore khakis" and "New Datsun 610 Wagon: An original portrait by Dalí."

It is the difficulty in interpreting surrealist images and the absence of obvious connections between the images and the products advertised that intrigues viewers of the ads. It is intrigue, I would claim, that makes ads like the Coco Chanel one appealing in themselves, whether or not they induce us to buy perfume. The surrealists claimed that they took snapshots of the psyche in its dream state. If that is so, then it would explain why surrealist ads are so powerful. Simply put, they work on a dream level of mind.

REPRESENTATION

One of my objectives in the foregoing discussion has been to suggest that in modern consumerist cultures, it is becoming more and more difficult to determine what is art and what is not. Already in 1913, the French American artist Marcel Duchamp (1887–1968) produced an upside-down but otherwise unaltered bicycle wheel, asserting that it (or any other everyday object) constituted a sculpture if an artist declared it to be so. Duchamp soon followed the bicycle wheel with a bottle rack, snow shovel, and, most notoriously, a urinal. The attitude of Duchamp and other members of the so-called Dada movement who shared his views about art reemerged in the early 1960s through an international group of artists calling themselves Fluxus. Like the Dadaists, they sought to erode the barriers between art and life and allow randomness and chance to guide their work. The Dada movement led to the pop art movement, which in turn brought consumer objects into the realm of art.

In other words, the Dada movement has conditioned the modern psyche to see ads and commercials as art texts rather than as simple posters or Barnum-style sales manifestos. Decoding ads and commercials will be discussed in the next chapter. Here the focus is on the ways in which advertising texts represent products generally through the use of techniques that the Dadaists, pop artists, and surrealists would find laudable.

Anchorage

What does the expression on the face of the female in the Coco Chanel ad discussed previously represent? Why is the female looking at us in that way? The face is, in fact, a primary source of emotional communication. Looking in the eyes is a sign of love, affection, dare, or sexual interest. Looking away and closing one's eyes is a sign of something else (rapture, reverie, indifference, disinterest, and so on). Visual images in advertising texts are absolutely critical in how they create synesthetic or surrealist effects. In a text, they speak indirectly to the subconscious mind, suggesting diverse kinds of meanings by association. People can picture faces and images much more accurately and quickly than they can recall words. This is also the reason why cartoon characters, computer graphics, and the like are used to endorse or represent products. Mouthwash bottles dance across the screen, automobiles turn into animals, and these capture our fancy, becoming instantly memorable.

The word **text**, as it is used in semiotic theory, means something very specific. It literally designates a "putting together" of signs or sign elements to produce a message, consciously or unconsciously. The text can be either verbal or nonverbal or both. In order for the text to signify something, one must know the *code* or *codes* to which the signs used belong. What does this imply? Consider the following simple example. If one were to listen to a verbal language that one does not know, all one would hear are "disembodied signifiers"—sounds, intonations, and so on—that one intuitively knows cohere into words and phrases that carry some intended meaning but to which one has no access. The decoding of the verbal signifiers—that is, their linkage to meaning—occurs only when one comes to know the language code to which they belong (such as its phonetic system, grammar, and lexicon). Similarly, musical performances, stage plays, common discourse exchanges, dance styles, religious rites, ceremonies, and so on are texts that we regularly make, as individuals or groups, from the various codes that a culture puts at our disposal. Access to the meanings generated by such texts is possible only if the codes used to create them are known.

To the notion of code in advertising, Barthes (1977) added the concept of **anchorage**, or the notion that visual images in advertisements are polysemous (i.e., they have many meanings), which are anchored by viewers to specific socially meaningful texts (such as the Bible and ancient mythical stories). In other words, ad texts are constructed with visual cues that imply an endless chain of meanings from which the viewer can choose some and ignore others; that is, the text's meanings are anchored to specific signification systems by specific interpreters. As mentioned, the underlying meaning on which a text is anchored is commonly referred to as its subtext. Consider, again, the Coco Chanel ad. What is its subtext? Is the feminine form powerful because it is birdlike? Is she a mythical form generated by the perfume? Is that the source of her magnetism and her enslavement (symbolized by the rope around her ankle)? This series of questions would be literally "meaningless" in cultures that do not ascribe the same connotative meaning to females as birdlike creatures. This "female ornithological code" is what allows us to formulate, let alone contemplate, such questions. In other words, the subtext is anchored both in the interpreter and in the specific culture in which the interpretation takes place. The components involved in the act of interpretation—the interpreter, the text, the context, the code, the culture, the product, and so on—are inextricably intertwined or, to paraphrase Barthes, anchored in the same meaning terrain.

Fantasy

All of us have moments when we need to escape, as the expression goes. We can do so by reading (e.g., novels and comics), watching movies, and so on. We escape, in a word, through fantasy. Art is a form of fantasy. It allows us to fantasize momentarily on its content or mode of display. In advertising, the product is, clearly, the means through which the viewer's fantasy will be fulfilled. In beer ads and commercials, the fantasy world provided involves masculine desires. They often draw on pseudoartistic traditions where, such as in Jean Auguste Dominique Ingres's *The Turkish Bath*, multiple females are put on display for the pleasure and selection of the male viewer. In a recent Bud Light commercial, the scene begins with a male uttering the phrase "So I was having a Bud Light . . ." and then continues on to recount the story of a man at a bar who meets a group of female friends, charms them, selects the one he likes most, and then conquers her from the "Turkish Bath."

In effect, many ads and commercials are based on the representation of some fantasy world. The representation of male fantasies of beer ads is matched by the representation of female fantasies in perfume ads, by the representation of "back to nature" fantasies in soap and deodorant ads, and so on. Advertising has created or, more correctly, re-created a true fantasyland of the psyche to which anyone can have access by simply viewing ads and commercials. Much like children's fantasies—stories that involve beings and events that do not exist in real life—ads allow us to escape into the world of dreams where fantasies become real.

A fantasy that is as old as civilization is the one where death is conquered and one can remain "forever young." Oil of Olay ads tap into this fantasy constantly, allowing primarily female viewers to escape into this particular fantasyland. One ad shows a woman with reading glasses (suggesting that she is mature and probably highly educated) who has just grown out of "pimples" and now can easily eliminate "wrinkles" with the Olay moisturizer. This fantasy of a never-aging face is brought to the next stage when, as an older woman, she can wear both "bifocals and ripped jeans." In effect, this ad mirrors in a simple, direct, yet highly effective way the desire in society not only to stay and look healthier for a longer period of life but also to act and think young forever. Like the main character in Oscar Wilde's (1854–1900) ingenious novel *The Picture of Dorian Gray* (1890), the Olay ad campaign, like those of many other products, allows us to escape into Dorian Gray's fantasy, whose portrait ages and grows ugly in the attic while his actual appearance remains the same. The book contains a simple warning—the devotion to pleasure and beauty is destructive. It is, after all, a fantasy.

DESIGN

As mentioned at the start of this chapter, going into a store constitutes not just a buying experience, as it did in the days before packaging, logos, and brand names, when goods were in colorless bins and containers. It constitutes an aesthetic experience, involving some or all of the senses. In some department stores, for example, the smells of perfumes, the piped-in music, the colors of the perfume bottles and their shapes, and so on coalesce in our minds to provide a total sensory experience. A visit to any store, therefore, is akin to a visit to a multimedia art gallery. In this way, we can "experience" a product before buying it. Packaging and product design are part, clearly, of an unconscious perception of products as objets d'art. Who does not recognize a Coke bottle, a Campbell's soup can, or other familiar containers? These have become so familiar that they are hardly recognized any longer as having been designed specifically to promote product familiarity and appeal through design. They have become true artifacts in the archaeological sense—mementos of cultural lore.

Containers

Product design, like the brand name and logo, ensconces brand image effectively. This starts with the container (e.g., bottle or package) in the case of products such as drinks, perfumes, and the like. Take Coca-Cola again. The contour, hobble-skirted Coke bottle was created in 1915, becoming one of the world's most familiar bottle designs ever created. It is now even stored in museums and private collections. Tab-open tops for Coke were introduced during the mid-1960s, at which time the company also introduced its familiar can. Together with the logo on the bottles and cans, the Coca-Cola design has become an icon of contemporary consumerist culture.

Not all containers or packages have become so broadly familiar. Some are designed to be practical. Aerosol cans, easy-to-open detergent bottles with a tough plastic and durable design, lightweight containers for carryable products (e.g., pills and candies), and packages with images that show how to open or close a bag are all examples of designs that have a high practicality in their form (Hine 1995). However, for most brands container design is intended to do much more. For some products, in fact, the container (e.g., package or bottle) is the brand. Take, for example, perfume products, which seem to depend on bottle design to carve out their identity. Most of the bottle designs of the "high-class" perfumes and colognes range in style from the gothic and neoclassical to the modern and postmodern. Such bottles are hardly "throwaways." They have the same "timeless" look about them that precious artifacts or artworks have. As a practical illustration of the "lure of the bottle," consider the pitch-dark, elliptically shaped cologne of the Drakkar Noir cologne bottle (by Guy Laroche), mentioned briefly in chapter 3. First, the color of the bottle, black, and the name of the cologne are iconic counterparts. The bottle has a black color, connoting fear, night, and the occult—a design feature that expresses in visual form the meaning of the name *Noir* (French for "black"). The sepulchral name Drakkar is also congruous with the bottle's design at a suggestive level, reinforcing the idea that something scary but nevertheless desirous may happen by splashing on the cologne. The guttural Drakkar name is, in fact, suggestive phonetically of Dracula, the deadly vampire who mesmerized his sexual prey with a mere glance.

Needless to say, other readings of the bottle can also be envisioned, probably because the Dracula figure has come to symbolize other things in today's pop culture. One of these is the breaking of taboos. As represented in cinema,

Dracula challenges authority, putting forward a fine line between passion and power and resuscitating the mythical search for eternal youth and immortality. Bram Stoker's Dracula was the embodiment of evil, but the Dracula that finds its way into modern-day pop culture has evolved into a much more ambivalent creature—a reflection of the blurring of the boundaries between good and evil in modern society. Incidentally, the word *Drakkar* has a Viking origin, referring to the longship or dragon ship of Viking legend—a warship designed to carry the virtual warriors on their raids over a millennium ago. It is not possible to ascertain whether the brand has intentionally attempted to play on this ambiguity of Dracula and Viking virility. Nevertheless, the phonetic quality of the word itself unmistakably suggests Viking-like strength.

As another example, consider the bottle design of a Versace cologne product called Versus. The bottle displays a prominent V-shape figure, conveying at an iconic level the association between the cologne's name, Versus, and its manufacturer, Versace. But the word Versus and the V-shape intaglio connote much more at another level. The *V* is, in fact, suggestive of an "opening" into some mysterious yet desirous world. It is thus suggestive of femininity—presumably the object of male desire. But the interpretive path does not stop there. There are other side paths that the bottle design opens up. One can ask, in fact, whether the object of sexual desire is not really the "opposite" of females as the name Versus suggests implicitly. In other words, does the cologne allow men to descend even further into deeply hidden homosexual desires? Whether or not the interpretations put forward here are correct in any real sense is beside the point. The point is that both are seemingly possible (or at least plausible) because the design features of the bottle and its logo generate an entangled web of ambiguous connotations. In sum, the Versus bottle is a miniature work of art, with its allusion to "oppositional" tendencies in the psyche.

Aware of the power of design in the creation of a signification system for a product, the makers of Salem cigarettes attempted, in the late 1990s, to win over young smokers by creating a trendier image for their cigarette brand while at the same time striving to avoid the backlash from society that has beset the tobacco industry in the previous few decades. Using an abstract style to design the cigarette package, akin to that employed by symbolist or expressionist painters, Salem marketers tested the new-look product with an ingenious marketing campaign. The company mailed out a sample package along with four gift packages—a box of peppermint tea, a container of Chinese fortune cookies, a bottle of mint-scented massage gel, and finally a candle. Each package—on which a small notice contained the message *Mailing restricted to smokers 21 years of age or older*—came with a coupon for a free pack of cigarettes. The package's symbolist design, along with the occult nature of the gifts, imparted a mystical aura to the cigarettes, mirroring a "New Age" strain present in youth culture that Salem attempted to tap into. Salem also touched up its *S* logo and package typeface to reflect a New Age look, with gothic-looking fonts and shapes. It is no coincidence that the name of the brand itself is suggestive of the occult. The Salem witchcraft trials—the result of the largest witch hunt in American history—were held in 1692 in Salem, a town in the Massachusetts Bay Colony. Nineteen people, both men and women, were convicted and hanged as witches. About 150 other people were imprisoned on the witchcraft charges. The Salem trials resulted in the last witchcraft executions in America.

Packaging is, as mentioned at the start of this chapter, the sign system that gets people's attention when shopping. It is what allows shoppers to discern differences in products. As Neumeier (2006: 90) aptly puts it,

> In some retail environments, such as the supermarket, it's possible for a package to reach 100% of people shopping in that category. For several seconds, or even a few precious minutes, the shopper is completely focused on the differences among brands. Previous intentions to buy one product or another are suddenly put aside and memories of past advertising are shoved into the background as the competing packages go "mano a mano" for the shopper's attention.

Actual Product Design

The shape, size, and distinctive features of automobiles, for example, not only are identifiers of car make but also evoke a set of meanings that the manufacturer builds into them. Take, as a classic case in point, Ford's Mustang model, which was introduced on the market in 1964. Its design as a quasi-sports car, for the young (or young at heart), was indisputably the key to its success. Marketed as a low-price, high-style car, Mustang appealed instantly to a large segment of people, imparting a sense of "car artistry" that was associated only with luxury cars. In a phrase, its design was perfect for the market audience. People simply loved being seen driving it. It attracted men and women equally. Its design included elegant, narrow bumpers instead of the large ones popular at the time and delicate grillwork, which would jut out at the top and slant back at the bottom to give the car a forward-thrusting look. Visual interest was added by the air scoops on its sides to cool the rear brakes. Its hefty logo of a galloping horse adorned the grille, becoming a veritable iconic logo of pop culture. The name and car design matched perfectly—a "mustang," although small, is a powerful animal, as is the car; a mustang is a wild horse, as were the youths of the era at the threshold of the counterculture movement; and so on.

The Mustang story can be repeated throughout the manufacturing domain. The thing to note here is that product design is part of the overall semiotizing of the brand. It matches, or mirrors, the brand name, the logo, and the overall art used in ad construction. As a final example of product design, consider the new breed of designer dolls made to be intentionally grotesque in a cute sort of way (one-eyed, one-horned, and so on) (Budnitz 2007). Starting in the mid-1990s, toy manufacturers started tearing off and substituting appendages on traditional toys like G. I. Joe and Barbie with mangled body parts and selling the new hybrid dolls at comic book conventions. Thus were born the designer dolls. In a post–*Toy Story* and video game world, this comes as no surprise. The dolls have already made their way into art galleries, which are now places that no longer make a distinction between high, pop, advertising art, and toy forms. Influenced by Japanese anime style and by pop culture themes that range from skateboarding and gangsta rap to occultism and *South Park*, the toys are designed to fit in perfectly with the current Zeitgeist of futile satire, pastiche, bricolage, and theatrical mayhem. Who buys them? Adults raised on *South Park* and skateboarding, it would seem. They are literally "signs" of the times.

7

The Meanings of Ads

I have discovered the most exciting, the most arduous literary form of all, the most difficult to master, the most pregnant in curious possibilities. I mean the advertisement. It is far easier to write ten passably effective Sonnets, good enough to take in the not too inquiring critic, than one effective advertisement that will take in a few thousand of the uncritical buying public.

—Aldous Huxley, 1894–1963

As mentioned throughout this book, advertising is all about representing products. A fundamental semiotic "law of marketing" can, in fact, be posited as follows—the salability of a product or service correlates with the effectiveness of advertising to link it conceptually to some desire or need (erotic, social, and so on) or to some culturally and psychologically relevant theme or narrative through appropriate representation. The effectiveness of the techniques used to represent products (as already mentioned) is limited only by the ingenuity of the advertiser, by the limits of the various channels of communications used, by certain legal restrictions in place where the advertising messages are constructed, and by standards self-imposed by the advertising industry.

Ads and commercials, as discussed in the previous chapter, are works of pop commercial art. This is why we react to them in aesthetic ways. It is when we attempt an explanation of the meanings built into them that we enter into a critical mode of interpretation. As already discussed, hermeneutics is the term used in semiotics to refer to this mode of interpreting anything, from novels and symphonies to sports spectacles and print ads. The interesting and significant aspect of hermeneutics is that, as we saw in the previous chapter indirectly by illustration, it allows ample space for differences in the interpretation of any text, opening up a potentially fertile dialectic on its meaning. This chapter offers a particular set of "hermeneutic excursions" into the domain of meanings generated by advertising texts. It is hoped that these will engage the reader in an imaginary dialectic with the author of this book or, at the very least, lead him or her to reflect on the kinds of meanings generated by advertising in and of themselves.

DESIRES, NEEDS, AND EMOTIONS

Before discussing the meanings of ads, it is informative to take a brief look at the kinds of desires and needs that advertising attempts to tap into. As mentioned previously in terms of a so-called semiotic law of marketing, advertising effectiveness varies according to the degree to which it can access and activate the areas of the brain that control desires and needs. Using the kinds of representational techniques discussed in previous chapters (among others), advertising can be characterized, in effect, as the art of representing desire.

A Typology

A useful typology of desires, needs, and emotions that seems to underlie a vast panoply of advertising materials is the one provided by Straubhaar and

Table 7.1. Typology of Desires, Needs, and Emotions

Desire/Need/Emotion	Characterization
Achievement	the desire/need to achieve meaningful objectives in life
Affiliation	the desire/need to win acceptance
Consistency	the desire/need to ensure order and routine
Diversion	the desire/need to enjoy oneself
Dominance	the desire/need to exert influence in relations
Fear	any fear (of ostracism, marginalization, etc.)
Independence	the desire/need to be self-reliant
Novelty	the desire/need to have new things
Nurturing	the desire/need to care for others and be cared for by others
Pleasure	the desire to extract pleasure from life events
Popularity	the desire/need to win the attention of others
Recognition	the desire/need to be recognized
Security	the desire/need to be free from harm and threat
Sexuality	the desire/need to express sexuality
Stimulation	the desire/need to have one's senses stimulated
Support	the desire/need to receive support
Understanding	the desire/need to teach and instruct

Table 7.2.   Fear Factor Built into the Subtext of Television Commercials

Product	Fear Subtext
Ice cream, some beers, soft drinks	Not eating or drinking the products = fear of social marginalization
Shampoo, breath mints, mouthwash, deodorants	Not using the products = fear of ostracism because of bad body odor
Condoms	Not using the product = fear of being labeled by peers as reckless
SUVs built sturdily	Not driving the SUV = fear of putting one's loved ones at risk
Certain types of clothing	Not wearing the clothing = fear of having an unattractive body image
A certain brand of biscuits	Not buying the biscuits = fear of not providing the best for one's kids
Cell phones and iPods	Not having the items = fear of being left out of a peer group

LaRose (2000: 371). Table 7.1 reproduces that typology (with some additions of my own).

As we saw in previous chapters, these figure prominently in guiding the kinds of representational techniques used by advertisers, from logo design to the use of surrealist art in the creation of ads and commercials. Advertising strategy is based, by and large, on the implicit principle that people will be more inclined to buy things if they perceive them as satisfying some basic emotion, desire, or need. For example, some brands exploit fear or shame as their basic ploy. As a case in point, I recorded 50 television commercials on a variety of lifestyle and cosmetic products shown on American television in 2006. Of these, I concluded that 42 were structured around a subtext of fear—fear of marginalization, ostracism, and so on. A sampling is given in table 7.2.

A series of similar follow-up studies showed that the three main emotions tapped into by all kinds of products, not just lifestyle ones, are fear (of all kinds of things), sex, and popularity. Of 150 commercials I taped in early 2007, which were then assessed in terms of desire, need, or emotion both by myself and by 25 students independently, fear emerged again as the most prevalent emotion built into commercial subtexts, followed by sex and popularity. Percentages of commercials based on emotions are as follows:

Fear = 40% (60 of 150 commercials)
Sex = 28% (42 of 150 commercials)

Popularity = 26% (39 of 150 commercials)
Other = 6% (9 of 150 commercials)

In no way can it be claimed that these results are scientific since they were based on a random sampling of whatever programs came on at certain times of the day. Moreover, strict statistical methods were not employed. However, overall they seem to point in a general hermeneutic direction, given that follow-up studies produced similar results. As Diane Barthel (1988: 18) has aptly put it, the basic meaning built into advertising is about the ego and how people can identify it in the "personality" created for the product:

> Would-be advertising men are advised that the one word consumers never tire of is *me*. Advertisers simply tell them who that "me" is, and how to make it ever more attractive, comfortable, exciting, appealing. To do this, advertisers must do more than communicate information on a product. They must communicate image. Their task is somehow to position a product within a market of competing goods and to aim it toward an identifiable population. They must give it a personality.

Stimulating Consumption

As Danziger (2004) has cogently argued, the constant stimulation of desires, needs, and various emotions through a saturation of advertising has led to what can be called "consumption frenzy," that is, buying things for the sake of buying them, whether they are needed or not. There is little doubt that this frenzy is not due solely to a rise in general affluence alone but, as Danziger argues, to a perception of products as vehicles for satisfying desires—a perception that has been engendered by the quantity and ubiquity of advertising in our society. Everywhere one turns, one is bound to find some message designed to persuade people to buy some product. And ad messages are being constantly updated and renewed, creating a sense that they are evolving along with society generally. Budweiser beer, for instance, is constantly creating new humorous commercials for its brand, allowing it to keep in step with the changing times and with changing trends within its target market. The humor used, as mentioned in previous chapters, is in fact intentionally consistent with that used on television sitcoms, in cinema, and in pop culture generally. It is the kind of humor that makes the brand appear contemporary and relevant. Consumers can thus see that the commercials are put on for their enjoyment.

In a phrase, a dynamic interplay between advertising and lifestyle trends has emerged whereby one influences the other synergistically. As Twitchell

(2000: 1) aptly puts it, "Language about products and services has pretty much replaced language about all other subjects." Brands are no longer perceived to be just things for consumption; they are seen mainly as the means for securing a better job, protecting oneself against the hazards of old age and illness, attaining popularity and personal prestige, obtaining praise from others, increasing pleasure, advancing socially, having fun, and maintaining health. Today, they are also being seen more and more as bridges connecting the off-line and online worlds. For example, video games coexist in these two worlds since they can be played in both online and off-line versions. Moreover, some objects are now bought specifically in "dual world" terms, so to speak. For instance, the recent Webkinz craze of stuffed animals come equipped with a code that constitutes a password to a website allowing children to insert their animals into a virtual world, complete with name, bedroom, and so on.

All this shows the power of advertising to influence collective perceptions. Such things as Webkinz and even fast-food eateries would be inconceivable in nonconsumerist cultures and would have been unimaginable even in a consumerist one not so long ago. The popularity of fast-food restaurants is, as advertisers obviously know, tied to shifting social realities. Fewer and fewer modern-day families have the time to eat meals together within the household, let alone the energy to prepare elaborate dinners, as mentioned briefly in chapter 4. And even when they do, it is highly unlikely that they will perceive the eating event as a structured one aimed at preserving family harmony. Eating at fast-food locales is affordable, quick, and cheery; they are places where the family can eat together, at the same table, with no television or other distraction.

As Berger (2005: 77–79) has also argued, advertising has brought about a love of objects in themselves regardless of what they allow buyers to do with them. The increase in the number of collectors today bears this out. These are essentially people who enjoy buying certain things for the sake of buying them. And I must admit to the reader that I am a member of the collector ranks. My personal fetish is classical music CDs. Berger (2005: 79) puts it as follows:

> Collectors, we must realize, are a kind of consumer. But this element tends to be hidden by the other elements of collecting, which distract our attention from the fact that being a collector involves buying things. Thus, collectors get some gratifications from their behavior: the pleasure of buying things without any of the negative aspects involved in being a consumer; a kind of pride of ownership; and the development of an area of expertise, related to the objects that are collected.

ADS

Since the Drakkar Noir product has been discussed from various angles in previous chapters (chapters 3 and 6), it is logical to start off the discussion on how ads generate meanings by considering one of the print ads created for it—an ad found online and in magazines of various kinds a few years ago. The color of the bottle and the background are pitch black, making the brand name, tagline (*"La douce violence"* or sweet violence), and the male and female hands displayed in the ad stand out. The male hand tightly holds the bottle displayed in the ad at the same time that the female hand holds his hand, just as tightly but in a soft sensuous way. No other parts of the two bodies can be seen. What is going on? Why is he holding on to a bottle of cologne? What does the bottle symbolize? And what does the tagline allude to? There is little doubt that the ad evokes some sexual imagery enwrapped in diabolical (Dracula-based) symbolism. In fact, if one looks closely at the male hand, the jagged knuckles of which are most prominent, its contour and shape start morphing into the head of a devilish mask, complete with an outline of horns and of long-set dark eyes.

Putting together all these cues leads to a host of possible interpretations of the ad. Most of them, however, would probably involve some sense of the macabre or of symbolism that reaches deeply into a sense of fear mixed in with excitement—a dual perception that is typically associated with (first-time?) sex. Whatever interpretation we ultimately come up with, it is clear that the ad is not a simple description of the product. It is a representation of what the product is all about psychologically or socially, not what it does (provide scent).

What Is an Ad?

As mentioned in the opening chapter, ads have existed since the beginning of history in the form of posters, store signs, and the like. However, these were hardly the ads that we see today, such as the Drakkar one just described. They had no intention of representing or "semiotizing" products or services. Their purpose was simply to present information about them. They were what we call "classified ads" today. Signs on stores were also ads in the sense that they provided visual information on what was available in the store. A sign with a horseshoe on it indicated that the store offered the services of a blacksmith.

A modern-day ad can be defined semiotically as a text that presents a product not for what it is but, rather, for what subconscious desire, need, or emotion it can fulfill. An ad hides an implicit promise—namely, by using a product, psychological results will ensue. Advertising is, in a certain sense, a form of modern-day magic. The manufacturers of such products as Viagra and headache remedies create ads that boast of new, secret ingredients that will enhance sexuality or bring relief, like a magic potion. Ads may also indirectly suggest that a mouthwash or a toothpaste will magically transform an unpopular person into a popular one. People thus unconsciously buy products for the magic qualities suggested by advertising. Does this mean that those who view the Drakkar Noir ad are inclined to perceive the cologne as a kind of magical (diabolical) elixir of love? Probably; otherwise, the manufacturer would hardly create such an ad for the product.

In advertising theory today, the term *ad* includes *commercials*. Recall the 1984 Macintosh commercial discussed in chapter 4. The main thing to note about it here is that it unfolded like a mini-Orwellian novel. Orwell's novel *1984* portrays a terrifying totalitarian society of the future that punishes love, banishes privacy, and distorts the truth. Ridley Scott's commercial portrays a similarly terrifying society of automatonic male employees who are enslaved by their jobs and to whom the truth is distorted by their leader—"Big Brother"—who speaks to them on a screen. Orwell set his novel in an imaginary world dominated by three police states continually at war with each other. Scott sets his commercial in a world dominated by a PC police state. The hero of Orwell's novel searches for truth and decency, leading him to rebel against the totalitarian government. Joining him in his rebellion is a young woman who becomes his lover. In the Scott commercial, it is a young woman by herself who shatters the totalitarian order with a sledgehammer, an action that eliminates both Big Brother and the totalitarian world of his employees.

This is a remarkable example of a commercial, one that launched the new Mac product brilliantly. Other commercials are not as dazzling, but they nonetheless have similar characteristics. They are mininarratives that imbue a product with psychologically and socially relevant meanings. The Mac commercial was a clever attack on conformity in the male-dominated business world. It spoke of a new age, much like Scott's own *Blade Runner*.

A commercial can be defined, simply, as a narrative created to represent a product. As mentioned previously in this book, the commercial is an offspring of early radio. Since radio reached masses of people, print literate or not, radio commercials, which often included catchy jingles, became highly influential as techniques for disseminating product imagery throughout society. With the advent of television in the late 1940s, the commercial was adapted to the new visual medium. As households across North America started acquiring television sets en masse in the mid-1950s, commercials became so familiar that perception of brands became inextricably intertwined with the style and content of the commercials created to promote it. Television toy commercials, for instance, started the trend of inducing parents to believe that certain toys had educational value. Commercials designed to sell insurance, fire alarms, cosmetics, and vitamin capsules were designed (and continue to be designed) to evoke fear (of sickness, crime, loss of social standing, impending disaster, and so on). Television also gave visual form to fictitious radio cartoon characters, such as Mr. Clean and Speedy.

By the mid-1960s, the boundaries between television programming and commercials that sponsored them became increasingly blurred. Advertising agencies produced nearly all network programming. Stations often sold agencies full sponsorship, which included placing a product name in a show's title (e.g., The Texaco Theater). The ratings system used in broadcasting arose, in fact, from the sponsors' desire to know how many people they were reaching with their "brand placement" strategies. The A. C. Nielsen Company, which had been surveying audience size in radio since the mid-1930s in the United States, eventually became the dominant television ratings service.

The Connotative Index

There are, of course, many ads and commercials today that have primarily an informational intent, much like the ancient posters. Ads for household products, for example, provide mainly information about what a product can do. Adopting semiotic method again, the content of such ads can be said to be highly denotative. In contemporary semiotics, the terms *denotation* and *connotation* are used to refer to meaning content that is, respectively, informational and representational (to use terms consistent with the ideas being discussed in this book). For the sake of accuracy, however, it should be mentioned that other terms are used, such as literal versus figurative, reference versus sense, and so on. But for the present purposes, denotation and connotation will suffice. Consider the word *cat*. At an informational level, the word elicits an image of a "creature with four legs, whiskers, retractile claws," and so on. This is its denotative meaning, which is intended to point out what distinguishes a *cat*—a mammal with "retractile claws," "long tail," and so on—from some other mammal. This allows us to determine if something real or imaginary under consideration is an exemplar of a "cat." Similarly, the word *square* refers to a figure characterized by the distinctive features "four equal straight lines" and "meeting at right angles." It is irrelevant if the lines are thick, dotted, two meters long, 80 feet long, or colored differently. If the figure has "four equal straight lines meeting at right angles," it qualifies as a square.

All other senses associated with the words *cat* and *square* are connotative—that is, they indicate what these two represent in psychological and social terms. Some connotative uses of *square* can be seen in expressions such as the following:

She's so *square*. = "old fashioned"
He has a *square* disposition. = "forthright," "honorable"
Put it *squarely* on the table. = "evenly," "precisely"

Connotation encompasses all kinds of senses, including emotional ones. Consider the word *yes*. In addition to being a sign of affirmation, it can have various emotional senses, depending on the tone of voice with which it is uttered. If one says it with a raised tone, as in a question, "Yes?" then it would convey doubt or incredulity. If articulated emphatically, "Yes!" then it would connote triumph, achievement, or victory. Connotation is the operative meaning mode in ads such as the Drakkar Noir one. And, indeed, this is borne out by the fact that their hermeneutic decipherment, as we have seen, leads us to ask what the text represents in psychological and social (not informational) terms.

The way in which the ad has been put together is suggestive, in a representational sense, of the myth of Dracula, as we have seen. But this is not the only nondenotative meaning that could have been enlisted to make sense of the ad text. The dark animal power of olfactory attraction is another one—a power that brings about "la douce violence." Indeed, in a classroom exercise with my students a few years ago, we came up with eight discernibly different interpretations of the ad. It is not important that any one or the other interpretation of the ad is the correct one; what counts is that so many interpretations are possible in the first place. In fact, the more interpretations there are, the more likely is the effectiveness of the ad, as I discovered empirically through several research projects (see Beasley and Danesi 2002). This suggests a corollary to the semiotic law of marketing enunciated previously—namely, that the effectiveness of an ad varies according to the number of suggestive connotations it generates; the more it generates, the more effective it tends to be, thus apparently enhancing product recognition and allure (and probably sales). The term **connotative index** (CI) can be used to refer to the relative number of connotative interpretations—high, average, low—that an ad or commercial tends to produce. These can be determined in a relatively simple way, as I did by asking subjects what they see in a certain ad and then recording the interpretations. Counting the interpretations is tantamount to counting the number of different connotations built into the ad. Typically, ads for home products and services (e.g., insurance or detergents) have low to average CIs, whereas those for lifestyle products have average to high CIs. The CI can be conceived to fall on a continuum, with 0 connotation (pure denotative or informational content) at one end and maximum connotation (open-ended, ambivalent, ambiguous content) at the other. Classified ads, ads in trade manuals, and the like tend to fall in the sector of the continuum nearest to the 0 end point, whereas lifestyle ads tend to fall in the sector that becomes progressively more connotative—the 1 point. My research on the validity of the CI (Danesi 2006) has tended to support the general notion of the CI.

As Barthes (1957) correctly pointed out, the notion of connotation is of great importance to the study of advertisements because in a cultural system it is this form of meaning that constitutes a veritable "fund of knowledge" into which an ad or commercial taps. Specific colors at certain times of the year, for instance, connote traditions, values, and belief systems. In some cultures, *white* is often symbolic of "cleanliness," "purity," and "innocence," whereas *dark*, its paradigmatic counterpart, symbolizes "uncleanness," "impurity," or "corruption." The study of advertising is, in a sense, a study of connotation as it manifests itself in this particular form of representation and communication.

DECODING ADS

The semiotic concept of code was introduced in the previous chapter. Essentially, a code is a set of meanings that are built into something. For example, a "gender code" contains the meanings that a culture ascribes to the male and female genders so as to keep them differentiated. The notion of CI suggests that there are likely several codes utilized by ad makers to represent products. Decoding is, therefore, the process of fleshing out the codes. So, in the Drakkar Noir ad, we fleshed out two possible codes built into the text by suggestion—a "Dracula (or vampire) code" and an "animal instinct (olfactory) code."

The CI can now be revised and expanded to refer to the relative number of codes that are suggested by an ad and interpreted as such in terms of the connotations they generate. The higher the CI, the more codes built into the ad and, arguably, the greater its "hidden appeal."

What Is Decoding?

The term **decoding** is used throughout advertising studies. As it is used here, it refers, simply, to the unraveling of the codes used by advertisers. For example, in chapter 4, the Mac line of products was discussed in terms of an "Eve code." What are the characteristics of this code that the Apple Computer Company has seemingly utilized to represent its Mac product? Without going into detail here, suffice it to say that the code has biblical and womanhood connotations that are self-explanatory. By using the concept of opposition

Table 7.3. The "Eve Code" Built into Mac Products and Ads

Mac Products	PC (IBM) Products
Mac computers generally have a feminine (stylish) quality in their design	PCs generally have a more masculine (rigid) quality in their design
Ads and commercials (such as the 1984 Super Bowl one) emphasize the role of women in the "new world order"	Ads and commercials emphasize the role of IBM in the largely male-dominated world of computer science
The logo recalls the Eden scene	The logo bespeaks of no-nonsense scientific rigor
The Mac guy commercials suggest that real men today can be as creative and trendy as women; that is, they can (and should) be in touch with their "feminine side"	In the same commercial the PC guy is portrayed as out of touch with the "feminine side" of his psyche

(chapter 1) and thus pitting Mac products against PC ones, the elements of this code can be easily fleshed out (see table 7.3).

Decoding any ad involves a similar type of reasoning. In effect, we are relating two levels that are implicit in representational texts—a surface and an underlying one. The surface level constitutes the physical depiction or representation itself with which an ad is created. State Farm ads, for instance, invariably show situations of family-based need that are met by the company through the intervention of friendly and neighborly agents who are always there (as the company's jingle puts it) in difficult times. The different ads are, in effect, surface variations of an underlying "rural code" structured around such meanings as "security," "safety," "family values," "friendliness," "trustworthiness," and so on. The CI for State Farm ads is relatively low since I can perceive mainly the rural code built into them. However, it is obviously an effective code when it comes to this product because the company has never changed it over the years. It is the central feature of its image.

As we saw previously, connotative suggestions were gleaned from the Drakkar Noir ad by taking into consideration the various cues shown in the surface text. Suggestion is, in effect, the result of five main cue-detecting processes:

- Similarity (the shape of the male hand is similar to the shape of a mask)
- Difference (the different hand types suggest male and female participants)
- Contiguity (the location of the female hand below the male hand in the ad suggests a supine orientation of the bodies)

- Intensity (the male and female body parts against the dark background in the ad emphasizes them)
- Association (the grip of the hands is associated with sexual joy)

These cues often work in tandem in the generation of connotative interpretations. Suffice it to say that, from a psychological standpoint, the human mind seems predisposed to link meanings together in some way that has its own culture-specific "suggestion logic."

Decoding the Text

Let's take another ad for a lifestyle product. Consider the one used in the mid-2000s by Gucci to promote one of its purse products. First, the Gucci name itself, which is featured prominently in the center of the visual text, evokes an aura of artistry, craftsmanship, fashionability, and superior quality to the product, given that the product is the "work" of an Italian style artist—Gucci—not just an assembly-line product for common folk to wear. This connotation can be seen in the artistry of the ad itself, making it appropriate for the brand. The ad's primary visual elements—black snakes (or snakelike leather cords) surrounding a delicate, small purse—suggest a chain of mythic meanings that are associated with black snakes, including fear, darkness, and evil. This can be called the "snake code." Since ancient times, snakes have been feared in many cultures for their deadly venom. They have been used as symbols with this meaning in narratives of all kinds. But they have also been used with connotations of phallic symbolism in the traditions of many cultures. This can be called, logically, the "phallus code." These two codes seem to be built into the visual imagery of the ad, which shows slithering snakes in an embrace, suggesting phallic copulation, since snakes come into close proximity only when they form "mating balls," in which they frantically try to mate with a single female.

The chainlike handle of the purse and the metal handcufflike clasp in the center are visual cues that suggest a "sexual fetish code," given the sexual bondage connotations associated with chains and handcuffs. Conversely, the same cues may also suggest an image of the female protecting herself against the slithery males. This can be called the "female protection code." Needless to say, none of these codes can be proved to be in the ad in any empirical way. However, by asking a group of 50 students during a recent class exercise, most of the connotations discussed here came up (without any prompting on my part). They are probably implicit because they are ancient mythic codes associated with basic human emotions and desires, such as sex. Clearly, ads of this type are aesthetically powerful because they bestow on a brand the

Table 7.4.   Possible Codes Built into the Gucci Ad

Textual Cue (signifier)	Connotations	Implicit Code
entangled black snakes	fear, darkness, and evil	"snake code"
shape of the snakes	phallic symbolism	"phallus code"
chainlike handle	sexual bondage	"sexual fetish code"
handcuff cues	protection from the snakes	"female protection code"

timelessness and universality that we associate with primordial mythic codes. Whether this ad will induce consumers to buy the purse is open to question. It is certainly not the point of semiotic analysis to determine this. Nor is it the goal of semiotics to criticize makers of such ads. On the contrary, a semiotician should, in theory, approach an ad like he or she would any text. To the semiotician, advertising provides an opportunity to examine how mythic codes manifest themselves in contemporary textual forms.

It should also be pointed out that the interpretation of any advertising text is just that—one possible interpretation. Indeed, disagreement about what something means is not only unavoidable but also part of the fun of doing hermeneutic semiotics. Differences of opinion fill the pages of the semiotic journals and lead, like in other sciences, to a furthering of knowledge in the field. The point of the previous analysis has been simply to illustrate the technique of decoding, not to provide a definitive interpretation of the ad. The key to unlocking the underlying codes built into the text is to consider the surface signifiers as clues or cues, just like a puzzle, in order to see what hidden code(s) they suggest. Possible codes built into the Gucci ad are shown in table 7.4.

The representation of a product in ads and commercials can now be defined more specifically as the use of codes (consciously or unconsciously) to capture, portray, simulate, or relay impressions, sensations, perceptions, or ideas that are deemed to be culturally meaningful. Both the maker of an ad or commercial and the interpreter must have access to the same codes; otherwise, the ad would convey no meaning. Now, what distinguishes ads with high and low CIs? The research on this topic (mentioned previously) has given partial

Table 7.5.   Features of Ads Correlated to CIs

Low to Mid-CIs	Mid- to High CIs
Straightforward cues related to the product	Cues that seem unrelated to the product
Abundant use of descriptive language and taglines	Little or no use of accompanying language texts
Factual information about the product (price, design, etc.)	Little or no information about the product
Product shown in some practical context	Product highlighted as an objet d'art

answers to this question. Patterns or features in ads that seem to correlate with CIs are shown in table 7.5.

As the analyses of the Drakkar Noir and Gucci ads reveal, the advertising that has a high CI tends to have a basis in myth—the Drakkar Noir subtext alludes arguably to the myth of vampires and the Gucci subtext to some version of the snake myth. Mythic subtexts are powerful because they act on the primordial parts of the psyche. And, indeed, the themes of the first myths have not disappeared from modern cultures; they continue to work at an unconscious level. As mentioned in chapter 2, Roland Barthes (1957) cleverly demonstrated that these myths are recycled over and over in modern-day spectacles and advertising. In Hollywood westerns, for instance, the mythic "good" versus "evil" opposition was symbolized by heroes wearing white hats and villains black hats or the reverse. The mythologist Mircea Eliade (1961: 204–5) has also claimed that many of the activities that characterize modern-day life are really reflexes of ancient mythic traditions or concepts, such as the "fight between hero and monster, initiatory combats and ordeals, paradigmatic figures (the maiden, the hero, the paradisal landscape, hell, and so on)," which crop up in television spectacles, movies, and best-selling novels, among many other things.

Other kinds of codes are, of course, used to create effective ads. Consider one for Camel cigarettes. The camel depicts the socialite smoothness and finesse represented by 1930s and 1940s cinema stars, especially Humphrey Bogart in *Casablanca*. The lure of the "desert adventure code" is perpetrated mainly by Hollywood with such blockbusters as *Casablanca* (1943) and *Lawrence of Arabia* (1962). The code consists of virile, debonair, courageous, self-effacing men who have a "matinee idol" appeal (at least in the imagination). Smoking was—and continues to be somewhat—part of that appeal.

There are, of course, other ways to decode texts other than the purely semiotic–mythic way based on the concepts of text and code. Citing Berger (2000: 107), the other ways include the following:

> *Psychoanalytic Analysis*. How does the text tap into the psyche or unconscious regions of the mind? What emotions (fear, sexuality, anxiety, and so on) does it elicit?
> *Sociological Analysis*. What does the text contain that relates to class, gender, race, age, and so on? What does the ad and product reflect about social concerns?
> *Historical Analysis*. How have advertising and its methods evolved over the years? How does this specific ad fit into the evolutionary process?
> *Political Analysis*. What does the ad reveal about the state of politics, or how does it relate to the political process? Is it part of a generic propa-

ganda or culture industry designed to promote goods and services in and of themselves to pacify people, as Marxist theorists have often argued?

In my view, these approaches all have a role to play in the overall understanding and study of advertising. But they are derivative to semiotic method in the sense that they focus more on the effects of advertising in psychological, sociological, and political terms, not on the meaning structures that may underlie these effects.

REALITY ADS

Recall the Dove set of reality ads discussed briefly in chapter 2, which promoted real women with real curves starting in the mid-2000s. Like reality television, the campaign used real people (not paid actors) to represent "real women." In contrast to professional actors who are chosen because they are attractive and ultrathin, the Dove models seemed to hit closer to home with female consumers. The campaign was wildly successful, receiving accolades from the media and political personages alike. The real women used in the campaigns also became stars themselves, featured on such television programs as *Oprah*. Like the real people in *American Idol*, they became instant celebrities by virtue of the fact that they were seen through the filter of advertising and the media.

The ploy was a transparent one. It was part of what I called a Cinderella subtext (chapter 2). It can be called, more accurately, a Cinderella code—a code that makes the implicit promise that common women can be transformed into "beauty princesses" overnight with Dove products.

But reality advertising is not a product of the age of reality television. Nor is it an invention of Dove. It has always been a major technique in the creation of ads and commercials. From testimonials using celebrities to represent the implicit qualities of a product to the technique of "jumping on the bandwagon" to support causes, including causes that are (on the surface) detrimental to sales of the brand (e.g., antismoking campaigns), reality advertising has always been a major player in the game.

What Is Reality Advertising?

Reality advertising can be defined, simply, as the creation of ads and commercials that 1) use real people in them (rather than actors chosen on purpose for them), 2) use celebrities to promote the product, 3) support social causes, or 4) blur the lines between real and imagined communities of users.

The Dove set of ads and commercials is a perfect example of technique 1. The concept behind the campaign is, simply, to use real women with "imperfect bodies" in ads and commercials. The Dove "street casting" technique, as it can be called, is being adopted more and more by other brands. It gives the impression that ads are designed to be informational rather than representational (in the sense defined in this chapter). But, in effect, they turn out to have a high CI because they tap into the Cinderella code. They are part of a new form of media-based reality fantasizing—the same type of fantasizing that is seen on reality television programs. It is not a matter of chance that the women used in the ads are not obese or unattractive. Like professional models, they are pretty, young women. They hardly constitute a cross section of American women.

A recent example of technique 2 is Reebok's set of "I am what I am" ads and commercials. The campaign features athletes and pop entertainers who celebrate their individuality and authenticity. It is a brilliant campaign, tapping into both celebrity and reality television culture at once. Basketball star Allen Iverson, rap artist Jay-Z, and move icon Lucy Liu—all used in the campaign—stand out in people's minds because they are perceived by them as being true to themselves, challenging the status quo, and doing things their own way (at least according to the ads and commercials). In a "do-it-yourself" world, Andy Warhol's maxim that everybody will seek to have his or her "15 minutes of fame," no matter who a person is initially, is the code that underlies the Reebok campaign. This "Warhol code," as it can be called, is designed to talk directly to a generation raised on digital technology and the potential it bears for self-realization, regardless of traditional social systems set up to screen talent and to provide opportunity. Reebok has also launched an online forum (www.reebok.com) where consumers will have the opportunity to create their own "I am what I am" ads, in line with the Warhol code.

Some brands attempt to blur the lines between reality and themselves by showing themselves to be involved in, or sensitive to, social issues (technique 3). For example, Natural American Spirit Cigarettes (Santa Fe Natural Tobacco Co.) put the following politically correct acknowledgment on its packages in the early 2000s: "We make no representation, either expressed or implied, that these cigarettes are any less hazardous than any other cigarettes." This was a transparent ploy to convey an image of itself as a concerned and socially responsible brand. The cigarette packs also contained fliers featuring endangered species and supporting statements of small-scale farmers. Similar kinds of "social bandwagon" campaigns have been mounted by other cigarette brands and by companies such as Benetton.

Creating communities of users (technique 4) is also a common one in reality advertising. Contemporary consumers are warier of the branding ploys that were used with their parents and grandparents, given that they have been exposed to mass marketing since birth and given the fact that schools now teach about deceptive and persuasive advertising in all kinds of courses. The marketing savvy of consumers today makes them shy away from campaigns that tell them that their lives will be changed by adopting a certain brand. This is why brands such as Smirnoff Vodka now promote their products by entreating people "to join the party," implying that they would otherwise be marginalized socially. Honda too inveigles consumers to join the "in crowd" by becoming a member of Honda's "Civic Nation," with its hip-hop music commercials and images of street racing. Apple warns consumers that without possessing an iPod they might be left, by implication, out of the "nightclub scene," where the iPod itself brings people together in a bacchanalia of fun and friendship suffused with the promise of sexual activities.

As Douglas Atkin (2004) argues, ads and commercials now strive to develop a cultlike effect on people, endeavoring to turn them into devotees in ways that are not unlike those utilized by real cults. The salient feature of the recent approach by brands such as Smirnoff and Apple is that they promise to unite people through a shared experience and trust—the exact same promise that attracts people to religions and cults. Advertising has clearly replaced (or at least complemented) religion. Cult brands such as the iPod seem to answer the need for gregariousness by creating virtual and real communities. Providing the comfort of real communities are brands such as Mary Kay cosmetics, Saturn automobiles, and Snapple beverages, aided by clever campaigns that emphasize that users of the brands form a specific type of community—Saturn drivers, Snapple drinkers, and so on. The companies thus organize get-togethers, complete with food and festivities, so that consumers can meet each other and feel that they are part of a larger reality.

The Spread of Reality Advertising

Reality advertising is now everywhere one looks. A similar deployment of the Warhol code, for instance, can be seen in Noxzema's nationwide search for the next "Noxzema Girl," open to all women between the ages of 18 and 34. The winner will receive money and, more importantly, a contract to star in Noxzema's own campaigns. Women can enter online submitting photos and a personal statement. As Neumeier (2006: 101) asserts, this kind of advertising allows advertisers and consumers to enter into any imaginary dialogue that, in turn, simulates real-world communication:

> Real-world communication is a dialogue. I say something to you, you say something back. You may ask it only to yourself, like when you read a magazine ad,

but your brain is nevertheless an indispensable component of the total communication system. You respond by buying the advertised brand, or by mentally storing the information for future use, or by simply turning the page.

As Neumeier suspects, dialogue is a crucial part of human reality, and it is our need for this reality that contemporary advertising taps into. The link between dialogue and human reality was established in the ancient world by the great teachers and philosophers of that world, from China to the Middle East, from north to south, east to west. It is probably the oldest implicit principle in human history of how we gain understanding, and its validity is evidenced by the fact that it is still part of education and most forms of philosophical inquiry in all parts of the world today.

Studying what dialogue is, therefore, is no trivial matter, if it indeed constitutes a format for reality advertising. It was used by Socrates, after all, in the form of a question-and-answer exchange as a means for achieving self-knowledge. Is that what the reality ads surreptitiously promise to give us, namely, self-knowledge? Socrates believed in the superiority of dialectic argument over weighty writing, spending hours in the public places of Athens and engaging in dialogue and argument with anyone who would listen. The so-called Socratic method is still as valid today as it was then, betraying the implicit view that it is only through dialogue that it becomes possible to grasp truths about the world and about ourselves. Through dialogue, in fact, we come to understand our own ignorance, which entices us forward to investigate something further. There really is no other path to understanding than the dialogic one—so it would seem.

Dialogue goes on all the time in human life. It is so instinctive and common that we hardly ever realize consciously what it entails in philosophical and psychological terms. It manifests itself in conversations, chats, and even internally within ourselves. As the Russian psychologist Lev Vygotsky (1962, 1978) showed in his pioneering work on childhood development, "internal dialogue" surfaces in early childhood as a means for the child to come to grips with the nature of language and its cognitive functions. In effect, when children speak to themselves as they play, they are engaging in true investigative dialogue, testing out meanings and concepts as they are imprinted in the phonic substance of words. Dialogue also manifests itself in the theatrical and narrative arts, from drama and comedy to poetic texts of all kinds. It is a linguistic act that requires an ability to understand both the nature of information and the role of human participation in shaping incoming information into usable knowledge.

The modern-day intellectual who certainly understood this was the late Russian philosopher and literary scholar Mikhail Bakhtin (1895–1975). His concept of the "carnivalesque dialogue" is especially relevant to the study of reality advertising. The festivities associated with carnival are tribal and popular; in them, the sacred is "profaned," and the carnality of all things is proclaimed through the theatricality of spectacles. At the time of carnival, everything authoritative, rigid, or serious is subverted, loosened, and mocked. Carnival is part of popular and folkloristic traditions that aim to disrupt traditional connections and abolish idealized social forms, bringing out the crude, unmediated links between domains of behavior that are normally kept very separate. Carnivalesque genres satirize the lofty words of poets, scholars, and others. They are intended to fly in the face of the official, "sacred world"— the world of judges, lawyers, politicians, churchmen, and the like.

For Bakhtin, carnival is the context in which distinct voices can be heard and where they will flourish through "polyphonic" expression. For Bakhtin, therefore, carnival is the basic form of real (everyday) human dialogue. People attending a carnival do not merely make up an anonymous crowd. Rather, they feel part of a communal body. At carnival time, a unique sense of shared time and space, in fact, allows individuals to become emotionally involved in a collectivity, at which point they cease to be themselves. Through costumes and masks, individuals take on a new bodily identity and are renewed psychologically in the process. Reality advertising is, clearly, a carnivalesque rite of sorts. It gives polyphonic dialogue (a dialogue among many) a context in which it can occur—the ad campaign. It is irrelevant whether the dialogue is perceived to have meaning. It is sufficient to know that it can occur. It is impossible to enter into a polyphonic dialogue with the Drakkar Noir ad discussed previously; it is much easier to do so with the Dove ads. The dialogue in the latter case does not occur in actual fact; it occurs in an ersatz fashion through identification with the women in the ads—a dialogue that can become real by going to Dove's website and posting questions to the actual women and the manufacturer online.

As mentioned in chapter 3, it was the late Jean Baudrillard who pointed out that the borderline between our symbolic creations and reality has virtually vanished in today's media and advertising world, collapsing into a simulacrum, a mind-set where the distinction between fantasy and reality has broken down completely. We seem, in effect, to enjoy our dream (surreal) worlds more than we do harsh reality. Reality advertising taps perfectly into this cognitive mode, allowing us to enter into a carnivalesque dialogue with the advertiser.

In the past, the more ads and commercials represented worlds that transcended reality, the more people were inclined to see the products as vehicles for fantasizing and grasping a larger-than-life reality. Until the Dove and Reebok campaigns, it is accurate to say that ads tended to shun, not encompass, reality. Representing the world "as it is" goes seemingly contrary to this long-established trend. The new Volkswagen Jetta campaign is a case in point. The campaign emphasizes safety features, but it does so without the usual crash test dummies. Rather, it uses real Jetta drivers and their passengers driving along safely until a crash occurs, involving them in a "real accident." The subtext is a transparent one—accidents happen, and when they do, driving a Volkswagen Jetta will allow you to emerge from them with not a single scratch. In effect, this is "shock treatment" advertising. But is it really real (no pun intended)? Or is it just tapping into our collective state of simulacrum and our need for polyphonic dialogue?

In my view, such advertising is really nothing more than a clever new technique—a technique that blends in perfectly with trends in media and pop culture. Reality advertising is hardly real. It is advertising that simply uses "the techniques of the real," as they may be called. It is still all about fantasy and escape. The instant that so-called reality representation is no longer perceived as a means of escape, the advertiser will drop the reality dialogue and adopt different techniques.

8

Marketing

The real persuaders are our appetites, our fears and above all our vanity.
The skillful propagandist stirs and coaches these internal persuaders.

—Eric Hoffer, 1902–1983

To say that marketing is, today, one of the most important industries for maintaining and expanding capitalist economic systems would be an understatement. Simply put, it is a vital cog in the global economic machine. The United States has the largest marketing and advertising industry partnership in the world, with its center in New York City, where many of the major agencies have their headquarters. There are more than 6,000 advertising agencies in the United States, ranging in size from one-person organizations to huge agencies with several thousand employees. It is clear that, in the first decade of the twenty-first century, marketing, advertising, and business have become three equal sides of an economic triangle.

Marketing is all about getting the brand message out into society. So accustomed are we to marketing ploys that we no longer see them as such. Product names, logos, and messages are placed absolutely everywhere, from the boards in hockey rinks to T-shirts and theater tickets. Without the dissemination of brand image through such ploys, the product is bound to fail in the contemporary marketplace. The main priority of marketing is, in fact, the so-called ad campaign, which is designed to do exactly that—to get the message about a product out as broadly as possible. The second main concern of marketers is testing the efficacy of campaigns and of other advertising techniques, from the choice of brand name to the design of the product. Marketing has become so important that about half the cost of goods and services results from the marketing process. More people work in marketing than in production.

There are, of course, other tasks that marketers carry out to make products and services attractive to customers, from helping to devise pricing strategies to developing an agenda of promotional gimmicks (store samples, free trials, and so on). But the focus here is on those related to ad campaigns and to the testing of advertising efficacy since these are the ones that are germane to the purposes of this book. Thus, the objective of this chapter is primarily to look at the ways in which marketers get the message out and insert brand products into unconscious social groupthink. One of these, as mentioned, is the ad campaign; another is the use of multiple media to deliver campaigns; another still is called "placement," or the insertion of a product into general cultural activities by locating it in spectacles or media as a prop in them, not as an advertised item.

MARKETING

As Twitchell (2004) has cogently argued and illustrated, the success of product **marketing** has led to the spread of marketing science across society. Religions, celebrities, politicians, and sports organizations, among others, are now being promoted in the same way and with the same set of strategies and techniques that consumer products are. And this is not just a metaphorical use of the word *marketing*. Such individuals and organizations are literally being "marketed" as if they were products.

Market researchers handle a wide range of tasks. Marketers estimate the demand for products and services, describe the characteristics of probable customers, and measure potential sales. They also determine how prices influence demand, and they test the effectiveness of present and proposed advertising. A market research study begins with a statement of the problem that the client wants to solve. This statement leads to a detailed definition of the information to be gathered. There are two types of market research data: primary and secondary. The former are data that are obtained through questionnaires, interviews, retail store shelf audits, the use of electronic scanners at retail checkout counters, direct observation in stores, and the like. The latter type of data are statistics and other information that are already available from such sources as government agencies and universities.

Marketing Research

As mentioned, the primary task of marketing research is to determine the appropriate individuals or groups who are most inclined to react positively to a certain kind of ad campaign on the basis of age, sex, income, occupation, and other demographic and psychographic variables. Such research attempts to find out, as a corollary, why people buy certain products so as to find the most effective style to use in their advertisements. Marketing research also involves measuring the size and makeup of radio, television, and Internet audiences at different times of the day; circulations of publications; and the popularity of certain websites. Advertisers then use information on audience size and makeup in selecting media in which to place ads, preparing a media plan that will give an effective combination of *reach*—the number of people who will see or hear the advertisement—and *frequency*—the number of times that they will see or hear it.

In the product promotion world, marketers aim, first and foremost, to determine who the probable users of a product or service will be and what kinds of advertising styles are appropriate for specific types of individuals. The results from the relevant research are then used for product development, including which products are to be manufactured. This type of research has, over the years, led to the segmentation or classification of people according to demographic (age, gender, class, economic level, and so on), geographic (where people live), and psychographic, or personality, profiles. This has made possible the following standardized characterization of individuals within the marketing world:

- The "chief shopper," or the individual in a household who does the shopping for the household
- The "enthusiast," or any individual who loves ads and commercials for their own sake
- The "reformer," or the person who wants products that will improve the quality of his or her life rather than products that appeal to his or her sense of lifestyle
- The "succeeder," or the person who wants products that will enhance his or her quality of life, social position, and so on
- The "acquiescent," or the person with an easygoing attitude toward advertising who is more likely to be impressed by humorous, clever, or eye-catching ads and commercials
- The "aspirer," or the individual who wants products that improve his or lifestyle image
- The "impresser," or the person who buys certain products to impress or keep up with neighbors

Information such as this provides the basis for determining the kinds of people at whom to aim advertisements, the types of meanings to build into ads, and in which media to place the ads.

Testing Advertising Efficacy

To gain an estimate of the efficacy of an ad campaign, marketers have developed a series of techniques, ranging from questionnaires to the use of devices such as the Galvanometer. The main ones are the following (in no particular order):

- The values and lifestyles questionnaire (abbreviated commonly to VALS), which allows marketers to assess how certain consumers feel about a product and how an ad campaign successfully represents their specific lifestyle aspirations
- The "copy testing" technique, which allows researchers to measure the effectiveness of advertising messages by showing ads to specific types of consumers
- The recognition test, which allows marketers to check how well someone can recall an advertisement, with or without prompting
- The "benchmark measuring" technique, which involves measuring a target audience's response to the early stages of an advertising campaign so as to test the probable efficacy of the campaign
- Evaluation questionnaires, which allow marketers to assess how well an ad campaign has met its original aims
- The "commutation test," which consists of changing an image or word in an ad, replacing it with another one to see what kind of reaction the change generates
- The "consumer jury test," which involves asking consumers to compare, rank, and otherwise evaluate advertisements in an ad campaign
- Forming a "consumer panel group," which reports on products they have used so that manufacturers can improve them on the basis of what the group reports
- The DAGMAR technique (full form: defining advertising goals for measured advertising results), which allows marketers to identify the effects advertising has on consumers in stages, from awareness of the product to action (purchasing)
- The "day-after-recall test," which is designed to ascertain how much someone can remember about an advertisement or commercial the day after it was broadcast
- The "diary method," whereby respondents are asked to keep a written account of the advertising they have noticed, the purchases they have made, and the products they have actually used
- The "eye tracking" technique, whereby the eye movement of subjects is recorded in order to determine which parts of the brain are activated while viewing some ad or commercial, or the technique of following the

eye movements of Internet users in order to determine what they look at and for how long so that Web page designers can improve the effectiveness of their sites

- The "forced exposure" technique, whereby consumers are brought to some facility to view and provide commentary on some television program complete with the new commercials
- The Galvanometer test, which measures physiological changes in consumers when asked a question or shown some stimulus material (such as a print ad)
- The "keyed ad" technique, which asks subjects to write down a specially coded address that will indicate where they saw an ad, thus helping advertisers glean the effectiveness of advertising in some particular newspaper, magazine, website, or other medium
- "Motivational research" techniques investigating the reasons why individuals buy specific types of merchandise, why they respond to certain advertising appeals, why they watch particular kinds of television programs, why they listen to certain radio stations, and so on
- The "response method," whereby the efficacy of Internet advertising is evaluated by the way people respond to it through such mechanisms as direct clicking
- "Tachistoscope testing," which measures a person's recognition and perception of various elements within an ad by means of different lighting and exposure techniques (the tachistoscope is a device that projects an image at a fraction of a second)
- Voice-pitch analysis, whereby a subject's voice is analyzed during his or her responses so as to assess the subject's emotional reaction to an ad

Perhaps the best way to test efficacy is simply to assess the level of sales that results from an ad campaign or to observe the length of time that an ad campaign is successful. For example, the "Mmm Mmm good" campaign for Campbell's soup has been and continues to be a successful one; otherwise, it would have been replaced a long time ago.

THE AD CAMPAIGN

Most businesses hire advertising agencies to create their ads and place them in the various media. In most cases, the individual ads form part of an *advertising campaign*—a systematic method of media-based advertising that may run for several months or more. The objective of the campaign may be to demonstrate a product's superiority over competing brands, to change the image of the product or company, or to achieve some other goal. The agency must also determine the target market—the people who are likely users of a product and at whom the advertising will be aimed.

Ad campaigns have been a part of American society since at least the turn of the twentieth century. They are the equivalent of the town crier, but it is a town crier with a vast technological voice. Some have become so familiar that they are now part of cultural lore. Here is a highly selective handful of examples of famous ad campaigns through the years—campaigns that have involved not only advertising per se but also the deployment of such strategies as product placement (which will be discussed later in this chapter):

- In 1892, the Coca-Cola logo appeared across the country, painted as a mural on walls, displayed on posters and soda fountains where the drink was served, and imprinted on widely marketed, common household items (e.g., calendars and drinking glasses).
- In 1904, the Campbell's Soup Company began its highly successful advertising campaign featuring the rosy-cheeked Campbell Kids and the slogan "Mmm Mmm good." The campaign is still ongoing today.
- In 1970, McDonald's launched its highly successful "You deserve a break today" advertising campaign that made fast-food eateries part of a larger social reality rather than places for teenagers to hang out.
- In 1985, Nike signed basketball player Michael Jordan as a spokesman, marking the beginning of a dramatic growth for the company. Nike marketed the Air Jordan line of basketball shoes and clothes with a series of striking ads and commercials with the slogan "Just do it" featuring football and baseball star Bo Jackson and motion picture director Spike Lee. The campaign boosted Nike's profits considerably. In 1997, Nike entered a new period of high-profile product imagery when company spokesman Tiger Woods became the first African American (and also the first Asian American) to win the Professional Golf Association's Masters golf tournament.
- In 1991, the American Medical Association criticized RJR Nabisco for using the Joe Camel cartoon character in its advertising campaign, claiming that the campaign was targeted at children. In 1992, the U.S. surgeon general asked the company to withdraw the ads, and this request was followed by more government appeals in 1993 and 1994. The company responded to public concerns by promoting a campaign that encouraged store merchants and customers to obey the law prohibiting the sale of tobacco products to minors. In 1997, under increasing criticism, the company ended its Joe Camel ad campaign.
- The growth of the Gateway 2000 computer company in the 1990s was helped, in large part, by an unusual advertising campaign featuring em-

ployees standing in cow pastures. The company also shipped its computers in boxes splattered with black spots like those of Holstein cows, reflecting its midwestern roots.

- Famous early 2000 ad campaigns included the "Think outside the bun" campaign of Taco Bell and the "I'm lovin' it" campaign of McDonald's. These brought the ad campaign into the purview of a new generation of consumers brought up on video games and self-indulging fantasies.

What Is an Ad Campaign?

There is little doubt in my mind that the modern-day ad campaign traces its roots to the strategies of P. T. Barnum (chapter 5) and especially his technique of putting posters throughout the countryside—note that the word *campaign* derives from the Latin for "countryside"—so that he could reach as many people as possible. The "door-to-door" salesman was just around the corner. To this day, campaigns of all sorts, from political to social, involve some form of visitation to where people live and some form of posting or allocating appropriate materials.

An ad campaign can be defined as the systematic creation of slightly different ads and commercials based on the same theme, characters, jingles, and slogan. It is comparable to the theme and variations form of music—where there is one theme with a number of variations. The primary function of ad campaigns is to ensure that the product is advertised as broadly as possible and, often, that it can be integrated or featured in cultural spectacles or various social venues. Another function is to guarantee that product advertising is in step with the times. As discussed in chapter 5, perhaps no one more than Pepsi has been successful at understanding the importance of this function. The Pepsi product was invented in 1898 by an American pharmacist named Caleb Bradham, who gave it the brand name Pepsi-Cola to highlight the fact that the pepsin in it was a digestive product. In 1903, Bradham produced the first ads for the product. These announced its pharmacological function simply as "Exhilarating, invigorating, aids digestion." To boost sales, however, in 1906, Pepsi started changing its image with the slogan "The original pure food drink," emphasizing that the drink was not a chemical product but a "pure" substance. In the 1950s, Pepsi was among the first companies to adopt youth culture trends and symbols and make them its own. It has, since then, employed teen stars and young celebrities in its commercials. Starting in 2001, it created its "Forever young" campaign, mirroring the desire in society not only to stay and look young for a longer period of life but also to act and think differently than "older" people. In effect, Pepsi has always reflected social changes in it ad campaigns. There is little doubt that these have affected how people perceive the brand. Pepsi was created as a medicinal drink to aid digestion. But through its campaigns it has lost this meaning completely. It has become the elixir of youth. As Holt (2004: 2–3) aptly puts it, "Although the product has a name, a trademarked logo, unique packaging, and perhaps other unique design features, the brand does not yet truly exist" until it becomes part of society and develops a history for itself that meshes with the history of society during the same period of time.

Ad campaigns are now part of an unconscious process that transforms products into historical artifacts. Coca-Cola bottles from the turn of the twentieth century or Parker pens from the end of the nineteenth century, for instance, have become prized collectibles, having almost as much value as ancient artifacts or works of art. In a fascinating book titled *Twenty Ads That Shook the World* (2000), James Twitchell argues this very point. He discusses 20 ad campaigns that have become, in effect, part of the broader social history of America. As he aptly puts it (2000: 8), "They got into our bloodstream." The ads are as follows:

1. P. T. Barnum's publicity techniques (1870s)
2. Lydia E. Pinkham's Vegetable Compound campaign (1880s)
3. Pears' Soap campaign (1888)
4. Pepsodent's "Magic" campaign (1920s)
5. Listerine's "If you want the truth" campaign (1924)
6. Queensboro's use of radio (1920s)
7. New Haven Railroad's "The kid in upper 4" ad campaign (1942)
8. De Beers' "A diamond is forever" campaign (1948)
9. Hathaway's "Hathaway man" campaign (1951)
10. Miss Clairol's "Does she or doesn't she?" campaign (1955)
11. Marlboro cigarette's "Marlboro man" campaign (1950s)
12. Anacin's "Hammer-in-the-head" campaign (1950s)
13. Volkswagen's "Think small" campaign (1962)
14. Coca Cola's "Things go better with coke" campaign (1964)
15. Lyndon B. Johnson's campaign for the presidency (1964)
16. Revlon's Charlie campaign (1970s–1980s)
17. Absolut Vodka's "Larceny" campaign (1980s)
18. Apple's "1984" commercial (1984)
19. The advent of the infomercial (1995)
20. Nike's Michael Jordan campaign (1990s)

The techniques introduced by Barnum have been discussed in this book several times already, as have Apple's 1984 commercial and Nike's Michael Jordan campaign. They require no further commentary here. I will start, therefore, with Lydia E. Pinkham's Vegetable Compound ad campaign of the 1880s, designed to promote remedies for female uterine infections. This was among the first ad campaigns to use the product character concept to promote the product. Its logo of the grandmotherly Pinkham became, subsequently, a kind of cultural emblem throughout America, standing for reassurance and feminine wisdom.

As one of the first to adopt a brand name, the Pears' Soap Company produced a truly captivating ad campaign in 1888, using the picture of a lonely child with the following accompanying tagline:

> A specialty for improving the complexion and preventing redness, roughness and chapping, recommended by Mrs. Langtry, Madame Patti and obtained 15 international medals as a competition soap.

This "portrait of childhood" mirrored the maudlin sentimental view of childhood that prevailed in a Victorian society; that is, the child's angelic face nicely captured the view of children as innocent creatures. In the 1920s, Pepsodent toothpaste mounted one of the first true scare tactic ad campaigns featuring a man and a woman seated at a restaurant with the implicit warning that this kind of "romantic scene" would not be possible without "pretty teeth." A similar scare tactic technique was employed by Listerine in its 1924 campaign, which featured the slogan "If you want the truth—go to a child" and the picture of a child reacting adversely to his mother's bad breath. The use of radio to promote a product was initiated by the Queensboro Corporation in the 1920s. As mentioned previously, the radio commercial transformed advertising radically. With the use of catchy music, the employment of narrative dialogue, and other dramatic devices, the radio commercial gave the advertiser's message the kind of theatrical power that print could not possibly give to it. Entire radio programs became associated with products as a consequence.

New Haven Railroad's The Kid in Upper 4 ad campaign of 1942 opened the door to the strategy of deflecting negative attention away from a product or service. The ad showed a young man in an upper berth, awake, pondering something. In the berth below him, two other young men could be seen sleeping. The tagline revealed what the youth in the upper berth was thinking— "Leaving behind the taste of hamburgers" and "the pretty girl who writes so often." The campaign wanted to shift people's attention away from the lousy train service of the era. It worked beyond expectations, as train use went up considerably after the ad campaign was mounted. The "kid in upper 4" became an icon—a topic of magazines such as *Life*, *Newsweek*, and *Time*; a character in an MGM movie short; and the subject of a popular song. The ad campaign showed clearly the extent to which advertising was starting to become integrated into the larger cultural system.

De Beers' 1948 campaign utilizing the catchy phrase "A diamond is forever" was a clever strategy linking love, marriage, and diamonds. It is relevant to note that, in the mid-2000s, De Beers altered its campaign message somewhat. In an age of high divorce rates and personal indulgence, the new De Beers ads were designed to appeal to women with the financial means to take individual ownership of the "diamonds are a girl's best friend" tradition. The 1948 campaign portrayed the diamond ring as an engagement symbol. The new campaign was designed instead as a pitch to women directly, portraying a diamond ring as an expression of personal taste rather than as connected symbolically to courtship and marriage. The diamond ring thus morphed into something that women could give to themselves without any expectations of love and commitment. The tagline in the ads claimed that the time had come for "Women of the world" to "raise your right hand." At one level, the statement was a play on the expression "Workers of the world, unite!" a rallying cry for oppressed people. However, at another level, it suggested that by putting the ring on the right hand rather than the left (the one reserved for engagement and wedding rings), women now had the power to declare their independence.

The 1950s and 1960s brought with them the entrenchment of many contemporary advertising practices. In 1951, Hathaway shirts were promoted as distinctive brands, entrenching the use of "signature clothing" items as identifiers of personality once and for all. Miss Clairol's highly successful "Does she or doesn't she?" campaign of 1955 introduced the gossip technique into advertising. The creation of a fictitious product character by Marlboro cigarettes, called the Marlboro Man, became a symbol of American manhood. And for some people he remains so to this very day. Anacin showcased the power of synesthetic advertising by creating ads and commercials in the 1950s portraying pain inside the human head as comparable to the clanking sound made by a banging hammer and the harrowing sensation produced by an electric charge. The campaign, it is said, made people react physically (as if they had a headache). Volkswagen's incredibly successful "Think small campaign" (1962) promoting its Beetle model and Coca-Cola's similarly effective "Things go better with Coke" (1964) campaign were classic examples of how brand advertising and social trends were beginning to mirror each other more and more. In 1964, aware of the success that advertising had reaped for President Dwight Eisenhower before him, Lyndon Johnson's campaign team decided to use an ad campaign designed to tap directly into the dominant fear of the era—extinction through the atomic bomb. The ad campaign showed a little girl in separate frames—as in a comic book sequence. The girl was annihilated in the last frame by an atomic blast. The tagline "We must love each other, or else die" completed the ad. Many political pundits claim, to this day, that it got Johnson elected because it conveyed a concern for an issue that was felt strongly at the time.

Revlon's Charlie ads of the 1970s and 1980s reflected trends brought about by the feminist movement of the era. One ad showed a female dressed in business attire, carrying a briefcase, and, in a clear reversal of roles, touching the derrière of a handsome young man. This "role-reversal" method left a permanent imprint on advertising technique. The first infomercial appeared in 1995; since then, television channels promoting goods and services all day long have become common throughout the world. Bluntly, these glorify consumerism as part of a "philosophy of life."

Since Twitchell's book came out, various other ad campaigns would merit being added to the list. Some of these, like Dove's "Real women" and McDonald's "I'm lovin' it" campaigns, have already been discussed. One trend, however, merits a brief comment here. Starting in 2002, car commercials generally adopted the surrealistic feel of the computer screen as captured by the 1999 movie the *Matrix*. Such commercials attempt to create a feeling of "escape from reality" into a fantasy world of "total control," imitating video games. In one, by Mazda, we see a young boy looking at cars as if they were on a screen, turning to his audience with the childish exclamation "Zoom, zoom," an onomatopoeic word for toy car movement. The subtext is transparent—in today's computer, video game culture, nothing is as exciting as doing your own thing through technology. In effect, the trend today is to look at what is going on in pop and technological culture and then mirroring it in ad campaigns. In a fundamental sense, all advertising today is "reality advertising." The campaigns retell us the ongoing cultural stories on their own terms, and we perceive them as indistinguishable from the stories.

Co-Option

The most effective type of ad campaign is, in fact, the one that co-opts social themes. The word *co-option* was introduced into advertising studies by Thomas Frank in his insightful 1997 book *The Conquest of Cool*. Frank proposed it to describe the dominant strategy of big-brand advertising in the 1960s to appropriate the symbols of counterculture lifestyle as their own, adapting and recycling them on their own consumerist terms. Counterculture clothing fashion was thus quickly converted into mainstream fashion by clothing companies such as Levi jeans; counterculture music style became the code adopted by the big record brands, making it mainstream music style; and so on. By decade's end, this strategy led to the crystallization of a social mind-set whereby every individual could feel that he or she was "part of the scene." All the individual had to do was buy the appropriate clothing or record.

As a marketing strategy, co-option was a truly brilliant one. Marketers decided it was in their best interest not to fight youth insurgency or transgressive symbolism but rather to embrace it outright. The main technique of the co-option approach was the development of an advertising style that mocked consumerism and advertising itself. It worked beyond expectations. Through advertising, being young and rebellious came to mean having a "cool look"; being antiestablishment and subversive came to mean wearing "hip clothes." The corporate leaders had cleverly "joined the revolution," so to speak, by deploying media images of youthful subversion to market their goods and services. "Young" and "different" became the two key words of the new advertising lexicon, allowing consumers to believe that what they bought transformed them into ersatz revolutionaries without having to pay the social price of true nonconformity and dissent. Campaigns such as the Coca-Cola "Universal Brotherhood" one directly incorporated the images, rhetoric, and symbolism of the counterculture movement into their style and content. With the emblem song "I'd like to teach the world to sing in perfect harmony," the campaign showed the extent to which the counterculture message had become branded. The Dodge Rebellion and Oldsmobile Youngmobile campaigns followed the soft-drink one, etching into the nomenclature of the car brands themselves the powerful connotations of hippie rebellion and defiance. Ironically, by claiming to be a part of the social revolution, the big brands created their own real revolution—a revolution in how they marketed and advertised their products. Since the late 1960s, the worlds of advertising, marketing, and entertainment have become totally intertwined with youth lifestyle, both responding and contributing to the rapid fluctuations in social trends.

A perfect example of a brand that has consistently used co-option as a strategy is the Gap, a company founded in 1969 in San Francisco. The name, in fact, was coined in reference to the "generation gap" between young and old people. One of the company's first slogans was "Fall into the Gap." Not surprisingly, Gap products are now marketed to all ages. It too has co-opted the "forever young" theme. This is why their commercials feature musical artists from the present and the past. The subtext of the commercials is an obvious one: "Your age and musical preferences are irrelevant; we are all in the gap (the same lifestyle) together." Here is a sampling:

- 1998: "Khakis swing" featuring *Jump, Jive, an' Wail* by Louis Prima (a jazz artist of the 1940s and 1950s)
- 1999: "Everybody in cords" featuring *Mellow Yellow* by Donovan (a star of the hippie era)
- 2001: "Give a little bit" featuring *Give a Little Bit* by Supertramp (a popular rock band of the 1970s and 1980s)

- 2005: "How do you wear it?" featuring *Lady* by Lenny Kravitz (a 1990s music star)
- 2006: "The skinny black pant" featuring *Back in Black* by AC/DC (a hard-rock band popular in the 1980s but making a comeback in the mid-2000s)

Co-option is now the primary strategy in ad campaigns. The synergy phenomenon discussed in chapter 1 is largely a result of co-option. But the broader consequences have been substantial. Co-option may, in fact, be one of the primary causes in the obliteration of the crucial emotional difference that traditional cultures have always maintained between the social categories of young and old. Today the rhetoric of youth is quickly transformed by advertising into the rhetoric of all, the fashion trends of the young are recycled and marketed as the fashion styles of all, the fluctuating musical aesthetics of youth culture are quickly incorporated into the musical aesthetics of society at large, and so on. Youth has become a social norm. The many self-proclaimed rebels of the 1960s counterculture, who genuinely thought they were bringing about a radical change to the mainstream consumerist culture, ended up becoming the incognizant trendsetters of the very culture they deplored, providing it with features of lifestyle and discourse that the brand power brokers have been able to adapt and recycle into society at large.

Passively, we now accept the fact that we are classified by marketers into "taste groups," "lifestyle groups," "market segments," and the like. In the semantic system of this language, the individual human being is hardly envisioned as a being with a unique character but rather as a nameless entity whose behavior can be inferred from the laws of Gaussian statistics and thus easily manipulated. As Frank emphasizes, the conquest of cool has had a radical surreptitious effect on the psychology and sociology of the contemporary world.

The lesson learned from the success of the co-option strategy by big business is that the road into any marketplace is paved not only by economic savvy but also by cultural savvy. In a sense, the co-option strategy has brought about a demise of the original form of capitalism, intended for the benefit of the bourgeoisie, transforming it into one of market populism. Today, being cool implies not being subversive politically but rather knowing all about technology and its magical gadgetry. And this new cool is a by-product of a social world in which values and lifestyles are intertwined with objects and gadgetry. The counterculture reformers saw the Western world's all-pervading sense of alienation and of rootlessness as caused by materialism. This, they claimed, had undermined the human values shared by common folk, leading to a loss of social stability and to individual feelings of anxiety and dissatisfaction. The hippies felt that they were doing something meaningful to combat alienation. They fought against misery and oppression. They sought to reestablish the spiritual over the material. But as it turned out, they ended up being the unwitting instruments of the materialists. The hippies did not pull the plug on capitalism; they merely allowed market populists to give it a new and highly appealing dynamism.

Co-option could not have worked as successfully as it did in the first place unless there already existed in the "social genes" of the Western world a built-in tendency toward consumerism. The causes of the hippie revolution were provoked by human sentiments—by an abhorrence of social injustice, by a disgust over discrimination against specific groups (such as African Americans and women), and so on—not by an aversion to capitalism. Sooner or later, the same sentiments will provoke other revolutions. It is ironic to note that the very images of Western capitalism that the hippies deplored were adopted by the youths of communist countries two decades later as they successfully brought down communism. That, in my view, is the greatest paradox of all and something that no one can really fathom. Life is really much more complicated than any critical analysis of capitalist ideology will allow.

THE MEDIA–TECHNOLOGY PARTNERSHIP

Ad campaigns have become sophisticated not only in their content but also in the way they use technology to deliver their messages. As mentioned in chapter 2, there always has been a partnership between advertising and new mass communication technologies, with advertisers being among the first to use them. The use of multiple media to deliver ad campaigns is now a standard strategy of all the big brands. Traditional or off-line media (print, radio, television, signs, direct mail, displays, and so on) are now used in tandem with new satellite and online technologies, which include such new marketing techniques as pay-per-click advertising, banner ads, e-mail marketing, and blog marketing.

Getting the Message Out

Print ads, as discussed in chapter 2, reach people primarily through newspapers and magazines. They require no further commentary here. Another way of getting the message out through print and related technologies can be called *display advertising*. This includes using such devices and procedures as outdoor signs, leaflets, brochures, posters, painted bulletins, transit signs, window displays, and point-of-purchase displays. The print medium bolstered by the use of illustrations, color, photography, and so on is a semiotically powerful one. As we saw in chapter 6, it is particularly amenable to the use of aesthetic techniques in the making of ads and narrative ones in the making of commercials. The artwork and dramaturgy in such ads and commercials are the main elements that enhance the image of a product, and, thus, its marketability.

Also as mentioned in chapter 2, radio advertising has always been used in getting the message out because it has the advantage that people can listen to it while doing other things. Radio programming today also makes it easy for advertisers to direct their pitches to the right consumers because radio audiences, in general, are specialized and thus come already precategorized for the marketer. Television advertising is the most popular medium for delivering ad campaigns. Network television reaches a vast, nationwide audience, and, for this reason, is still the choice of most advertisers. The Internet, however, is quickly taking over as the primary medium for ad campaign delivery. Internet marketing began in the early 1990s with websites that simply offered product information. It has now evolved into a sophisticated market universe all its own. Companies like Google, Yahoo!, and MSN offer advertising to all kinds of businesses. As a consequence, anyone with a product or service to offer can reach the widest audience possible. E-commerce and e-stores, as they are called, are burgeoning, and e-marketing is gradually replacing direct-mail pitches as well as radio and television ad campaigns and infomercials. Virtually any product or service can now be ordered from Internet sites by clicking the appropriate icons or cues.

Since usage of and reaction to digital advertising is much easier to track than that of traditional off-line advertising, Internet marketing offers many advantages. It has also had a large impact on several industries, including music and banking, not to mention the advertising and marketing industries themselves. Downloading MP3s over the Internet instead of buying CDs has become a dominant way in which music sales now occur. Banks currently offer the choice to carry out banking tasks online. Currently, over 50 million people in the United States bank online.

Online Advertising

As discussed in chapter 2, online advertising offers a host of new possibilities to the advertiser. These include banner ads, which are graphic images or animation displayed on a website; interstitial ads, which move across the screen or float above it; ads that change size and may alter a Web page (known as expanding ads); ads that change the background of the Web page being viewed (called wallpaper ads); video ads, which display moving video clips; and ads that look like dialog boxes with buttons, simulating an alert (known as trick banners). Other online advertising techniques (among many others) include the following:

- Polite advertising, whereby a large ad is downloaded in pieces to minimize disruption of the content being viewed
- Pop-ups, whereby a new window opens in front of the one being viewed, displaying an advertisement
- Pop-unders, whereby a new window is loaded or sent behind the window being viewed so that the user does not see it until closing one or more active windows
- Mobile ads, which are ads sent to an SMS device or cell phone

Needless to say, the Internet has also become a major source for co-option and other kinds of pivotal advertising campaign strategies. For example, in 2001, the carmaker BMW hired several famous directors to make short digital films featuring its cars. The movies were viewable only on the Web but were also promoted through television spots. Those films clearly blurred the line between art and advertising, showing how a true continuity had emerged between the larger cultural order and the advertising domain. More and more brands are using similar techniques online, co-opting trends and celebrities to promote their products. People can now go to websites and discuss ads, products, and campaigns. In early 2000, *Vogue* and *W* magazines created the website Style.com, where people can click on to get the latest gossip about the fashion industry and get information about celebrities, fashion models, and the like. The site includes material from other companies. Such co-option strategies would have been unthinkable in a pre-Internet era.

BRANDING

Brand advertising and brand display methods are now everywhere, having become integral components in modern-day consumerist cultures. The "branding" of culture is, clearly, one of the most important marketing strategies, if not *the* most important. Branding can be defined, simply, as the general technique of ensuring that a brand is displayed prominently in some social context. Revlon, for instance, spent millions of dollars in the early 2000s for close-up shots of its products during the broadcasting of the American television soap opera *All My Children*. Similar schemes have been used by virtually all the big brands. Many brands, moreover, enthusiastically sponsor socially significant events, from demonstrations against poverty to sporting spectacles. In a phrase, branding has become a major marketing technique.

What Is a Branding?

The showcasing of brands in movies and television programs is known more specifically as *brand placement*. This will be discussed in the next section. Placement is just one of the branding techniques used today, which include the sponsoring of events (as mentioned), the ownership of such organizations as sports teams, and the making of donations to worthy causes (among others). The intent is to tap into social trends and systems or to be noticed by society not simply as a brand but as something much more. Supporting worthy causes is a particularly effective branding technique. For example, as a family-oriented company, McDonald's started sponsoring Ronald McDonald House Charities a few years ago. The organization operates hundreds of Ronald McDonald Houses worldwide in which the families of critically ill children may stay when the young patients undergo medical treatment away from their homes.

Sometimes, the product itself becomes such a fad that it shapes trends in society. This phenomenon can be called *reverse branding*. In the 1950s, for example, Silly Putty, Slinkies, and Hula Hoops became so popular that they were the inspiration of songs and narratives. Silly Putty was introduced in 1949 by advertising marketer Peter C. L. Hodgson, who discovered a substance developed by General Electric researchers looking for a viable synthetic rubber. The useless silicone substance could be molded like soft clay, stretched like taffy, and bounced like a rubber ball. Slinky was a coil toy that could be made to "walk" down a staircase by itself by placing it on a higher step in a specific way. The Hula Hoop was a light plastic hoop that could be whirled around the body for play or exercise by the movement of the hips. These products became icons of pop culture, remaining so to this day because they were promoted constantly through the media.

In the 1940s and 1950s, brand placement was a simple matter. In radio and television programs such as *Texaco Theater*, *General Electric Theater*, and *Kraft Theater*, the program itself was associated exclusively with one sponsor. Children's programming, like the *Mickey Mouse Club* (which premiered in 1955), was similarly sponsored. The show used young actors hired by Disney who became themselves icons of child culture, promoting the whole Disney brand of products. But this form of sponsorship was not applicable to all kinds of programs and formats. In its lieu, other branding strategies soon crystallized and spread across media. Often, the sponsor would be included as part of the script, thus making the distinction between program content and a sponsor a blurry one. The movies entered the branding fray in 1982 when the extraterrestrial creature in Stephen Spielberg's *E.T.* was seen snacking on Reese's Pieces—increasing sales for the product enormously. That event started the trend of brand placement in Hollywood. In 1983, for example, movie actor Tom Cruise donned a pair of Wayfarers (Ray-Ban sunglasses) in *Risky Business*, and sales for the product shot up, as did generally the wearing of sunglasses to convey a "cool look."

Another type is called *cobranding*, which can be defined simply as some form of cooperation among the brands. For example, the Pillsbury Doughboy was used by the Sprint Corporation in 2004 and 2005 to promote its product in a campaign in which he paired up with the Sprint Guy. Similarly, the Maytag repairman turned up in an ad for the Chevrolet Impala, and the Taco Bell Chihuahua appeared in an ad for Geico. Examples such as these now abound. Various bookstore chains, for example, have joined forces with coffee giants such as Starbucks. The subtext that this partnership promotes involves the image of individuals who enjoy the finer things in life and who are cultured in a well-rounded way. The association of brands with intellectualism and the arts is a long-standing one. Those with political, religious, or economic power have always attempted to promote themselves as cultured by becoming patrons of the arts. Sponsoring arts events is a way to gain respect and authority and to reveal concern for the culture in which a sponsor exists. In the past, artists (such as classical music composers) would dedicate their works to a benefactor or sponsor, acknowledging the benefactor's help and support.

Placement

Placement is without doubt the most effective of all branding strategies. It is now so common that it goes largely unnoticed. Its main objective is to amalgamate brand identity with pop culture, spectacles, and media. A good example of this amalgamation was the launch of the teenage-directed television serial *Dawson's Creek* in January 1998. All the characters in the program were outfitted in clothing and accessories made by J. Crew. They appeared, in fact, to be models that had stepped out of the J. Crew catalog, and the actors were featured in the catalog that very same month. Two seasons later, as the "cool look" changed in society, the characters got a makeover and a new wardrobe from American Eagle Outfitters. And, once again, the company used the actors as models for their own purposes, featuring them on their website and in-store promotions.

With new media, placement is becoming easier and easier to realize. The toy maker Mattel, for instance, started a Planet Hot Wheels website in the early 2000s from which one can download a game. Hot Wheels are small toy cars made to resemble real cars. They are cheap and highly popular with young boys. The website was intended to impart a "cool image" to the brand so as to attract teenagers and so-called tweens (prepubescent children) to whom little children look up to. The site offered upgrades for "virtual vehicles" and a motocross 1950s drag race game, which were free with a Hot Wheels purchase. The Mattel case constitutes a new form of placement called *embedding*. Embedding can also involve cooperation among brands. The website www.neopet.com is a case in point. Offering a host of recreational and educational activities to children, in 2004 it created a virtual McDonald's site, a Lucky Charms game, and other brand embeds in it.

Placement is the natural outgrowth of the branding–pop culture partnership that started decades ago. Psychologically and socially, this has had a number of consequences. Being a part of an "in crowd" today entails sensitivity to the right brand of shoes, T-shirt, jeans, and so on. Through the brand, we now symbolize our own "brand" of lifestyle. This is why brand names are so powerful—they provide a "coded" membership entry card to a lifestyle sector. In the 2000s, iPods were such entry cards, designed to be tucked away but also displayed on the body as accessories.

The celebrity endorsement of brands can also be seen as a form of placement. It is an effective strategy because it transfers what people perceive in the celebrity to the product. So too is the creation of fictitious characters to promote specific brands (as mentioned previously). Many of these have become pop culture celebrities themselves, independently of the products they represent. Mr. Clean, Uncle Ben, Charlie the Tuna, and Hostess's Twinkie the Kid have become such an intrinsic part of cultural lore that they were even featured (as mentioned) in cameo roles in a 2001 animated film called *Foodfight*. And in the same year, Barbie became a ballerina in the movie *Barbie in the Nutcracker*.

9

Advertising and Society

> Consumer wants can have bizarre, frivolous, or even immoral origins, and an admirable case can still be made for a society that seeks to satisfy them. But the case cannot stand if it is the process of satisfying wants that create the wants.
>
> —John Kenneth Galbraith, 1908–2006

There is little doubt that modern advertising, with all its sophisticated techniques, has had an impact on people and especially on the enormous rise of consumerism over the past century. People no longer buy things because they need them but because shopping itself is fun. Shopping has become as much a part of entertainment culture as spectacles such as sports events and blockbuster movies. There is now fantasy buying, frenzy buying, hysteria buying, recreational buying, impulse buying, and the list could go on and on. There are also consumer "diseases," so to speak, called addictive buying and obsessive buying. As a consequence, perhaps nothing else has caused as much controversy as has advertising. In the past few decades in particular, it has generated a truly bitter debate in society at large: Does it influence attitudes and behavior? Is it a valuable contributor to a free market economy? Is it a form of artistic expression? Does it induce people to overeat and live beyond their means? Such questions have been touched on in this book. In this brief concluding chapter, I will address them by looking at the relevant issues and studies.

The question that most of the studies have entertained, without answering it in any definitive fashion, is whether advertising has become a force molding people's behavior and worldview or whether it constitutes no more than a "mirror" of preexisting tendencies within capitalist societies. Many of the studies contain moralistic subtexts, warning us that we are on the road to perdition with our neomania, as Barthes called it (chapter 1). But to what extent are the warnings of such pure-minded scholars accurate? Is advertising to be blamed for causing virtually everything, from obesity to spiritual nihilism? Has advertising spawned the contemporary world? There is no doubt, as mentioned here and throughout this book, that advertising has played a significant role in bringing about consumerism. It has been good for the economy but maybe not so good for people and the environment (given the waste that rampant consumerism has generated). However, in my view, although people mindlessly absorb the messages promulgated constantly by advertisements and although these may have some effects on behavior, people accept them by and large because they can, both financially and psychologically. Advertisements are not in themselves disruptive of the value systems of the cultural mainstream; rather, they simply fit in with them. In a manner of speaking, without the capitalist economic hardware running society, advertising could not work as cultural software.

I am of two minds on this whole issue. On the one hand, I can see the devastation that mass consumption has wreaked on the environment and how fragile the world's economies have become, depending almost entirely on the obsessive demand for new goods, new objects, new gadgets, new *everything*! On the other hand, I enjoy shopping for the sake of shopping every once in a while. I also enjoy the odd hamburger and fries. In effect, I am like the very subjects that scholars investigate—I know that the state of the contemporary world is both good and bad. But, then, maybe it has always been that way.

SOCIAL EFFECTS

To repeat, advertising has been good for economics. Advertising pays all the costs of commercial television and radio, making it possible for everyone with a television and radio to get free entertainment and news programs. Advertising also pays for three-fourths of the costs of newspapers and magazines. Without advertising, readers would have to pay a higher price for newspapers and magazines, and many of them would go out of business. Given the dependence of media on advertising, some social critics have come to question whether it is really advertisers who control the media and not the other way around. And, in fact, in order to sell advertising time at high prices, all broadcasting media try, understandably, to attract the largest possible audience for their sponsors. Critics argue that television stations therefore broadcast too many general entertainment programs and not enough informational and cultural programs.

These attacks on advertising are not new. Ever since Vance Packard's 1957 indictment of advertising as a surreptitious form of persuasion (chapter 1), the entire enterprise has come constantly under attack in the academies and in some social and political circles, although no consensus has ever been reached by researchers as to its effects on the ethos and attitudes of people living in consumerist cultures. Yet the critiques continue unrelentingly. Some have, of course, an element of truth in them. Since the end of the nineteenth century, advertising has succeeded, more so than any economic process or sociopolitical movement, in promoting and ensconcing consumerism as a way of life. By proposing consumption solutions to emotional and social problems, it has become a form of pseudoreligious discourse. Ads and commercials now offer the same kinds of promises and hopes to which religions once held exclusive rights—a better life, personal prestige, social advancement, better health, happiness, and so on. Advertising is, in effect, a modern-day form of magic. The manufacturers of such products as gasolines and headache remedies boast of new, secret ingredients—in the same way that magicians would use secret charms, spells, and rituals in seeking or pretending to cause or control events or to govern certain natural or supernatural forces. Advertising promises implicitly to produce marvelous effects.

Hidden Effects

Are there really "hidden effects" on society brought about by advertising? Perhaps. Above all else, critics have accused advertising of surreptitiously inducing a hedonistic and epicurean worldview in most people today—to greater or lesser extents. Lifestyle advertising in particular, they suggest, filters and even interprets reality for us. The subtext of such advertising conveys the message that the only meaningful thing in life is the fulfillment of desires. In the past, the casual use of many of today's cosmetic products, for instance, would have been considered either a sin or a manifestation of vanity. Advertising is also trenchantly criticized for bombarding us with messages of assurance that consumption in itself can solve human problems. The gist of the anti-advertising argument is that advertising may have shaped the modern psyche. The basic claim is that viewing the world through a television commercial or through magazine ads is bound, eventually, to transform people's perception of the real world into a mindless gaze that interprets it as if it were a scene in an ad. Day in and day out, advertising's fragmented images of life are bound to impart a simplistic materialistic view of life, namely, that satisfying desires is the only thing that counts. At least that's how the anti-argument story generally goes.

It is also claimed that the language of advertising has also had a hidden effect on the language of ordinary communication. Advertising style reduces thoughts to formulas, stock phrases, jingles, and slogans. Its conceptual system is not tied to a larger social or philosophical grammar. It is instantaneous, geared to encapsulating fleeting images and condensed thoughts. Traditionally, the socially meaningful forms of discourse, such as gospels, catechisms, philosophical treatises, and poems, have always attempted to pose and answer the great questions of humanity: Who are we? Why are we here? and so on. Advertising instead constitutes a form of discourse that merely celebrates consumption. Its categories announce, "If you buy this or that, then you will be eternally young, sexy, happy, and so on." No wonder, then, that mythic themes pervade modern advertising. As advertisers obviously know, we need myth in order to understand who we are and how we are tied to the history of our species. Advertising has also developed its own form of historiography. Retro ads, for instance, constitute historical self-reference. With computer techniques, images from 1950s commercials are incorporated into modern-day television commercials that document the history of a product.

Such strategies are persuasive because they are logical. But whether there really are hidden effects on people emanating from the advertising domain is an open question for the simple fact that they cannot be proved or demonstrated in any empirical way. However, there is little doubt that advertising, like any representational activity, has unquantifiable effects. A particularly critical assessment of advertising in this regard came from the early feminist camp in the 1970s and 1980s, which saw it essentially as a sexist form of art, representing (or, better, misrepresenting) women as either sex goddesses or housewives. In a phrase, the early feminists argued that ads were degrading to women. Some of the critiques of the early feminists were well founded, given the effusion of images of women as either "sexual cheerleaders" or "motherly homemakers" in many early ads. But advertisers have shown themselves to be extremely clever in deflecting such criticism. They answered it, in fact, with such ad campaigns as the Charlie one discussed in the previous chapter. Moreover, advertisers have come forward to claim that by portraying women as liberated in many of their ads and ad campaigns, they have actually played a critical role in liberating women from seeing themselves as constricted to the roles of housekeeper and mother. Women can in fact enjoy cosmetics and beauty mystiques without feeling guilty, thanks to advertising.

Globalization

As mentioned early on in this book, McLuhan had predicted already in the 1950s that the spread of electronic media would eventually turn the world into one electronic "global village" where Coca-Cola, McDonald's, and other brands would morph into "global brands." With the advent of satellite television and the Internet, McLuhan's prophetic vision has become a reality. The greatest hidden effect of advertising may, as it turns out, be the fact that it has help spread consumerism throughout the global village through technology. Across the globe, people are now buying the same products, reacting to the same kind of advertising pitches, and speaking a similar kind of "ad speak." Individuals can now feel that they are participants in a larger virtual community—a community extolled by brands such as Coca-Cola (with its universal brotherhood campaign) and Benetton (with its united colors of humanity campaigns). All they have to do is wear the right kind of clothes, listen to the right kind of music, and talk the right kind of talk.

However, taking an aside, I would like to suggest that it is far too easy to blame advertising for the rise of consumerism throughout the world. One must not forget that this very rise might be an innate human tendency, called the "pleasure principle" by philosopher John Locke (1632–1704). Given the increase of general affluence (in relation to the past) and the growth of the production of goods, it would seem that people across the globe now have the opportunity to gratify an instinctual drive to seek maximum pleasure or gratification and minimum pain. According to Freudian psychology, this principle originates in the libido and is the force that governs the id. Without accepting the Freudian perspective outright, there is little doubt that the pleasure principle is what probably directs a large percentage of human behavior and shapes human needs. It is, as Stuart Ewen (1988: 20) aptly puts it, a tendency "that is closely interwoven with modern patterns of survival and desire." Rather than talk of hidden effects, it is more accurate to say, in my view, that the images that advertising produces on a daily basis reinforce the desire to fulfill the pleasure principle. If advertising has become so effective, then, it is primarily because it taps into this deeply ingrained proclivity.

The crystallization of McLuhan's global village is a result of technology. Starting already in the Renaissance with the advent of print technology, materials became affordable through mass production, and as a consequence print literacy was sought by more people than ever before in history. Print literacy impels people to separate the maker of knowledge from the knowledge made since the maker is not present as the reading process occurs. And this in turn leads to the perception that knowledge can exist on its own, spanning time and distance. Because of this, McLuhan characterized the emerging world shaped by print literacy as the "Gutenberg Galaxy," after the German printer Johannes Gutenberg, the inventor of modern movable type. Through books, newspapers, pamphlets, and posters, McLuhan argued, the printed word became, after the fifteenth century, the primary means for the propagation of knowledge and ideas. More importantly, given the fact that print materials could cross political boundaries, the printing press set in motion the globalization of culture. Paradoxically, this process did not simultaneously lead to the elimination of all the distinct cultures that had previously existed. On the contrary, he claimed that "tribal tendencies" continued to resonate within people, creating even further tensions between peoples. As hinted at in the opening chapter, the Gutenberg Galaxy transformed advertising into a new verbal art form, that is, not just a form of information but one of persuasion.

By the start of the twentieth century, the great advances made in print technology led to an increasing standardization in the conduct of various human activities, from diplomacy to the scientific method. But the technological event that truly made the global village the reality that it is today was the astounding advance in the science of electronics and, a little later in the century, in computer science. Print technology opened up the possibility of founding a world civilization; electronic and digital technologies have brought that possibility closer and closer to realization. In today's "Digital Galaxy," as it can be called, the images seen on television and on computer screens in any part of the world have become images available to people across the globe, no matter where they live and what language they speak. Advertising images in particular are powerful because they cannot be neatly evaluated as true or false or pigeonholed into distinct slots. They are emotional artifacts to which people react in an imaginary way. There is, of course, a positive side to this whole new situation. Without satellite and Internet communications, many conflicts, wars, and horrific cases of poverty would go unnoticed. Digital technologies have brought these situations literally into focus, creating universal human concern and empathy. So, while the global village may have had some purportedly deleterious effects on the human psyche (at least according to some social critics), it has not stifled human empathy or altruism.

The global village has, of course, been very good for business, providing the electronic means for spreading advertising through the world and, thus, for providing the conditions for brands to achieve global status. A casebook example of a brand that has been successful because of the global village is Lux Toilet Soap, whose slogan is "The toilet soap of the stars." Lux (Latin for "light") has been a top-selling soap for over seven decades around the globe. Using well-known Hollywood stars along with local cinema and television stars to promote its products, the brand has guaranteed itself a niche in the global village, promoting itself as being "global" and "community based" at the same time. It is this double brand identity that secures placement in the virtual village.

Two other textbook cases are McDonald's and Disney—both of which have reached multinational status and are, practically, household names worldwide.

The sociologist Alan Bryman (2004: 25–26) refers to "McDonaldization" as the process "by which the principles of the fast-food restaurant are coming to dominate more and more sectors of American society as well as the rest of the world" and "Disneyization" as the correlative process "by which the principles of the Disney theme parks are coming to dominate more and more sectors of American society as well as the rest of the world." Like Lux, both companies have adopted the new global village strategy of blending into both the global and the local culture in tandem. One marketing study, cited by Eric Schlosser (2001: 34), found that the Golden Arches are now more recognizable across the globe than the Christian cross. As a symbol of unabashed American capitalism, it is little wonder that the fast-food eatery has been the target of demonstrations, vandalism, and attacks around the globe. People react to symbols emotionally.

The success of Lux, McDonald's, Disney, and other global brands is explainable in straightforward semiotic terms. By co-opting local symbolism and meaning systems, they have blended into them seamlessly. McDonald's has done this in part by allowing its menu to vary according to religious and social traditions across the world. In India, for example, the eatery serves Vegetable McNuggets and a mutton Maharaja Mac—culinary adaptations that are necessary in a country where Hindus do not eat beef, Muslims do not eat pork, and Jains eat no meat at all. This "blending of signification systems" is the strategy that turns products into global brands. Success in the global village is measurable, in fact, on the ability of a brand to be adaptive and sensitive to cultural differences.

A GLANCE AT THE STUDIES

The question of whether advertising has had effects on society has been investigated from all kinds of scientific angles. Some studies have shown that advertising does indeed seem to produce concrete effects on people. Others have shown, instead, that there is little correlation between advertising and mass behavior (including consumerism). The studies can thus be divided into those supporting and those contesting an "effects model"—that is, any model sustaining that advertising has negative effects on people, assuming that consumerism and epicurean lifestyles are "negative things" in the first place.

Studies and Views Supporting an Effects Model

The severest critiques of advertising, pop culture, and media (all wrapped into one cultural bundle) have come from the Frankfurt School (full name: the

Frankfurt Institute for Social Research), which was founded at the University of Frankfurt in 1922. The school was the world's first Marxist institute of social research. Its leading members included internationally famous scholars such as Walter Benjamin (1892–1940), Max Horkheimer (1895–1973), Herbert Marcuse (1898–1979), Erich Fromm (1900–1980), Leo Lowenthal (1900–1993), and Theodor Adorno (1903–1969). The aim of those psychologists and philosophers was to understand the ways in which human groups created meaning collectively under the impact of what some of them called capitalism's "culture industries." Overall, the Frankfurt School was highly pessimistic about the possibility of genuine individuality under modern capitalism and condemned most forms of popular or mass culture as a type of incessant propaganda system that indoctrinated the masses, disguising genuine social inequalities in the process. The school's main contention was that media representations and advertising were essentially vulgar, functioning primarily to pacify ordinary people.

Adopting Italian Marxist Antonio Gramsci's (1891–1937) concept of *hegemony*, they claimed that the domination of society by the group in power occurred mainly through the manipulation of mass communications systems. Gramsci had used the term in reference to his belief that the dominant class in a society used social "instruments" of control, which varied from outright coercion (e.g., incarceration, the use of secret police, and threats) to gentler and more "managerial" tactics (e.g., education, religion, and control of the mass media) in order to gain the unconscious (and thus more enduring) consent of common people. The concept of hegemony has found its way into current-day culture studies, where it is used to refer more to the cultural manufacturing of consent by politicians in power than it is to forms of coercion in the Gramscian sense.

Although not affiliated with the Frankfurt School, some contemporary critics of contemporary pop culture and media draw heavily on the general arguments made by it. Closely aligned with the basic tenets of the school is the propaganda model, associated primarily with Noam Chomsky (1928–) of the Massachusetts Institute of Technology. Chomsky and his followers claim that those who control the funding and ownership of the media determine how the media select and present their news and events, making the media nothing more than a propaganda system putting forward only one point of view. As this shows, Marxist theory has clearly left residues. But its main line of argument ignores a basic question: Why has modern-day consumerist culture brought about more favorable changes to the social status of common folk than any other cultural experiment in history, including (and especially) Marxism? The emotional appeal of pop culture and consumerism generally, moreover, cannot be logically dismissed in a cavalier fashion as mere instruments of pacification.

A second category of "pro-effects model" studies are, in fact, called just that—media effects studies. These are classified generally under the rubric of "magic bullet" or "hypodermic needle" theories because they see representations in media as influencing individuals and/or societies in some negative way—either like a "magic bullet" constituting a "killing force" of people's minds or a "hypodermic needle" that enters their minds directly. These theories are now largely discredited but still find their way into academic discourses and popular condemnations of advertising from both the political left and the political right. One of the most discussed types of studies supporting some degree of effects on people is known as *cultivation theory*. The theory is associated with the work of two American researchers, Paul Lazarsfeld (1901–1976) and George Gerbner (1919–2005), both of whom put forward the idea that the worldviews that the media construct, whether true or not, become the accepted realities over time.

So, has advertising had effects on people? The jury is still out on this question. However, even at a rudimentary level of analysis, it is hard to deny the fact that it has had some tangible effects. For one thing, it has certainly shaped how we do business. Advertising now plays a major role in the distribution of goods from manufacturers to consumers, providing, as we have seen in this book, an effective way for manufacturers to inform buyers about products. Advertising also helps the economy grow by stimulating demand for new products, making modern economic systems virtually reliant on advertising for their continued existence. However, some economists suggest that the money spent on advertising is wasted, arguing that much advertising simply leads consumers to switch from one brand of a product to another brand. Brand switching may increase the profits of a particular firm but has no positive effect on the overall economy.

Perhaps the most important social effect of advertising is that it supports the mass communications media and, thus, has made mass forms of entertainment available to virtually everyone. So, it may have shaped trends within entertainment and pop culture generally. At the very least, a synergy exists between advertising and the media, with one depending on the other. Many critics also charge that advertising persuades people to buy products they do not need or want through the use of the various techniques discussed in this book. Advertisers reply that they do not have the means to make people buy unwanted products. They claim that people freely choose what to buy or what not to buy. Most researchers agree, however, that advertising is particularly persuasive to young children, who do not have the ability or experience to judge advertising critically. For this reason, the Federal Trade Commission in the United States has strict regulations governing advertising aimed at children.

Studies and Views Contesting an Effects Model

In contrast to studies supporting the belief that advertising has negative effects on people, a large group of researchers has shown that people are not passive consumers of advertising representations but rather that they use them for their own purposes and are thus largely immune from the potentially conditioning factors that may issue forth from being exposed to ads. Known as *uses and gratifications theory*, it is associated primarily with the work of American sociologist Elihu Katz (1926–). Many related studies have corroborated Katz's basic contention. I myself cannot help but concur since I tend to use both the media and advertising pitches according to my own needs and desires. I use advertising, in other words, in a conscious and practical way. I suspect that most people do the same.

It has been found, moreover, that media and advertising impacts are indirect and are modulated by a series of social variables. A number of studies have shown, for example, that audiences get out of media and advertising content what they are already inclined to get. Known as *selective perception theory*, the gist of the research in this regard has found that the perception of content is often mediated by "leaders." Lazarsfeld (mentioned previously) and Katz had argued as far back as the mid-1950s that people tend to come up with interpretations that are consistent with the values of the social class or group to which they belonged. People are participants in interpretive communities—communities that crystallize from real communities such as families, unions, neighborhoods, and churches. In such communities, there are members, called "opinion leaders," who mediate how the other members will interpret media and advertising content. So, in contrast to hypodermic needle theories, which see advertising impact as a one-step flow reaching a homogeneous audience directly, selective perception theory sees it as a two-step flow in which the first step is through the opinion leader(s) who takes in the content, interprets it, and then passes it on to group members (the second step).

A third major anti-effects theory has been put forward by British cultural theorist Stuart Hall (1932–). Hall argues that people do not absorb texts passively but rather *read* them (interpret them) in one of three ways, known as preferred, negotiated, and oppositional readings. The *preferred* reading is the one that the makers of texts have built into them and that, they hope, people will take from them. The *negotiated* reading is the one that results when audiences agree with or respond in part to the meanings built into texts. And an *oppositional* reading is one that is in opposition to what the maker of the text had intended. A simple way to understand the difference between the three types is to consider a comedian who has just told a joke on stage. If the audience laughs wholeheartedly, then the joke has produced the preferred reading. If only some of the audience laughs wholeheartedly, while others chuckle or sneer, then the joke has brought about a negotiated reading. Finally, if the audience reacts negatively to the joke, with resentment, then it has produced an oppositional reading. Advertising is designed to elicit a preferred reading. But studies have shown that this reading unfolds mainly in target or fragmented audiences. By and large, there is always some negotiation in the processing of an advertising text. For this reason, advertising is probably not as effective as it is claimed to be, even as this book has suggested it is in previous chapters.

CULTURE JAMMING

Believing that advertising has become a threat to spiritual and ecological survival, there has been a considerable backlash against the whole capitalistic, corporate culture that it serves in the past few years. In *Culture Jam* (2000), for instance, the Canadian activist Kalle Lasn makes a persuasive case against the globalization of consumerist culture. As a leading voice in the so-called culture-jamming movement, Lasn (who is also the founder of *Adbusters* magazine, which satirizes ads and commercials) is at the front of a movement that decries the mindless consumerism of modern society at the cost of psychic and environmental disaster.

In the past decade or so, the culture jammers have been spearheading (or at least influencing) calls for boycotts of global brands throughout the world. Together with demonstrations and attacks against brand outlets, it is obvious that the success of the branding movement has spawned an antibranding one. The basic approach is to unmask the signification systems of brands so that more and more people can gain critical understanding of the images that advertising generates on a daily basis and thus to provide people with "cognitive immunity" against them.

What Is Culture Jamming?

Culture jamming is based on a simple technique. Take the slogan by Benson and Hedges "I'd rather fight than switch." It is loaded with cultural meanings related to feminism, smoking, and so on. How does one "jam" this system of connotative meanings? That is, how does one bring it down to a level that deprives it of its metaphorical strength? Easy. Just finish the slogan with a phrase bringing out what the product can potentially do in a harmful sense: "I'd rather fight than switch and get cancer on my own terms."

Culture jammers are a loose global network of media activists aiming to change the way media and corporate institutions wield power. Lasn believes that corporate America is no longer a country but one overarching "brand" shaped by the cult of celebrity and the spectacles that sustain it. Culture and marketing have, according to Lasn, become one and the same. Lasn's fears are not unfounded. There are a small number of colossal media conglomerates that run the global economy (Disney, Time Warner, Bertelsmann, Viacom, News Corporation, PolyGram, NBC, MCA, Sony, and a few more). Global advertising is now under the control of, basically, a handful of advertising agencies based in New York, London, Paris, and Tokyo. Aware of the social dangers that such a state of affairs poses, Lasn issued a "Media Manifesto," in obvious parallelism with the many other manifestos that have been issued and that have "changed the world" (of which Karl Marx's is probably the most famous). The manifesto has five main resolutions that culture jammers are determined to maintain:

- "We will take on the archetypal mind polluters—Marlboro, Budweiser, Benetton, Coke, McDonald's, Calvin Klein—and beat them at their own game."
- "We will uncool their billion dollar images with uncommercials on TV, subvertisements in magazines and anti-ads right next to theirs in the urban landscape."
- "We will take control of the role that the tobacco, alcohol, fashion, cosmetics, food and automobile corporations play in our lives. We will hold their marketing strategies up to public scrutiny and set new agendas in their industries."
- "We will culture jam the pop culture marketeers—MTV, Time Warner, Sony—and bring their image factories to a sudden, shuddering halt."
- "On the rubble of the old media culture, we will build a new one with a non-commercial heart and soul."

The various issues of *Adbusters*—a name evocative of both the "busting" of advertising and the title of the 1984 movie *Ghostbusters* and thus also evoking the sense of the elimination of the "ghosts" of capitalism—are designed to bring about the aims of the manifesto. Subvertisements are ad texts that literally subvert the meanings of the brand messages in them. They take the signification systems of ad texts and turn them on their heads.

In a sense, the culture-jamming movement takes its impetus from the common view of consumerist culture as a huge distraction factory, aimed at uprooting the traditional forms of art and meaning making. But the basic assumption on which culture jammers operate, a number of whom have come out of my own classroom, is not completely true. The distraction factory has, actually, had a beneficial effect on human cultural evolution by engendering a "democratization of art." By this I mean that, today, anyone can buy a CD of any piece of classical music or a DVD of any classic movie or acquire any novel he or she desires—opportunities that were not available in a purported idyllic preconsumerist era to which culture jammers seem so nostalgically attached, even if such an era probably never existed. Even television, with its focus on distraction, has a good side to it. It provides comfort and companionship for many people, especially elderly ones, during long solitary evenings, not to mention stimulating social commentary in the form of documentaries and news programs that have, frequently, mobilized social activism.

Since the Industrial Revolution, a host of influential thinkers have pointed their collective finger at capitalism and the mass media as "perverting influences" of true cultural evolution. The German philosopher Jürgen Habermas (1929–), for instance, has claimed that capitalism has created cultures that exist solely in the service of economic efficiency. Semioticians like Roland Barthes, as we have seen, have blamed the brand–media partnership for inculcating materialistic values. Since the late 1950s, brand and media bashing has become common from both the right and the left of the intellectual and ideological spectrum. Global branding, advertising, and marketing are blamed for causing everything from street violence and family breakups to philosophical nihilism throughout the world. Even the present author recently joined the fray in a study of the "juvenilization of culture" (Danesi 2003). But are the critics (including the present one) right?

The view that specific cultural activities and forms of representation influence behavior is, actually, an old view and not a discovery of anti-advertising groups such as the culture jammers. Already in the ancient world, the Greek historian Herodotus (ca. 484–425 B.C.E.) claimed that Egyptians thought differently from the Greeks because they wrote their books from right to left rather than from left to right, as did the Greeks. Herodotus thus put forward the notion that the characteristics of the codes used by a culture to carry out its representational activities influenced how the members of that culture understood the world. A similar view was articulated by the fourteenth-century Algerian scholar Ibn Khaldun (1332–1406), who wrote a truly fascinating treatise in which he noted that the subtle behavioral differences that existed between nomadic and city-dwelling Bedouins were due to their differences in language and in how they used such differences to speak about reality. The same type of view was reiterated centuries later by Johann Gottfried von Herder (1744–1803), Wilhelm von Humboldt (1767–1835), Georg Wilhelm Friedrich Hegel (1770–1831), and Martin Heidegger (1889–1976). These intellectuals claimed that worldview is a product of culture and influences from the social environment.

The culture-jamming movement has taken the view of such intellectuals one step further through what may be called antisemiotizing activism. So, on

posters for McDonald's, the slogan "I'm lovin' it" might be modified by a culture jammer (through defacement) to read "I'm lovin' it, as my veins clog up
with cholesterol." In a semiotic sense, the culture jammer takes the connotation out of the message, rendering it literal and thus openly revelatory. The argument put forward by the culture jammers is based on the view that the kinds
of content that brand promotion activities contain have perverting effects on
people because of their metaphorical content. Some culture jammers also link
shopping addiction with advertising. People go to malls not just to shop but
also to engage in a form of socialization. The mall has replaced the town
square and the piazza. It is now a part of everyday life, as was any other meeting locus of the past, and a locus for self-expression through shopping. Some
may not like this aspect of modern-day lifestyle, but it is a fact of life for many
who clearly do.

Counterargument

If the culture jammers are correct, then Orwell's Big Brother has, seemingly,
taken over the globe. However, many questions arise with regard to the culture jammer's overall outlook. After all, it has always been easy to blame big
business and the media for thwarting the more "noble goals" of life that people would otherwise purportedly pursue. This would mean, of course, that the
"blamers" have some secret knowledge of what those goals are and, more importantly, of why people should pursue them. But, as at any other period of
human history, it is difficult, if not impossible, to pinpoint what is "en-
nobling" and what is "demeaning" from the current slate of human activities
and systems of belief. The consequences of the reckless globalization of mass
manufacturing and mass marketing especially for so many frivolous products
are, needless to say, greatly worrisome with global warming and the depletion
of the earth's natural resources reaching dangerous levels, not to mention the
deepening of existing inequalities related to policies and conditions engendering the social exclusion of various peoples. But are the brands to be
blamed exclusively for all this? Is everyone else an innocent victim of their
clever manipulations? Hardly.

The culture jammers' view that the brand–media partnership is indelibly altering human psychology is actually a version of the magic bullet or hypodermic needle theories. The claim that media representations are capable of
directly swaying minds has simply not been demonstrated in any empirical
fashion. The popularity and spread of junk food is often cited in support of
this view. Promoted by effective advertising campaigns, junk food has become part of the common diet. But the consequences on health have been dis-
astrous. The inordinate consumption of junk food is, in fact, one of the main

factors contributing to the rise in obesity. And this has created a psychologically damaging situation for those who become obese since their body image
is at odds with the ultraslim body images that the media perpetrate as the
norm for attractiveness. This disjunction of fact and image, which psychologists call "cognitive dissonance," has likely generated culture-based crazes,
such as dieting and fitness crazes. But the hypodermic needle view ignores
the historical record. The ravages of overeating or undereating are not just
contemporary phenomena induced by exposure to advertising. They have always been symptomatic of the excesses of affluent lifestyles in the case of the
former and of strictly religious ones in the case of the latter. Fasting, for instance, has been practiced for centuries in connection with religious ceremonies. Originally, it was one of a number of rites in which physical activities were reduced or suspended, resulting in a state of quiescence
symbolically comparable to death or to the state preceding birth. Fasts were
also part of fertility rites in primitive ceremonies.

Finally, the culture-jamming movement does not provide an alternative.
After all, it is up to the individual in a consumerist culture to simply say "No."
There is nothing more effective, in my view, than personal choice. This is one
of the main reasons why I wrote this book in the first place. Even the widespread use of cosmetics has been useful socially, as Kathy Peiss (1998) has
shown, because it liberated women to express their sexuality—something that
traditional, preconsumerist cultures have always tended to strictly forbid. The
founders and early leaders of the "cosmetic movement" were simple
women—Elizabeth Arden (1884–1966), a Canadian, was the daughter of
poor tenant farmers; Helena Rubinstein (1870–1965) was born of poor Jew-
ish parents in Poland; and Madam C. J. Walker (1867–1919) was born to former slaves in Louisiana. While it is true that advertising has preyed on social
fears associated with "bad complexions," "aging," and so on, it has nevertheless allowed women to assert their right to emphasize their sexuality, not conceal it. The paradox of our current "Oil of Olay culture" is that it has been
both good and bad. So be it.

In the end, it may be true that advertising may be reshaping the world in
more ways than we might think. A culture mediated so pervasively by advertising images is probably asking for trouble. What Kubey and Csikszentmihalyi (1990: 199) had to say about the psychosocial effects of television almost two decades ago applies, in my view, as well to advertising:

> Because consciousness is necessarily formed by exposure to information, media
> fare helps define what our most important and salient goals should be. Being an
> intimate part of the consumer society, television tells us that a worthwhile life is
> measured in terms of how many desirable material objects we get to own, and

how many pleasures we get to feel. To achieve such goals complex skills are unnecessary. Even though some people spend a great deal of attention in trying to find bargains, in monitoring prices and sales, in developing culinary taste and fashion sense, in keeping abreast of new models and new gadgets, for the most part consumption does not require much disciplined effort and therefore does not produce psychological growth.

The answer to the dilemma of advertising is, in my view, to become aware of the subtexts that brands, logos, ads, and commercials generate with the help of semiotic analysis. When the human mind is aware of the hidden codes in texts, it will be better able to fend off the undesirable effects that such codes may cause. Semiotics can help to demystify advertising creativity and make the process of meaning creation on the part of advertisers accessible and thus virtually harmless.

Ultimately, the culture-jamming movement raises the question of what content is appropriate and, more importantly, who has the right (if anyone) of deciding what goes into cultural representations. The danger in attacking advertising as "harmful" and other kinds of representations as "acceptable" smacks of ideological bias. Moreover, most people can easily distinguish between what is appropriate for living a meaningful life and what is not. It is useless, in my view, to propose drastic measures to censor or repress advertising expressions of any kind in order to counteract any purported hypodermic needle effect. For one thing, representations produce such an effect only if individuals are already predisposed toward their content, and, for another, brand moguls will find ways around such measures. More and more groups have started to suggest censorship as a means of gaining control over the levers of the media and, especially, over the advertising messages that permeate the entire social order. But the answer is not to be found in censorship or in any form of state control. Even if it were possible in democratic societies to control the contents of media and the promotional activities of the brands, this would hardly solve the "problems of humanity." Immunization against any deleterious effects that the brand–media partnership may be having on us is, in my view, to become aware of the signification systems that are spread by this partnership. In this way, we will be better able, as individuals, to fend off any undesirable effects that advertising may cause.

Having attempted to rebut the aims of the culture jammers, I must admit that theirs is a just and noble goal. Everyone is indeed appalled by images of poverty in the global village and by the exploitation of the human and ecological resources that unbridled capitalism brings, as the many images in *Adbusters* constantly emphasize. But the antibrand view of the capitalist system is blind to history. It was, after all, the very capitalist system that culture jammers assail that brought democracy to Europe during the late medieval period by allowing the bourgeoisie to gain independence from both the religious and the aristocratic oligarchies through opportunities to invest saved capital. The bourgeoisie consisted originally of the free residents of European towns during the early Middle Ages. The term was extended in the late period to anyone who was able to become "free" through entrepreneurship. Although it has become itself a "new world" religion, strangely blending religious values with pop culture mores, bourgeois capitalism has provided the conditions for anyone to gain wealth, not just those born into it.

The belief of anti-advertising individuals today is really no more than a modern-day version of antibourgeois sentiments expressed over the centuries in various forms and in political and social movements. The underlying assumption of all such movements is that bourgeois capitalism, in its relentless aim to guarantee profit (at any cost), is insensitive to basic human concerns, promoting an unbridled form of materialism that has affected societies negatively. Lifestyle consumerism is considered to be a symptom of this fundamental bourgeois aim. But this is an ideological assumption, not a fact. One can argue, on the contrary, that the lifestyles crystallizing from democratic bourgeois capitalism have produced positive results that could never have been achieved under any other system.

As Heath and Potter (2004) have recently argued, the culture-jamming movement to create "brand-free" economies will not work because ultimately it constitutes nothing more than a way to promote no-brand and no-logo products. To emphasize their point, they refer to a 2003 *Adbusters* announcement that it would be selling its own brand of subversive shoe, the Blackspot Sneaker, to counteract the success of the Nike brand product. In effect, Heath and Potter argue, the Blackspot Sneaker ad employed the same kinds of advertising style as Nike. The irony of the whole exercise was that this very fact seems to have escaped the attention of culture jammers. Culture jamming turns out to be no more than an appealing form of self-deception, argue Heath and Potter. It is relevant to note that the culture jammers rarely go after the "small brands," just after the successful ones, defending the smaller and local brands against the "biggies" in the global marketplace. Moreover, an examination of the issues of *Adbusters* does not show any subvertisements against brands that may be said to have "cultural content," such as bookstore companies and record labels of classical music or jazz. This suggests a rather selective and elitist view of branding, not a truly subversive one.

The same irony applies to other antibrand groups. Take, for example, the vociferous religious right groups in the United States who are wont to blame the media and open sexual representations in advertisements for all that ails the country. Yet the leaders of those very groups use advertising and the media to great advantage themselves to purvey their ideas and their own products (books, DVDs, and the like) promising salvation and comfort to all their followers. Televangelism is a perfect example of how the very people who condemn the media use it for their own ends. With slick ads of their own and aggressive sales pitches, the televangelists peddle their wares and spectacles through the television screen with the same techniques that product advertisers utilize.

As Alissa Quart (2003) has observed, the real problem with the branding process is that both the critics and the defenders of it are right. The goal of capitalist systems is to promote a consumerist lifestyle so that profits can be ensured. To do so, they base their business strategies on selling images and their meanings rather than products in themselves. Therein lies the paradox of life today.

SO, WHY DOES IT SELL?

The title of this book is *Why It Sells.* Its purpose has been to try and show exactly that. The underlying theme has been that to sell a product effectively, advertisers and marketers promote it as something other than what it is—a simple product. In a phrase, successful selling involves a set of techniques that range from giving products names to placing them in movies and television programs as props within them.

Because of advertising, products are now perceived both as physical objects and as mental objects, or, in semiotic terms, denotatively and connotatively. In human life, there is virtually no object or artifact that is not imbued with meaning. The jewelry, clothes, furniture, ornaments, tools, and toys that the marketplace makes available would be perceived as practical or functional objects without advertising. The advertiser raises them to the level of meaningful signs by linking them through representation to cultural traditions, values, rituals, and so on.

In a phrase, the representations that advertisers make are powerful because they have social and cultural relevance. Take beer one more time as an example. Beer is beer, with varying nuances of flavor to it. But beer has social meaning that goes well beyond gustatory sense. Because it is a drink that is commonly used in social situations, especially among friends and peers, the advertiser taps into this meaning through a host of techniques that range from humor to chic lifestyle images. What kinds of people drink Budweiser, Stella Artois, Miller, or Corona beer? Answers to this question would typically include remarks about the educational level, class, social attitudes, worldview, and so on of the consumer. The one who drinks Budweiser is perceived by people as vastly different from the one who drinks Stella Artois. Why? Because the former is portrayed in advertising campaigns as a youngish down-to-earth male who simply wants to "hang out with the guys"; the latter is portrayed instead as a more sophisticated type (male or female) who appreciates the finer things of life. The two beer brands speak directly to different types of individuals so that they can see their own personalities mirrored in the lifestyle images created by advertising campaigns and thus identify with one or the other beer brand.

Advertising and marketing add a dimension to products that was absent from the marketplaces of the past—cultural meaning. And the more such meaning can be built into a brand, the more likely it will become itself socialized. The cultural meanings of brands can, however, hardly be pinned down exactly. They can only be inferred. They are, in a phrase, mental constructs, that is, culturally shaped forms that come to mind in relation to a specific brand. Take, as a case in point, the Amazon.com name—originally a Web-based bookstore with a database of millions of titles. The Amazon part of the name suggests at least two meaning levels. At one level, it reverberates with mythic overtones. In Greek mythology, the Amazons were a race of warlike women who excluded men from their society. The suggestion of a bold new world of strong women who possess secret knowledge and abilities is not a casual one. There are few people who will perceive in that name anything to the contrary. This is why speakers of English use it metaphorically to describe females who are tall and gigantic ("She's an Amazon"). At another connotative level, the Amazon name evokes an image of one of the earth's largest natural and still largely unexplored areas, the Brazilian Amazon region, thus challenging computer users to enter by analogy into its own unexplored world and navigate it. Of course, we do not see in our mind the Amazon jungle or gigantic women controlling a certain domain of cyberspace. We get, instead, a vague image or sense of the power of the website to get us what we want. We can, of course, bring the "Amazon imagery" to consciousness by reflecting on it. But such reflection is rare. Brand names suggest images, but these are never specific or clear-cut. They are understandable only within larger associations of cultural meaning. In a phrase, the difference between a brand and a product is a strategic one that has rather profound psychological implications. A product has no identity; a brand does. It garners one through its name, its association with cultural meaning, its dissemination through mass advertising campaigns, and other strategies designed to give it "cultural relevance."

It is relevant to note that advertising is among the most strictly regulated enterprises in North America (and in other parts of the world). This is a consequence of the "awareness raising" that the many critical social scientific studies on branding and advertising have brought about in recent years, some of which have been discussed in this chapter. But legislation is hardly the most effective way of protecting people against the purported persuasive power of advertising. Real immunization comes from understanding the semiotic nature of advertising and its techniques. If these are indeed effective, then, like the culture jammers suggest, all we have to do is literally jam advertising messages by ourselves to wring out of them all the hidden connotations and mythologies they might conceal.

Marketers are keenly aware of the magic of myth and symbolism. The list of the mystical meanings associated with ads and commercials, as discussed in this book, is a truly mind-boggling one. The marketer's craft works its unconscious magic on modern-day humans, making them see, for example, products as necessary for success or creating distinctions between better or worse—be it body shape, hairstyle, or brand of blue jeans. It is the symbolism of brands that creates allegiances to them. This explains why such things as older Coca-Cola bottles, pet rocks, and other such apparently trivial artifacts are preserved by common people and why they now have historical value.

The modern world is hardly utopia. Some have even written it off as an anti-utopian social order characterized by human misery and oppression. But utopias are figments of the imagination. After all, the capitalist system in which we live not only besieges us with brand images but also provides the services and products that ultimately help the "common person" to survive longer than ever before; and, of course, it also provides the means to achieve a degree of affluence that has never been attained by so many at any other time in history. Change will not come about by simply blaming capitalism for all our problems, as the Frankfurt School theorists and culture jammers have done with great efficacy. There are no simple answers, no easy solutions. Economics alone, as history informs us, will not run a society forever. In the meantime, I cannot but conclude this book by quoting the controversial writer Camille Paglia (1991: 25). In my view, she is right on target pointing out that it is profoundly hypocritical of anticapitalist intellectuals "to enjoy the pleasures and conveniences of capitalism, while sneering at it."

Glossary

advertising: (from medieval Latin *advertere*, "to direct one's attention to") any type or form of public announcement designed to promote the sale of specific commodities or services

aesthesia: the ability to experience sensation; in art appreciation it refers to the fact that our senses and feelings are stimulated by the art form

alliteration: the repetition of the initial consonant sounds or features of words

anchorage: Roland Barthes's notion that images in advertisements are polysemic (having many meanings); however, they are anchored to particular meaning domains by specific interpreters

brand image: the "personality" created for a product through a name, a logo, a style of packaging, and so on

brand name: name given to a product

code: a system of meanings that determine how we interpret something (gender, products, and so on)

communication: social interaction through messages; the production and exchange of messages and meanings

conceptual metaphor: the generalized metaphorical formula that defines a specific abstraction (*love is a sweet taste*)

connotation: the extended or representational meaning built into an ad or commercial; the symbolic or mythic meaning of a sign

connotative index: degree of connotation associated with an ad or a product itself

consumer advertising: advertising directed toward the promotion of some product

context: the environment (physical and social) in which ads, products, and so on are interpreted

decoding: the process of deciphering the underlying code-based meaning(s) of an ad

denotation: the primary or informational meaning of a sign; the process of presenting information about a product

fetish: an object that is believed to have magical or spiritual powers or that can cause sexual arousal

hermeneutics: the science or art of interpretation

icon: sign that has a direct (nonarbitrary) connection to a referent

image: the result of representing a product or service so as to enhance its value aesthetically, socially, and so on

index: sign that has a relation-based connection to a referent (indicating that something or someone is located somewhere)

interpretant: the meaning gleaned from a sign, ad, text, and so on in terms of personal and social experience

intertextuality: the allusion within a text to some other text that the interpreter would have access to or knowledge of

jingle: simple rhythmic catchy tune composed about a product or service

logo: distinctive product or company visual signature, trademark, colophon, motto, nameplate, and so on

marketing: the business of positioning, promoting, and distributing goods and services

medium: the technical or physical means by which a message is transmitted

message: any meaningful text produced with signs belonging to a specific code (or codes)

metaphor: the signifying process by which two signifying domains (A, B) are connected $(A\ is\ B)$ explicitly or implicitly

metonymy: the signifying process by which an examplar is used to refer to the category to which it belongs (*Scotch Tape* for any adhesive tape)

myth: any story or narrative in early cultures that aims to explain the origin of something

mythology: the study of myths; the recycling of myth in advertising

narrative: something told or written, such as an account, story, or tale

onomatopoeia: formation of words to represent something by imitating one or several of its sound properties (*drip, boom*, and so on)

opposition: comparison of two forms to determine if they are differentiated meaningfully (*night* vs. *day*, *good* vs. *evil*, and so on)

political-social advertising: advertising used for special political or social purposes

positioning: the placing or targeting of a product for the right people

product character: any character (real or cartoon) representing a product

propaganda: any systematic dissemination of doctrines, views, and so on reflecting specific interests and ideologies

public relations: the activities and techniques used by organizations and individuals to establish favorable attitudes and responses toward them

publicity: the craft of disseminating any information that concerns a person, group, event, or product through public media

referent: what is indicated by a sign (any object, being, idea, or event in the world)

repetition: technique of repeating an ad in different media

representamen: Charles S. Peirce's term for signifier (form)

representation: the process by which a product is portrayed as something other than itself

rhetoric: the study of the techniques used in all kinds of discourses, from common conversation to poetry

semantic differential: technique for fleshing out connotations associated with a product image through contrasting scales

semiotics: the science of studying signs

sign: something that stands for something (someone) else in some capacity

signification: the process of generating meaning through the use of signs

signification system: system of meanings established for a product or service through various techniques such as brand naming, creation of a logo, and so on

signified: that part of a sign that is referred to; a synonym for *referent* and *object*

signifier: that part of a sign that does the referring; the physical part of a sign

slogan: catchword or catchphrase used to advertise a product and that becomes closely linked with the product

structure: any repeatable or predictable aspect of signs, codes, and messages

subtext: a text (message) implied by connotation within a text

symbol: a sign that has an arbitrary (conventional) connection with a referent

synesthesia: the evocation of one sense modality (e.g., vision) by means of some other (e.g., sound)

tagline: any catchy statement used in advertising a product

testimonial: any ad that uses people to give testimony about the ad

text: a message with its particular form and contents

trade advertising: advertising that is directed toward dealers and professionals through appropriate trade publications and media

References

Allen, G. 2000. *Intertexuality*. London: Routledge.

Altman, L. 2006. *Brand It Yourself: The Fast, Focused Way to Marketplace Magic*. New York: Portfolio.

Arnheim, R. 1969. *Visual Thinking*. Berkeley: University of California Press.

Atkin, D. 2004. *The Culting of Brands*. New York: Portfolio.

Barthel, D. 1988. *Putting on Appearances: Gender and Advertising*. Philadelphia: Temple University Press.

Barthes, R. 1957. *Mythologies*. Paris: Seuil.

——. 1977. *Image-Music-Text*. London: Fontana.

Beard, A. 2001. *Texts and Contexts*. London: Routledge.

Beasley, R., and M. Danesi. 2002. *Persuasive Signs: The Semiotics of Advertising*. Berlin: Mouton de Gruyter.

Bell, S. 1990. Semiotics and Advertising Research: A Case Study. *Marketing Signs* 8:1–6.

Bendinger, B. 1988. *The Copy Workshop Workbook*. Chicago: The Copy Workshop.

Berger, A. A. 2000. *Ads, Fads, and Consumer Culture: Advertising's Impact on American Character and Society*. Lanham, Md.: Rowman & Littlefield.

——. 2005. *Shop 'Til You Drop*. Lanham, Md.: Rowman & Littlefield.

Bergin, T. G., and M. H. Fisch. 1984. *The New Science of Giambattista Vico*. Ithaca, N.Y.: Cornell University Press.

Bryman, A. 2004. *The Disneyization of Society*. London: Sage.

Budnitz, P. 2007. *I Am Plastic: The Designer Toy Explosion*. New York: Abrams.

Cook, V. 2004. *Why Can't Anybody Spell?* New York: Touchstone.

Crystal, D. 2006. *Language and the Internet*. 2nd ed. Cambridge: Cambridge University Press.

Danesi, M. 2003. *Forever Young: The "Teen-Aging" of Modern Culture*. Toronto: University of Toronto Press.

——. 2006. *Brands*. London: Routledge.

Danziger, P. 2004. *Why People Buy Things They Don't Need: Understanding and Predicting Consumer Behavior*. Dearborn, Mich.: Dearborn Trade Publishing.

Davenport, G. 1984. *The Geography of the Imagination*. London: Picador.

Dyer, G. 1982. *Advertising as Communication*. London: Routledge.

Eliade, M. 1961. *The Sacred and the Profane: The Nature of Religion*. New York: Harper.

Espes Brown, J. 1992. Becoming Part of It. In *I Become Part of It: Sacred Dimensions in Native American Life*, ed. D. M. Dooling and P. Jordan-Smith, 1–15. New York: HarperCollins.

Ewen, S. 1988. *All Consuming Images*. New York: Basic Books.

Frank, T. 1997. *The Conquest of Cool: Business Culture, Counterculture, and the Rise of Hip Consumerism*. Chicago: University of Chicago Press.

Frankel, A. 2004. *Word·Craft: The Art of Turning Little Words into Big Business*. New York: Three Rivers Press.

Goodman, A. 2005. *Winning Results with Google Adwords*. New York: McGraw-Hill.

Heath, J., and A. Potter. 2004. *The Rebel Sell: Why Culture Can't Be Jammed*. New York: HarperCollins.

Henry, J. 1963. *Culture against Man*. New York: Vintage Books.

Hine, T. 1995. *The Total Package: The Secret History and Hidden Meanings of Boxes, Bottles, Cans, and Other Persuasive Containers*. Boston: Little, Brown.

Hoffman, B. 2002. *The Fine Art of Advertising*. New York: Stewart, Tabori & Chang.

Holt, D. B. 2004. *How Brands Become Icons: The Principles of Cultural Branding*. Boston: Harvard Business School Press.

Karmen, S., 1989. *Through the Jungle: The Art and Business of Making Music for Commercials*. New York: Billboard Books.

Key, W. B. 1972. *Subliminal Seduction*. New York: Signet.

———. 1976. *Media Sexploitation*. New York: Signet.

———. 1980. *The Clam-Plate Orgy*. New York: Signet.

———. 1989. *The Age of Manipulation*. New York: Holt.

Kilbourne, J. 1999. *Can't Buy My Love: How Advertising Changes the Way I Feel*. New York: Simon & Schuster.

Klein, N. 2000. *No Logo: Taking Aim at the Brand Bullies*. Toronto: Alfred A. Knopf.

Kubey, R., and M. Csikszentmihalyi. 1990. *Television and the Quality of Life*. Hillsdale, N.J.: Lawrence Erlbaum Associates.

Lakoff, G., and M. Johnson. 1980. *Metaphors We Live By*. Chicago: University of Chicago Press.

Lasn, K. 2000. *Culture Jam: The Uncooling of America*. New York: Morrow.

Leiss, W., S. Kline, S. Jhally, and J. Botterill. 2005. *Social Communication in Advertising: Consumption in the Mediated Marketplace*. London: Routledge.

Lévi-Strauss, C. 1958. *Structural Anthropology*. New York: Basic Books.

———. 1978. *Myth and Meaning: Cracking the Code of Culture*. Toronto: University of Toronto Press.

Lindstrom, M. 2005. *Brand Sense: Build Powerful Brands through Touch, Taste, Smell, Sight, and Sound*. New York: Free Press.

Marks, S. 2005. *Finding Betty Crocker*. New York: Simon & Schuster.

Merrell, F. 2007. *Processing Cultural Meaning*. Ottawa: Legas.

Neumeier, M. 2006. *The Brand Gap*. Berkeley, Calif.: New Riders.

Ogden, C. K., and I. A. Richards. 1923. *The Meaning of Meaning*. London: Routledge and Kegan Paul.

Packard, V. 1957. *The Hidden Persuaders*. New York: McKay.

Paglia, C. 1991. *Sexual Personae*. New York: Random House.

Panati, C. 1984. *Browser's Book of Beginnings*. Boston: Houghton Mifflin.

Peiss, K. 1998. *Hope in a Jar: The Making of America's Beauty Culture*. New York: Metropolitan Books.

Pollio, H., J. Barlow, H. Fine, and M. Pollio. 1977. *The Poetics of Growth: Figurative Language in Psychology, Psychotherapy, and Education*. Hillsdale, N.J.: Lawrence Erlbaum Associates.

Quart, A. 2003. *Branded: The Buying and Selling of Teenagers*. New York: Basic Books.

Roy, M. 2000. *Sign after the X*. Vancouver: Advance Artspeak.

Savan, L. 2005. *Slam Dunks and No-Brainers: Language in Your Life, the Media, Business, Politics, and, Like, Whatever*. New York: Alfred A. Knopf.

Schlosser, E. 2001. *Fast Food Nation*. Boston: Houghton Mifflin.

Siegel, D. L., T. J. Coffey, and G. Livingston. 2004. *The Great Tween Buying Machine*. Chicago: Dearborn Trade Publishing.

Straubhaar, J., and R. LaRose. 2000. *Media Now: Communications Media in the Information Age*. Belmont, Calif.: Wadsworth.

Tash, M. 1979. Headlines in Advertising: The Semantics of Deviation. *Forum Linguisticum* 3:222–41.

Trout, J. 1969. Positioning Is a Game People Play in Today's Me-Too Market Place. *Industrial Marketing* 54:51–55.

Twitchell, J. B. 2000. *Twenty Ads That Shook the World*. New York: Crown.

———. 2004. *Branded Nation*. New York: Simon & Schuster.

Vygotsky, L. S. 1962. *Thought and Language*. Cambridge, Mass.: MIT Press.

———. 1978. *Mind in Society*. Cambridge, Mass.: Cambridge University Press.

Wheeler, A. 2003. *Designing Brand Identity*. New York: John Wiley & Sons.

Williamson, J. 1996. *Decoding Advertisements: Ideology and Meaning in Advertising*. London: Marion Boyars.

Wolfe, O. 1989. Sociosemiology and Cross-Cultural Branding Strategies. *Marketing Signs* 3:3–10.

Zipf, G. K. 1929. Relative Frequency as a Determinant of Phonetic Change. *Harvard Studies in Classical Philology* 40:1–95.

———. 1932. *Selected Studies of the Principle of Relative Frequency in Language*. Cambridge, Mass.: Harvard University Press.

———. 1935. *The Psycho-Biology of Language: An Introduction to Dynamic Philology*. Boston: Houghton Mifflin.

———. 1949. *Human Behavior and the Principle of Least Effort*. Boston: Addison-Wesley.

Further Reading

Andren, G. L., L. Ericsson, R. Ohlsson, and T. Tännsjö. 1978. *Rhetoric and Ideology in Advertising*. Stockholm: AB Grafiska.

Atwan, R. 1979. *Edsels, Luckies and Frigidaires: Advertising the American Way*. New York: Dell.

Barnouw, E. 1978. *The Sponsor: Notes on a Modern Potentate*. Oxford: Oxford University Press.

Barthes, R. 1968. *Elements of Semiology*. London: Cape.

Brierley, S. 1995. *The Advertising Handbook*. London: Routledge.

Danesi, M. 2007. *The Quest for Meaning: A Guide to Semiotic Theory and Practice*. Toronto: University of Toronto Press.

Danna, S. R. 1992. *Advertising and Popular Culture: Studies in Variety and Versatility*. Bowling Green, Ohio: Bowling Green State University Popular Press.

Driver, J. C., and G. R. Foxall. 1984. *Advertising Policy and Practice*. New York: Holt, Rinehart and Winston.

Forceville, C. 1996. *Pictorial Metaphor in Advertising*. London: Routledge.

Frith, T. K. 1997. *Undressing the Ad: Reading Culture in Advertising*. New York: Peter Lang.

Goffman, E. 1979. *Gender Advertisements*. New York: Harper and Row.

Goldman, R., and R. Papson. 1996. *Sign Wars: The Cluttered Landscape of Advertising*. New York: Guilford Press.

Hindley, D., and G. Hindley. 1972. *Advertising in Victorian England*. London: Wayland.

Jacobson, M. F., and L. A. Mazur. 1995. *Marketing Madness: A Survival Guide for a Consumer Society*. Boulder, Colo.: Westview Press.

Jhally, S. 1987. *The Codes of Advertising*. New York: St. Martin's Press.

Leymore, V. 1975. *Hidden Myth: Structure and Symbolism in Advertising*. London: Heinemann.

O'Barr, W. M. 1994. *Culture and the Ad: Exploring Otherness in the World of Advertising*. Boulder, Colo.: Westview Press.

Pope, D. 1983. *The Making of Modern Advertising.* New York: Basic Books.

Seabrook, J. 2000. *Nobrow: The Culture of Marketing—The Marketing of Culture.* New York: Knopf.

Sut, J. 1990. *The Codes of Advertising: Fetishism and the Political Economy of Meaning in the Consumer Society.* London: Routledge.

Vardar, N. 1992. *Global Advertising: Rhyme or Reason?* London: Chapman.

Vestergaard, T., and K. Schrøder. 1985. *The Language of Advertising.* London: Blackwell.

Wernick, A. 1991. *Promotional Culture: Advertising, Ideology, and Symbolic Expression.* London: Gage.

Williamson, J. 1985. *Consuming Passions.* London: Marion Boyars.

Online Resources

Adbusters
www.adbusters.org

Ad Council
www.adcouncil.org

Ad Forum
www.adforum.com

Advertising Age
www.adage.com/datacenter.cms

Advertising History
www.scriptorium.lib.duke.edu/hartman

Advertising World
www.advertising.utexas.edu/world

Adweek
www.adweek.com

American Association of Advertising Agencies
www.aaaa.org

Applied Semiotics
www.chass.utoronto.ca/french/as-sa/index.html

Cannes International Advertising Festival
www.canneslions.com

Clio Awards
www.clioawards.com

Product Placement
www.productplacement.co.nz

Semiotics for Beginners
www.aber.ac.uk/media/Documents/S4B/sem02.html

Index

About the Author

Marcel Danesi is professor of semiotics and anthropology at the University of Toronto. He is also director of the Program in Semiotics and Communication Theory at the university. He has written extensively on topics ranging from the origins of language to youth culture and advertising. He is currently the editor in chief of *Semiotica*, the official journal of the International Associational of Semiotic Studies. He became a fellow of the Royal Society of Canada, one of the highest awards given for distinguished work in academia by the Canadian government.